AARON McDUFFIE MOORE

An African American

Physician, Educator, and

Founder of Durham's

Black Wall Street

Aaron McDuffie Moore

BLAKE HILL-SAYA

With a Foreword by

U.S. Representative

G. K. BUTTERFIELD

and an Afterword by

C. EILEEN WATTS WELCH

THE UNIVERSITY OF NORTH CAROLINA PRESS Chapel Hill

This book was published with the assistance of the
Z. Smith Reynolds Fund of the University of North Carolina Press.

Designed by Richard Hendel
Set in Miller and Didot
by Tseng Information Systems, Inc.
Manufactured in the United States of America

The University of North Carolina Press has been a
member of the Green Press Initiative since 2003.

Jacket illustrations: (*front*) portrait in oils of Dr. Aaron McDuffie Moore, painted by
his daughter Lyda Moore in 1940 and now hanging in the lobby of the Stanford L.
Warren Branch of the Durham County Library; photograph of portrait by Cody Saya.
(*back*) North Carolina Mutual Life Insurance Company building; photograph courtesy
of the State Archives of North Carolina, Raleigh.

Library of Congress Cataloging-in-Publication Data
Names: Hill-Saya, Blake, author.
Title: Aaron McDuffie Moore : an African American physician, educator, and founder of
Durham's black Wall Street / Blake Hill-Saya ; with a foreword by U.S. Representative
G.K. Butterfield and an afterword by C. Eileen Watts Welch.
Description: Chapel Hill : The University of North Carolina Press, [2020] |
Includes bibliographical references and index.
Identifiers: LCCN 2019046688 | ISBN 9781469655857 (cloth : alk. paper) |
ISBN 9781469655864 (ebook)
Subjects: LCSH: Moore, A. M. (Aaron McDuffie), 1863–1923. | African American
physicians—North Carolina—Durham—Biography. | African American businesspeople—
North Carolina—Durham—Biography. | African American civic leaders—North
Carolina—Durham—Biography. | Hayti (Durham, N.C.)—History—20th century.
Classification: LCC R154.M725 H55 2020 | DDC 610.89/96073092 [B]—dc23
LC record available at https://lccn.loc.gov/2019046688

For

Deborah Chase Watts Hill, Ph.D.,

Charles DeWitt Watts, M.D.,

and Lyda Constance Watts,

who dreamed of this book and

who were our constant inspiration

CONTENTS

A gallery of illustrations begins on page 97.

FOREWORD

My relationship with Durham, North Carolina, spans many years, as an undergraduate and law student at North Carolina Central University and now as Durham's representative in the U.S. House of Representatives. Over these decades, I have embraced Durham's rich history. I especially enjoy the stories of those who transformed this outpost into a national leader in so many fields. For years, one name surfaced from podiums and pulpits, living rooms and community events, a name spoken with tremendous love and respect: Aaron McDuffie Moore.

As a student of history, I wanted to know more about this luminary. The more I learned, the more I found that Aaron and I shared identical priorities, including access to health care, educational opportunity, and economic empowerment. Where do you begin in describing a man who founded the state's first independent black hospital and nursing school, a library, a bank, an insurance company, a pharmacy, and, believe it or not, a Shakespeare society—and who kept a closet full of shoes to give to children too ashamed to come to Sunday school without them?

A persistent campaigner for broader educational opportunities for black children, Aaron cooperated with Booker T. Washington in persuading Julius Rosenwald to construct eight hundred rural Rosenwald Schools in North Carolina, most of which were in my congressional district. This book describes the contributions of Aaron and his Durham contemporaries during an often-overlooked period in North Carolina's history.

His accomplishments were local, statewide, and national in scope, but they began and ended with the welfare of individuals. A 2016 program sponsored by the North Carolina Governor's Office said Aaron Moore "almost single-handedly built one of the most prosperous black communities in the nation" and called him "a visionary ahead of his time with a strong commitment to helping others." All this from a humble, hard-working farm boy, grounded in faith and family.

Where do you begin? I wondered. Indeed, where do you stop? Aaron's accomplishments placed Durham alongside cities such as Tulsa, Oklahoma; Oberlin, Ohio; and Washington, D.C. as a beacon of black hope during the often-overlooked post-Reconstruction era of entrepreneurship, self-sufficiency, and civic progress by the newly emancipated. A man of tireless energy, relentless curiosity, and eternal optimism, Aaron Moore was not only Durham's first black physician but also Durham's own Renaissance man.

Aaron McDuffie Moore remains an icon in the Durham community. His is a story that goes beyond race. Although a commitment to "his people" was at the heart of every endeavor, that focus was never at the expense of others. He helped his neighbors—both black and white—understand each other and work together.

Aaron's inspiring narrative deserves to be told, and I am grateful to his great-great-granddaughter Blake Hill-Saya for telling it so well and giving us a glimpse into Aaron's humor, enthusiasm, impatience, and heartbreak. I am equally grateful to his great-granddaughter C. Eileen Watts Welch, who continues working to sustain the nonprofit Durham Colored Library, Inc., which Aaron Moore founded almost 100 years ago. The DCL board shared in her vision through its support of this book.

Get to know Aaron for yourself through the pages that follow. You will be richer through his acquaintance.

G. K. Butterfield

AUTHOR'S NOTE

Writing this biography of my great-great-grandfather Aaron McDuffie Moore has been my dream since I was a teenager. I was well into adulthood, however, before I realized the larger impact of being his descendant. I, who have kept a journal from the time I was nine, started wondering what it would be like to enter the similarly intimate, everyday world of my ancestors. I wondered not just about their more widely known accomplishments but also about the minutiae of their everyday lives and their inner monologues. I began hoarding photographs and collecting letters, books, and personal items, such as a pair of gloves and a few china cups. Anything I could find on the subject of my mother's family transported me and held the thrill of discovery. To this day I have a recurring dream that I stumble across some secret door to a new wing or room in my grandparents' house—it feels like discovering a shipwreck or the tomb of an ancient pharaoh—and suddenly all of my family mysteries are revealed to me.

Beautiful houses, such as the Moore residence at 606 Fayetteville Street—homes that were destroyed in Durham's Urban Renewal Project—haunt my imagination the most. Their era seems a lost world, a kind of Atlantis. Durham's Hayti neighborhood of 1900–1960 is a world that remains physically only in small part. It lives best in the memories of the families who resided there and in the surviving institutions.

As a biracial child, a classical musician, and a lifelong student of history and the humanities, I have often felt that I was born to be a bridge—between families, between the black and white racial experiences, between the stage and the audience, and now, I hope, between the voices of my ancestors and the hearts of my readers. I find that the more I work to bring Dr. Aaron McDuffie Moore's life into focus, the more my desire becomes simply to sit and visit with my great-great-grandfather. During my research, I have met many others who have encountered his story in their own work and have voiced that same desire: to know Aaron Moore better, to spend time with him, to better understand his world.

My task, therefore, has become to find a way to create this encounter with him, to explore the events and achievements that shaped his world in such a way as to offer a more complete and approachable sense of his life through the written word. I realize that this goal may blur the lines at times between the genres of memoir and historical biography. I feel, however, that both tones may best serve the story of a man whose outer achievements have been widely reported but whose more intimate life and personality have been less so. Many factual references, articles, and accolades have been written about this pioneering physician and entrepreneur. My aim is to collect that data and as much peripheral evidence as can be found and present it in one concentrated work. I have also tried to infuse those historical facts and references with his particular warmth, his passionate focus on his community, and his more personal existence. The occasional fictional scenes, informed by facts, are designed to engage the imagination and, in combination with the research, allow readers to fall into the story more deeply, to find that secret door to Aaron's lost world.

Aaron McDuffie Moore's imprint is truly in my DNA. I am driven, as he was, to ask, to know, to think, to pray, and to serve. I see these same traits in his many descendants. I share this call to service with C. Eileen Watts Welch, my mother's sister and my steadfast collaborator. I saw his curiosity and intelligence in my beautiful mother, Debbie, whose love of language and talent for research can now be with me and guide me only in spirit.

I want the world to know what made this humble country boy reach beyond all known boundaries and drive himself to accomplish what he did, not for just himself and his family but also for his community, his race, and the nation that he loved.

May the history we record preserve our loves as carefully as our struggles.

AARON MCDUFFIE MOORE

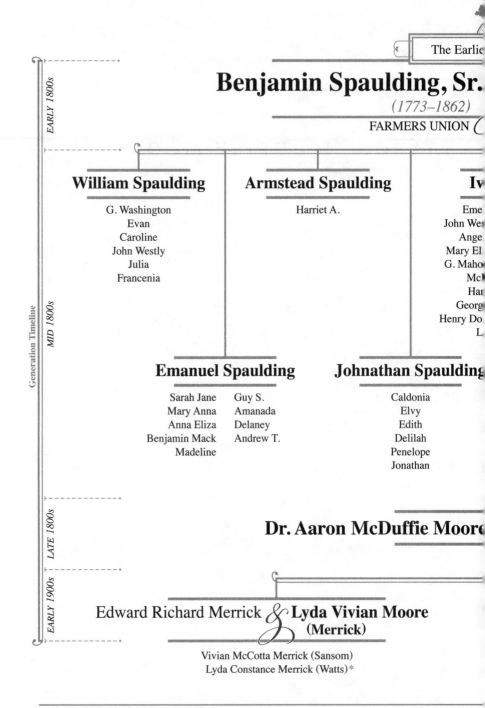

Benjamin Spaulding, Sr.
(1773–1862)

FARMERS UNION

William Spaulding

G. Washington
Evan
Caroline
John Westly
Julia
Francenia

Armstead Spaulding

Harriet A.

Iv

Eme
John We
Ange
Mary El
G. Maho
Mc
Har
Georg
Henry Do
L

Emanuel Spaulding

Sarah Jane   Guy S.
Mary Anna   Amanada
Anna Eliza   Delaney
Benjamin Mack   Andrew T.
Madeline

Johnathan Spaulding

Caldonia
Elvy
Edith
Delilah
Penelope
Jonathan

Dr. Aaron McDuffie Moore

Edward Richard Merrick *&* **Lyda Vivian Moore**
(Merrick)

Vivian McCotta Merrick (Sansom)
Lyda Constance Merrick (Watts)*

EARLY 1800s

MID 1800s

LATE 1800s

EARLY 1900s

Generation Timeline

---

* *Descendants of Lyda Constance Merrick (Watts):* Constance Eileen Watts (Welch) (*Daughter*),
S. Blake Hill-Saya (*Granddaughter*)

Edith Delphia Freeman (Spaulding)

(1786–1871)

NORTH CAROLINA

ulding	Benjamin, Jr. Spaulding	Henry Spaulding
aron Lomax	Francis E.	Callie Jane
oyd Leslie	Annie Madeline	Rhoda Columbia
sper F.	Bernard	Thomas J.
son C.	John Andrew	Louisa F.
abella	Annie Jane	Edith E.
onzo	Rhoda	Benjamin M.
mes Walter	Henry Ivan	Sharlee
meon C.	Bennie Mariah	John Henry
Josephine		Daniel A.
		Gertrude

Ann Eliza Spaulding (Moore)

		David Spaulding
Lewis	Daniel James	Robert Owen
Calvin B.	Israel, Jr.	Eliza E.
Mary Edith	Dephia Ann	Henry Deset
Margaret	Aaron McDuffie	Lucy Jane
Caroline		Annie Mariah
	Ann Eliza	David J.
		Mary E.

Sarah McCotta Dancy (Moore)

ichard Louise McDougald & Mattie Louise Moore (McDougald)

Virginia Louise McDougald (O'Daniel)
Arona Moore McDougald (Parker)

PROLOGUE *Imagined Reverie*

May 1916, a Sunday, around 7:00 A.M.[1] Light rain fell on the rooftops of Durham's Hayti with a familiar softness.[2] Dr. Aaron McDuffie Moore stood to one side of his dining table, his chair pulled back behind him, his left hand resting on the high curved back,[3] his coffee in its fine but plain china cup long since gone cold. He was gazing out beyond the wet porch pillars toward his beloved Fayetteville Street.[4] He could feel himself gradually resettling into his home, like a bird at the end of a long migration, gravity pulling him downward with a bit more force than usual. Travel always exacted from him a physical toll. He would have to get some rest. He would have to resist for one more Sunday the urge to fully reengage.

Two months of travel in Cuba, Puerto Rico, Haiti, and Panama, plus rough seas from Havana to New York and seventeen hours by train from Penn Station, had left him a bit weary.[5] As a physician, however, this kind of exhaustion had a familiar restlessness to it. He was used to operating at a high level no matter how tired he was, and he had to admit he liked it that way. The proverbial rocking chair would never be for him; there was far too much to be done.[6] He moved abruptly out of his reverie and pulled his watch out of his front vest pocket, pressing the stem to reveal its plain face. Folks would be gathering at White Rock Baptist Church soon. It would be good to hear that sweet bell ring again. It would be good to see his congregation and the familiar faces of home. It would be good to settle his soul and replace the troubles of the wider world with the tasks and tribulations of his local one. He breathed in, squaring his shoulders a little in his Sunday suit. He was anxious to get back to the hospital, to his office, to his Sunday school class, to all the various daily demands of his beloved home. His recent journey had reminded him of his place in the world and his determination to make a difference here in Durham—where he could and while he could. The world was a dangerous place, and politics were getting more dangerous for people of color with each passing year.

They had to work harder now to prove what was possible, to disprove the perception in America and the world that black people could not govern themselves or order their lives in productive and civilized ways. He looked for his leather case by the door and checked it for the postcards and souvenirs he was bringing for the children. Glancing at the oval mirror set into the hall tree,[7] he straightened his customary bow tie, with its subtle stripe, and smoothed a hand over his close-cropped gray hair. His passport application, issued in January, described him thus:

Age: 42 years
Stature: 5' 11"
Forehead: Broad
Eyes: Brown
Nose: Straight
Mouth: Moustached
Chin: Round
Hair: Brown
Complexion: Fair
Face: Oval

The corners of his mouth curved a little at the thought of how those words could be used to define a man, especially a man of color. He opened the inside door and then the heavier front door to get a sense of the temperature and rainfall. It was only a short walk next door, but he knew he would catch it from the womenfolk if he did not at least carry an umbrella.[8]

It smelled like spring today, muddy and fragrant and green. Soon flowers would be bursting open in the soggy grass. On a morning like this, he felt the urgency of the new life in those buried bulbs. It reminded him of his boyhood on the farm in Columbus County. The flowers' bright bells would soon ring in the season of resurrection. He lifted a hand and smiled at the first few church members to arrive, all under their umbrellas. He stepped back inside to find his own.

Still thinking of the urgency of life and spring, he wondered how he could include these sentiments in the travel anecdotes and comments he was developing for White Rock, the Women's Missionary Auxiliary, and the upcoming Lott Carey and Baptist conventions on his calendar. He usually deviated a little from his notes depending on the group. Every gathering was different; every event had a unique energy. He had gotten more accustomed of late to overriding his general preference for remaining in the background in order to speak on occasions like these.[9] Ultimately his aim would always be to inspire and mobilize the people, to give them a sense of pride in their accomplishments and citizenship in the world. Now more than ever he hoped to strengthen their will to plant more seeds and bulbs to burst forth in the springs of their future.

His heart, as always, was with the children. There was only so much he could do for children abroad. Here at home he was constantly planning, fighting, and worrying for them. What kind of society would receive their potential as these children reached adulthood? How could he best prepare them for a life of fulfilling work, good health, and strong moral character? How could he instill in them a love for the nation that did not seem to love or even value them in return? It was a constant inner battle to teach self-reliance when time after time he was unable to promise basic safety or prosperity. All he could do was keep trying, with the help of his fellow entrepreneurs, to build and maintain this tenuous structure in Durham's Hayti, where life, liberty, and the pursuit of happiness could be a reality and not a distant dream, to build the relationships on both sides of town that would hold that structure in place.

He pulled on his overcoat, basking for a moment longer in the comforts of home, and considered the band of his hat to determine back from front. He could hear the household start to rattle and move upstairs. His morning reverie would have to end.

Hundreds of miles away, across an ocean and amid the chaos of the U.S.-occupied black sovereign nation of Haiti, a small missionary center would stand as a reminder that the world was bigger than Fayetteville Street, that his and White Rock's and the Lott Carey Foundation's relentlessness on behalf of the black race could bear distant fruit.[10] For these efforts, let the people say Amen, for it was they who had donated their hard-earned wages and were building something good that they would never directly benefit from themselves, something that was a vote of confidence in their race. They had accomplished this through prayer, organized hope, thrift, and mutual sacrifice. No matter what the ultimate outcome of such a project would be, it was an expression of hope and morality in a troubled world. Let them say Amen. Let them say it now and evermore. And then, let this good work continue here at home. Let the people be lifted up.

PART ONE *A Country Boy*

GENESIS

Then God said, Let us make human beings in our image,
in our likeness, so that they may rule over the fish in the sea
and the birds in the sky, over the livestock and all the wild
animals, and over all the creatures that move along the ground.
—*Genesis 1:26*

Aaron McDuffie Moore was born on September 6, 1863, a Sunday. The Moores and their extended family lived in Sandy Plain, a section of Welches Creek Township north of the town of Whiteville in Columbus County, a rural region of southeastern North Carolina.[1] Within a few years the neighborhood would acquire the name it bears today, Farmers Union, taken from the soon-to-be-established Freedmen's Bureau school, where a young Aaron would begin his formal education.[2]

The exact time and details of Aaron's birth are unknown since there is no birth certificate on record. He was officially part of the family of Israel Moore and Annie Eliza Spaulding Moore in the federal census of 1870 and listed then as age seven.[3] No doubt, at the time of his birth, his parents entered Aaron's name in the family Bible after his older sister Delphia and before his younger sister, Eliza, who would follow just a few years later. Aaron was the ninth of ten children, five boys and five girls.[4] In the Moore family, one didn't get to stay the baby very long.

In early September, the weather remains mild in that region of North Carolina, and the leaves on the pecan trees that stood on either side of the family farmhouse would have still worn their late summer green.[5] The year 1863 in North Carolina was one of violently wet weather, following a year of intense drought. It was probably a very muddy season in the already swampy Welches Creek, which was bordered by "White Marsh" and "Brown Marsh" to the south and east.[6] Grain crops had not done well, and so those who had stores to spare bartered them, and all were living as frugally as possible.[7]

It is hard to imagine today delivering a ninth child with no modern conveniences or medical assistance other than a midwife, and doing so almost every eighteen months of one's life since marriage. Barring any complications, it is unlikely Ann Eliza Moore labored long before welcoming this new son. A baby boy was always good news on a farm, even if, in the short term, another mouth to feed might have been a worry. She and her husband named him Aaron after the biblical Aaron, a gifted priest who became the voice of his people, the Israelites, and helped his brother Moses lead them out of slavery. This was a poetic name indeed for a baby boy whose father was named Israel and who was born the year that had begun with President Lincoln issuing the Emancipation Proclamation. That very night, September 6, near Charleston, South Carolina, the besieged Confederate army gave up Forts Wagner and Gregg, a battle that would give the black soldiers of the 54th Massachusetts Volunteer Infantry a place of honor in American history.[8]

Columbus County, home to the Moores, was formed in 1808 and named for Christopher Columbus; the area owes much of its early settlement to the huge groves of longleaf pines covering the county and almost all of North Carolina's piedmont and coastal plain. Pines were tapped for their sap, or resin, which was used to make rosin, tar, rubber, pitch, and turpentine. These made up the naval stores industry. Furthermore, because of the Cape Fear region's natural network of waterways, namely the Cape Fear and Lumber Rivers, the naval stores industry became a mainstay of the region's fortunes as early as colonial times. North Carolina at one time supplied the British navy with enough naval stores to enable England to sell the excess to other nations across Europe. After the Revolutionary War, this region of North Carolina continued to supply the new United States with naval stores, and refinery operations began to spring up along the rivers and in ports such as Wilmington. Turpentine was used to make waterproof cloth, was burned in lanterns, and was even used to cure skin ailments and constipation. Rosin was used primarily in soap, while tar and pitch were used to keep wood and ropes from rotting in wet weather or at sea. By the time the Civil War broke out, naval stores were the South's third largest export, and North Carolina supplied 97 percent of those products. The trees held fortunes in their veins for those who knew how to tap and maintain them.[9]

Turpentine farmers and distillers had to be skilled and tenacious. The season was long, stretching from May to November, and each part of the process was intense. The trunk of the longleaf pine contains a complex system of "resin canals or ducts," like the veins in an arm or a leg. When the tree reaches a certain age, these passages "become lined with a tissue, the epithelium, from which resin is secreted. . . . Resin is not sap. The epithelium cells manufacture resin only when required to protect the tree."[10] So the tree must be constantly and carefully wounded in order to be tapped. Workers tapped these mature trees each season with a V-shaped wound. They then carefully reopened the cut about every week and monitored it closely as the precious resin flowed into "boxes" from which workers "dipped" the resin, or "gum." Workers then delivered the resin to a refinery, where it was rendered into all of its various and useful forms. By the Civil War era, lighter-weight copper casks made the refining process easier to perform closer to the harvesting site, whereas refineries originally had been near docks or train depots. We know that residents in the Farmers Union community owned such refining tools.[11] On a side note, the same refining equipment was often repurposed for spirits. There are legends still told today of the good liquor made on the sly in Columbus County and how the quality of it might have helped keep the black community safe from white neighbors, soldiers of both armies, and any local government interference.[12]

The more precise and skilled a turpentine farmer's team was, the longer his grove would last and the longer his trees would give the sap that so many livelihoods depended on. The faster he worked, the more he harvested and the more trees he could maintain and benefit from. Even the most carefully tended trees eventually died from the constant bleeding, and many of the longleaf pines are now gone from the region for that reason. It was dirty, smelly, sticky work and mastered only with training, experience, and a stubborn will. North Carolina natives, in fact, earned the nickname "Tar Heels" because of the sticky black stains on their boots and their ability to "stick" to this kind of backbreaking work.[13]

Aaron's grandfather Benjamin Spaulding was legally enslaved until his official manumission in 1825,[14] and there is no record of his receiving any inheritance from his white father and slave master, Samuel Swindell Sr. Ben began to purchase land the very next year in 1826 and became a "Tar Heel" himself, rolling barrels of tar by hand (there were no roads) to the Whitehall Dock on the Cape Fear River. The labor and initiative of this one man became the original spark of the Spaulding family fortune and would make them free landowners, with family deeds on record dating from the early 1800s.[15]

Benjamin chose "Spaulding" as his last name at his manumission, spelled "Spawlding" in the court record. The most prevalent family myth is that the name Spaulding came from an incident with an ax handle during Ben's youth when his master/father "knocked him *sprawling*" for being insolent.[16] Another theory is that he chose the name of a naval stores dealer with whom he did business in Wilmington. Both stories are unsubstantiated. According to the research of more current family historians like Luke Alexander of the Benjamin and Edith Spaulding Descendants Association, it seems equally possible that Spaulding took his name from a dynamic abolitionist preacher who was very active in that area of North Carolina.

However it came to be his, Spaulding was the name Benjamin proudly offered to Edith Delphia Freeman, a Native American woman (Waccamaw Indian) whose father was a local landowner and who added considerably to the family property with her dowry. What can be seen clearly on record are six tracts of land totaling 870 acres acquired by Edith Freeman in the Sandy Plain (Farmers Union) area from 1811 to 1823.[17] As an heir of Abraham Freeman,[18] she likely inherited more as time went on.

In marrying Edith Freeman, Benjamin Spaulding gained not only a dowry but also a steadfast and hardworking partner with whom to build his farming dynasty. Nine children later (William, Emanuel, Armstead, Johnathan, Iver, Ann Eliza, Ben Jr., David, and Henry),[19] they had turned a primarily naval stores business into a thriving farm with beef cattle, hogs, cotton, corn, and gardens able to produce whatever they needed to put on the table. They had their own cotton gin, sawmill, and blacksmith shop.[20] An 1850 Farm Schedule Report describes just one farm, that of Ben's oldest, son William Spaulding, as containing "30 improved acres, 670 unimproved acres, value $700. Implements valued at $25. One horse, 6 milch cows. 1 ox. 6 other cattle. 19 sheep. 15 swine. Livestock valued at $156. 125 bushels, Indian corn. 400 lbs., rice. Tobacco, 20 lbs. wool, 10 bushels. peas and beans, 100 bushels. Irish potatoes, 15 lbs. butter, Household utensils valued at $10. Slaughtered animals valued at $75."[21]

The 1860 census reports that Benjamin Spaulding, age eighty-six, and "Eady" or Edith Spaulding, age seventy-three, were owners of land valued at $1,500 and had a personal fortune valued at $600 (nearly $20,000 today).[22] It is also worth noting that "Old Ben" Spaulding was known for having a forceful personality that gave not an inch for laziness or laxity. He also seems to have been illiterate, usually signing his name with an X.[23] Several of his children, however, not only could read and write but are listed in census records as teachers. The extraordinary record of achievement of the many who have descended from Ben and Edith Spaulding, such as Congressman George Henry White, Dr. Aaron McDuffie Moore,

Charles Clinton Spaulding, Asa Spaulding, Richard McDougald, Cornelius McDougald, and literally hundreds of others, speaks to the effect of this rigorous environment and the important place that education held in the family's ambitions.[24]

When Benjamin Spaulding lay on his deathbed in 1862, one could argue he was dying freer and more accomplished than many men of his time of any race.[25] Around him stretched a Farmers Union that was "10 miles from east to west, five miles north and south, covering sixty-five thousand acres of land ... all owned by colored people."[26]

When Aaron was born in 1863, the family farm still depended largely upon turpentine-related work. The Civil War had increased demand for all turpentine goods, and the harvesting and refining workforce had dwindled as white farmers got drafted. The slaves of those white farmers fled the area after emancipation was announced or, in some cases, fought for the Union.[27] The pine groves remained for those who could tend to them and keep them yielding their precious "gum."

Even as Farmers Union and the Spaulding family were growing, Columbus County was not spared the horrors or the hardships of the war. The county lost many men to fighting and numerous women and children to disease and hunger. "Emancipation" was a word spoken with awe, hoped for in prayer, and paid for with blood. The Port of Wilmington and the Cape Fear River, not to mention the Goldsboro railroad line—making up the network through which the turpentine trade operated—became important targets for the Union during the early part of 1865, which must surely have affected the fortunes of Columbus County families, including that of the Moores.[28]

On April 17, 1865, two days after President Lincoln was assassinated, Confederate general Joseph E. Johnston and Union general William T. Sherman sat down at the Bennitt (Bennett) Place farmhouse near Durham, North Carolina, a town that would become Aaron McDuffie Moore's future home, and by April 26 they had signed the Confederacy's largest troop surrender, effectively ending the Civil War.[29] Aaron was eighteen months old.

As the national struggle that would be called Reconstruction began, the whirling rhythms of farm life wrapped themselves around baby Aaron. Little by little, things began to have names, and rules of conduct were made clear. He gathered up language in the ears that stood out from his head like question marks. He learned to use simple tools and began, like all children, to ask "Why?"

On a farm, every seed planted and every act of animal husbandry forges a human-to-animal, land-to-creature bond of interdependence. The security, food, and power that animals and plants provide reassure caregivers of their connection to the cycles of life. The latter half of the 1800s, particularly in the South and certainly in North Carolina, witnessed a shift in consciousness from the mindset of the farm to that of industry. Many of the minds that would move science and business forward in those years, such as Thomas Edison, Alexander Graham Bell, and Henry Ford, had rural beginnings. That farm-to-city transition held within it the seeds of our current culture. In that massive shift toward industrial progress, it can be argued that a certain degree of empathy was lost along with that connection with the natural world that the farm demands in exchange for survival.

These shifts in empathy and social consciousness both propelled and obstructed Aaron Moore's life path. In fact, it often seemed as if opportunity's ladder constructed its next rung mere moments before Aaron's foot stepped onto it, only to dissolve behind him as this unique window in history closed. But this phenomenon did not occur to Aaron alone; rather, it happened to a generation of black men and women who lived in a nation that briefly invested in their ability to contribute to society as emancipated and, ideally, equal citizens. The years between Aaron's birth and his entry into medical school in 1885 were some of the most complex yet promising in American history for a young black person. It is hard to believe now, in light of the failed experiment that was Reconstruction, that at that moment, great hopes seemed achievable for those of color who could and would strive for them. Young Aaron saw cousins and schoolmates who were just five or ten years older than him accomplish amazing things through education, respectability, and good connections. As an adult, Aaron would relentlessly try to hold this window of opportunity open and assist several generations that came after him in their education. As a young professional educated during Reconstruction, Aaron would witness the mechanisms of government begin to form in obstruction to the very success that his own upbringing, experience, hard work, and character had proven possible. That feeling of friction, where once he had felt freedom, would be flint striking on steel for Aaron McDuffie Moore and certainly would stoke the enduring fire that drove the deeds he is known for. His pace seemed ambitious from the first, as if there would never be enough time for him to learn and do and heal and build.

For now, however, we will just wonder: When did Aaron's quiet yet tenacious personality emerge? Was it in reaction to the sensory onslaught of his massive family and the relentless engine of activity on the farm? Was it because of his fascination with the achievements of his peers? When did his small fingers first reach for the pages of the family Bible? When was he able to let his curious mind dream or wander off on adventures, and where would he go in them? When did he begin to sense the urgency of each next step, those next rungs of his personal ladder, as they began to appear?

2

SANDY PLAIN

Two churches formed the early pillars of the spiritual and social life of Farmers Union: Rehobeth AME Zion Church and Sandy Plain Missionary Baptist Church. Oral tradition places Sandy Plain as the older, being founded circa 1840, while the earliest deed on record for Rehobeth is dated June 1859. Sandy Plain is listed as a part of the Lake Waccamaw Missionary Baptist Association, a collection of churches in Columbus County from 1884 to 1906.[1] The Moore family (and young Aaron) was associated with Sandy Plain Missionary Baptist Church and the greater Spaulding family with Rehobeth AME Zion Church.

It is simply impossible to separate the life and achievements of Aaron McDuffie Moore from the influence, inspiration, and support of the Negro Baptist church, starting with his home church of Sandy Plain. In stating this, however, we must also recognize the function of the church in black communities of this era and acknowledge the gravitational force and the organizational and institutional progress that both the Negro Baptist and the African Methodist Episcopal churches were able to foster, especially during Reconstruction. In that pivotal era, in which black communities lacked any unified system of social organization that was focused solely and benevolently on them, the Negro Baptist church and churches in general became a kind of central nervous system of infrastructure and social activism. The church environment fostered not only spirituality but also democracy. It made everyone who attended into a brother or a sister and provided a powerful platform for black leadership and ideas in the context of a regular gathering.

The Negro Baptist church was the result of the active inclusion, baptism, and religious instruction of enslaved blacks by the white Baptist churches of the master class in the early 1700s. Baptist churches were some of the earliest arenas in which abolition was preached.[2] Initially, white Baptist churches allowed blacks to attend and sit in separate sections on Sundays. Blacks sometimes had meetings in which their own people were allowed to lead them in prayer. While whites valued the respectability and moral character that they believed westernized religion encouraged in their enslaved populations, they did not, by and large, wish to worship simultaneously, so they allowed Negro Baptist churches to form around 1773–75.[3] After the formation of many Negro Baptist churches and the rise of black pastors and missionaries such as Lott Carey, whose work in Africa became the basis for many missions abroad, further organization of Negro Baptist churches into associations became necessary. The American Baptist Home Mission Society, a primarily Northern organization founded in 1832, was a powerful voice in the abolitionist movement.[4] When emancipation was finally declared, "the abolition of slavery as an American institution resulted in the nationwide formation of . . . local Associations, State conventions and larger groups. In 1866 a national convention, 'The Consolidated American Baptist Missionary Convention,' was organized. Its chief work was in the South and confined to the period of Reconstruction."[5] Aaron Moore was three years old when this last convention formed, and he was about to enter school.

One of the pillars of black education during Reconstruction in North Carolina was the Baptist Sunday school system. Sunday school was a weekly supplement to the schoolroom and an opportunity for both children and adults to become literate. In the schoolroom, books like *The Blue-Backed Speller* and *The New England Primer* were prized possessions. These schoolbooks also contained the catechism and were designed to go hand-in-hand with Bible studies on Sunday. In farming communities like Aaron's, where the school year was short, Sunday school was a regular weekly haven for learning and reconnecting to studious habits.

As the need to unite all of these Sunday schools under a more standardized curriculum became obvious, a county convention of chosen leaders and educators began to meet once a year around 1870 (the year Aaron turned seven). This convention evolved into the North Carolina State Convention and finally the North Carolina Missionary Baptist Sunday School Convention. The organization dispatched lecturers and monitors, called "Colporters," who were, essentially, mobile religious librarians. Funded by the American Baptist Home Mission Society, they traveled the state year-round and distributed standardized learning materials.

Students and adults who excelled at Bible study could earn diplomas and then teach classes themselves. We know that Aaron began to teach Sunday school in his early teens and also taught in his local school. Sunday school was important to him throughout his life, and it is easy to imagine that it was in the Sunday school environment that he first began to love learning.

The Negro church during Reconstruction became more than a place for worship; it offered human comfort and social services, mutual uplift, political information, self-improvement, literacy, and entrepreneurial encouragement. The church took on the task of restoring the self-esteem of a newly emancipated race through a powerful recipe of education, respectability, and service. Young Aaron Moore would benefit greatly from the success of, in particular, Baptist educational organizations.

We have not found any directly relevant accounts from the 1860s of what Aaron's early life was like, but we do have a detailed account from Aaron's second cousin Asa Spaulding, who was born in 1902 and grew up on a farm very like the Moore homestead in Farmers Union. Thirty years probably brought only minor changes to the rhythms of daily life on the farm, so it is worth diving into this vivid account and imagining Aaron's boyhood as having been very similar.

GROWING UP ON A FARM 1902–1918 IN COLUMBUS COUNTY
I was born on July 22, 1902, on the family farm.... Nearly all of the residents of Columbus County were farmers. Most of the families owned their homes and land, and the entire family helped with the farm work.... Everybody knew everybody else, and the children were raised to be obedient, polite and industrious. Whenever the temptation arose to stray from this childhood code of ethics, we could be sure that some parent or other relative would notice and set us straight again.... Bible reading was encouraged. My grandfather, John Wesley Spaulding, Superintendent of our Sunday school at Rehobeth AME Zion Church, offered ten cents to anyone in Sunday school who would read the Bible through.... Ten cents was a significant amount to a child.

Children reared in rural areas develop a sense of responsibility early because they are given chores to do from the time they are four or five years old.... My brother Fuller and I got up as early as four o'clock in the morning in the summer. We were responsible for feeding the mules, the cows, the hogs and chickens to get the farm day started.

We started to plow at sunrise.... We didn't have eight-hour days; they were from sunrise to sunset, or colloquially, "from can see to can't see." ... We raised corn, cotton, tobacco, cattle and hogs, and a good crop of scuppernong grapes.

We worked six days a week and went to church every Sunday.

The Sunday gatherings also provided opportunity for social contacts and visits. My father gave my older brother and me Saturdays off from our regular chores to make our own money and develop a sense of responsibility. He gave me an acre on which to plant cotton. ... I also teamed up with my brother cutting cross-ties for railroad track supports.... We'd load them on the wagon and take them to Rosindale for sale. Rosindale was on the railroad line,[6] in the turpentine producing area.... Rosin was produced in the area from the distillation of turpentine. My father had a distillery ... and he also produced pine tar in tar kilns, which he sold.

Sometimes we could mix work with play. At community corn shuckings, we would shuck bushel after bushel of corn while our picnic of chicken, sausages, spareribs and ears of corn roasted. We had persimmon and apple cider in the well keeping cool. When we took a break from corn shucking we would "eat, drink and be merry." The adults would engage in telling "tall tales" as some of them drank wine and cider....

In our farming community, school opened about the middle of October after all the crops were harvested. We started plowing for planting the next crops in late February.... The result was a very short school term, averaging about four-and-one-half months each year.[7]

From this vivid account we can extrapolate the daily rhythms of what must have governed Aaron's early boyhood as well. Thirty years earlier, amid the chaos of Reconstruction, times were probably a bit leaner for Aaron, less organized, and less prosperous.

Rehobeth AME Zion Church (the same as mentioned in Asa's account) was indeed the site of the original Freedmen's Bureau school where Aaron spent his earliest classroom years. Asa's account mentions that the two churches regularly mingled their activities, so there was no exclusivity about which church Aaron attended versus where he went to school.[8]

The community that Aaron grew up in was referred to as "Sandy Plain" between roughly 1860 and 1900. Therefore, Aaron would have called his home by the same name as his church for half of his life.[9]

THE COUNTY SCHOOL
Early Education and the Influence of Family, Politics, and Reconstruction

Autumn must have felt extra-special to Aaron as a boy because it started with his birthday, was full of the festivities and treats of the harvest season, and, best of all, marked the beginning of the school session. The leaves turning in the oak, maple, and pecan trees of Sandy Plain would usher in the short and coveted season of learning with rustling red and gold. The chill in the air after the long humid summer must have been a relief, as was switching the focus of his days from physical labor to the labor of learning. Aaron probably started school at five or six years old, and we know that he expressed very early that he wanted to be a teacher.[1] This was not an unusual wish for a boy who was a diligent student, which, by all accounts and indications, he was. The black community regarded teachers as a blessing, and to be an educator was the loftiest social goal anyone could have, besides being a reverend. It is worth including a few more of Asa Spaulding's memories at this time because we know he attended the very same school that Aaron did. Through Asa's eyes we can picture what that short but intense school term in the autumn and winter months might have been like for young Aaron.

> The courses offered in our one room Farmers Union School[2] were limited mostly to reading, writing, arithmetic, spelling and grammar, with some emphasis on geography and history. All classes were in the same room with studying going on at the same time class recitations were being conducted; you can imagine how much studying one could do with another class reciting in another part of the room. Beginning in third grade we had spelling contests with two teams at school. You were given three tries, and if you missed it after three times, you had to sit down. I had a reputation in the whole community for being a good student. I finished seventh grade at sixteen because of the short school terms.[3]

Learning was not an easy task in a one-room schoolhouse. It required dedication and focus. It is likely that in those leaner years, just after the Civil War, even more discomforts were present: vermin, not enough fuel to stay warm, fevers, sickness, and hunger.

We can also infer from Asa's account that the spirit of competition was used liberally as motivation to learn as well as inspiration to become known in the community as a good student. Other children who had excelled before and earned the respect of the community for their accomplishments could provide quite an aspirational example. Many of them were turpentine farmers as well. One of these older high achievers— and therefore a likely idol for Aaron Moore—was George Henry White, Aaron's older third cousin, who was born in 1852.

We know a bit about George's early schooling from his excellent and well-researched biography by Benjamin R. Justesen, and it would be logical to assume that a young George may have even taught some of the first classes that Aaron attended. George White's biography shares the following regarding his first teachers and the location of the school that Aaron almost certainly attended:

> The first [teacher] was W. B. Duncan, a white man who operated a subscription school in Sandy Plain before 1869 [notice he refers to Farmers Union as "Sandy Plain"]; Duncan's school may have been located on the Rehobeth Church site, which, according to county records, housed a series of such schools....
>
> George White may also have attended classes at the new Freedmen's Bureau school that operated in the Welches Creek area. ... The Rehobeth Freedmen's School was open under the supervision of John W. Spaulding of Rosindale [Aaron's uncle] ... who was later to become an active Republican leader in Bladen County. According to his 1869 report to the Wilmington Bureau office, Spaulding taught thirty-five black students that term, all but one under sixteen years of age [Aaron would have been six] and two-thirds of them male, but none of their names were listed. George White would have been nearly seventeen that fall.[4]

It seems likely that a nearly seventeen-year-old George H. White was the one student listed in that class "over sixteen" and that young Aaron would have also been present and beginning the early grades. Asa Spaulding's account says it took him until age sixteen to finish the seven grades offered in those short school terms. We also know that schools often asked talented students to teach or assist in teaching the other children; we know from family accounts that his own school asked Aaron to teach and that he did so for several years.[5]

Thirty-five students is a large number for a small one-room school, and it must have been a lively scene. It is inspiring to think that George H. White may have taught or assisted a six-year-old Aaron with some of his earliest lessons. At the very least, George was a boy to look up to throughout Aaron's early education, one with that coveted reputation of being a good student. He would go on to become not only one of the most powerful orators of his time but also a prosperous lawyer, an educator, a school principal, and ultimately a pivotal U.S. congressman.[6]

Another important educator in Aaron's family was William Luther Moore (1857–1930), a first cousin and the son of Israel Moore Sr.'s brother James Moore and Caroline Spaulding Moore. W. L. Moore started his teaching career in Columbus County in 1874. This would have been when Aaron Moore was around the age of eleven and still in the Rehobeth school. If W. L. Moore did not instruct Aaron directly at Sandy Plain, then he was yet another cousin who was teaching in the area and may have further inspired Aaron Moore to dream of also being a teacher. W. L. Moore later became a reverend and is credited with being one of the founders of the Croatan Normal School (contributing $200 of his own money) and the principal there from 1887 to 1890. The Lumbee Tribe at this time was also referred to by the Croatan name. W. L. Moore dedicated his life to the education and service of the Lumbee and Croatan community. The Croatan Normal School became the University of North Carolina at Pembroke, and to this day Moore Hall, which houses the Department of Music at the university, is named in Reverend W. L. Moore's honor. His example is further evidence of the dedication many in Aaron Moore's family showed to education and public service.[7]

It is important to note here the political climate that provided the setting and impetus for Aaron's early schooling. The Freedmen's Bureau — a Reconstruction-era organization established by the U.S. Congress on March 3, 1865, akin to a separate branch of government for emancipated blacks — and the churches combined their efforts for a short but intense period of time to protect, uplift, and educate.[8] Children like young Aaron Moore and George H. White, as well as many adults who wished to learn, stood to benefit. Education for the emancipated was deemed a national emergency of sorts. No party could successfully argue that the masses of former slaves and blacks in general did not deserve or could not be "improved" by education, especially when it led to a better workforce or a more advantageous voting bloc. The idea of blacks needing to improve themselves in order to be acceptable citizens was especially popular in the North, from which flowed much of the educational philanthropy. In the South, the attitude was more one of disbelief that the emancipated could learn. If they indeed could, then the more pressing questions concerned who would pay for it, what the content and political timbre of the curriculum would be, and where this schooling would take place. These questions became major points of contention in Reconstruction-era politics and have continued into the present day.

Abraham Lincoln, hailed in hindsight as the Great Emancipator, was in reality a reluctant one. His priority was always the preservation of the Union, and he finally came to believe that a moral cause such as emancipation was the only way to keep his abolitionist party's support and suppress the rebellion.[9] After emancipation was proclaimed in 1863 and Lincoln was assassinated in 1865 by a Confederate sympathizer, two political parties picked up where the bloody Civil War had left off: the Radical Republicans (the party of Lincoln, abolition, and the North) and the Southern Democrats (the party of the South and the plantation owners). President Andrew Johnson, himself a Southerner from a slave-owning family in North Carolina, moved hastily but vaguely into Reconstruction. Johnson significantly lowered the requirements for readmitting a Southern state to the Union and considering that state "loyal." He also refused to excommunicate defeated Confederate leaders from politics and instead issued many pardons. Under Johnson a state had to ratify the Thirteenth Amendment (abolishing slavery) to be readmitted to the Union but no more, and little caution was taken in rebuilding the newly readmitted Southern state governments.[10] In the wake of their defeat, many Southern states felt demoralized, driven by racism, ruined economically, and deeply afraid of retaliation by the emancipated. Because of these more lax Johnsonian terms, many Southern states hastily filled public offices with Confederate loyalists and generals and soon instituted a new system of laws, dubbed the "Black Codes," to govern the black population. Those codes, in many Southern states, added up to a new and thinly veiled government-sanctioned form of slavery. They also did not include black suffrage. In early 1866, North Carolina instituted a set of such laws, also called the "Black Codes." Though North Carolina's codes were milder than in many of the Deep South states, they restricted the movement of black people within and beyond state lines, banned interracial marriages, and made ownership of firearms by people of color nearly impossible.[11]

Frederick Douglass took it upon himself to remind Northerners why they had fought and died to abolish slavery in all of its forms and led a blistering campaign for black suffrage in the North. President Johnson argued that black suffrage should be left up to the states to decide. When Johnson was informed that many states in the South now had a black population that could change the political landscape, he expressed a worry that they would ally themselves with white elites and turn on poor whites. This would become a popular litany of white fear: that education, citizenship, and land ownership would lead to political power and representation, causing blacks to get "above themselves" and seek to "dominate" and disenfranchise their poor white neighbors.[12] Echoes of this racist belief would reemerge in 1898, after World War I, in 1932, and even in present-day politics.

In 1866 Congress passed the Fourteenth Amendment, which guaranteed equal protection under the law, and kept alive the Freedmen's Bureau. Washington deployed troops to the South to enforce and protect this new plan for Reconstruction and invited blacks in Southern states to send delegates to the state conventions, in which they would redraft their state constitutions. The new constitutions had to include black suffrage, or the state would not be seated in Congress.

In March 1867 the Reconstruction Act was passed. The act divided the South into five districts and put them under military rule, which dissolved nearly all state governments in the South. The act required North Carolina (along with all Southern states except Tennessee) to elect a delegation to redraft its constitution and to include in it the Fourteenth Amendment and the Fifteenth Amendment, which granted black men the right to vote. Freedmen, like those in Aaron's family, and teachers and members of the clergy were in particular made welcome to participate in the politics of their region.[13]

The Ku Klux Klan was also founded during this time period in Pulaski, Tennessee. Established as a secretive terrorist force, it was bent on subverting all military-enforced Reconstruction activities. Its focus was, above all, to intimidate blacks (and Northern sympathizers) through violence into not exercising their right to vote.[14] Black people, however, still bravely showed up and were involved in the political rebuilding of their home states.

By 1867's fall elections, which would choose delegates to reform the existing constitution, more than 70,000 new black Republican voters had registered. The result was a change in the majority makeup of Congress to Radical Republican, suddenly turning Johnson into a lame duck, and in 1868 he was impeached. The Radical Republican–held Congress swiftly drafted a new plan for "Radical" Reconstruction and also moved to ban any high-ranking Confederate officials from holding Southern office for several years.[15]

In North Carolina, the convention assembled in Raleigh on January 14, 1868, and adjourned on March 17, 1868. The Republican Party, now including fifteen black delegates, secured 107 of the 120 seats in the convention.[16] When they adjourned, blacks and whites, working together, had drafted a new North Carolina Constitution. North Carolina officially reentered the Union, and its Republican representatives took their seats in Congress.[17]

Aaron Moore's family participated diligently and prominently in this era of political change. As a result of the new constitution, which granted black men the vote and the right to serve in public office, on March 23, 1868, John Spaulding (Aaron's uncle) became a Republican candidate for the Bladen County Board of Commissioners. He was elected, confirmed, and installed.

County commissioner was a tremendously significant post, because the new state constitution had dismantled the county courts, which historically had been under the control of wealthy whites. The new system of elected commissions called for five commissioners per county. Aaron's uncle John Spaulding was the first person of color to serve in this new system of county commissioners in Bladen County.[18]

This was indeed a proud day for the extended Spaulding family and for black people and Native Americans all over Bladen County. At last they had representation in the courts that had been controlling their affairs for a century. Aaron was just four in 1868 and was probably learning his first chores on the farm. The excitement and gravitas of this event must have been evident on some level, even to a small child.

Political activism soon made landfall even closer to home. In 1872, Israel Moore, Aaron's father, was elected chairman of the Columbus County Republican Party. Aaron was now eight years old and well into his early schooling. Perhaps he was even able to read his father's name in the newspaper. It was printed in the *Weekly Carolina Era* as follows: "The Republicans of Columbus County assembled in convention at the schoolhouse in Whiteville on Monday, March 26, 1872. The convention was called to order by B. J. Spaulding.... A permanent organization was effected by the choice of Israel Moore for chairman and J. W. Spaulding for Secretary."[19] It is also interesting to note that this article lists George H. White's father, Wiley F. White, as part of the committee on resolutions. This evidence shows that Aaron Moore's father and George White's father were associates and were active together in local politics.[20]

During the late 1860s, after the attempt to integrate white universities was largely unsuccessful, mostly Northern philanthropists and churches founded black universities with teacher training, medical, law, and divinity schools. There were several lines of thought: segregationists wanted blacks to take care of their own, assimilationists wanted to "improve" blacks through white-led education, and antiracists wanted to eliminate racism and promote equal citizenship under the law. The assimilationist educators favored the classical/European model of university study; those who excelled at this kind of study could join the "higher" professions like law and medicine. Segregationists tended to favor technical schools and the allocation of black labor to the rural farming areas or blue-collar labor.[21] Regardless of philosophy, massive efforts backed by the Freedmen's Bureau, private donors, and the will of Radical Reconstruction Republicans were made to address the need to educate and prepare these recently recognized citizens for a new kind of life. Very quickly the governing bodies in the South began to better reflect their black populations. By the 1870s, black judges could preside in court, black lawyers could argue cases, and black mayors, congressmen, and governors began to serve.

As Reconstruction-era government began to be more integrated, the two political parties became more deeply entrenched. This time in the South is referred to as the "Carpetbag Government" era, and many of the social programs put in place during this brief time were clouded by controversy at best and tarred with the brush of corruption at worst.[22]

Southern Democrats—those of the former Confederate planter class—largely opposed all social services for blacks, any government-sponsored or integrated education, and the vote for blacks. They believed the Northern-run government of a forcibly reformed union needed to stay out of their business and let the states self-govern. They also feared an organized retaliation ("Negro Domination") for a century of slavery from this new group of suddenly equal citizens under the law.

Radical Republicans included Southern blacks and freedmen (families like Aaron's) along with many in the North and the majority of whites who were newly arrived in the South, dubbed "carpetbaggers." The Radical Republican Party was in favor of social services for all, equal suffrage, reparations, the seizure of Confederate goods and land to pay war debts, and a government big enough to represent and protect all under the law and to enforce such changes in the Southern states. The battle for what was going to define the expectations of citizenship for all in this newly mended nation had begun. It is easily argued that to this day the question of who can expect true equality under the Constitution has never been resolved. For Aaron and the children of his immediate community, however, it looked like the brightest future imaginable.

The new and energized bloc of black voters in the South was suddenly very important. On the national scale, the recently enfranchised could tip the balance between Southern Democrats and Radical Republicans and decide who would get to sit at the tables of power. As long as blacks were in the majority—and in some former slave states, they outnumbered whites three to one—blacks could sway the vote, and Radical Reconstruction would continue regardless of the voting demographics in the North. Such a situation was deeply alarming to Southern Democrats, who saw their accustomed positions of power blocked and their traditional way of life facing extinction. Vigilante attempts at black voter suppression by the expanding KKK increased.[23]

In 1868, the newly elected president, Ulysses S. Grant, a former Union general, was strongly allied with the Radical Republican agenda, and the hope was that he would make sure that the progress of the nation toward Reconstruction stayed on track. He used federal troops aggressively to enforce voting rights and to protect the freedoms of black citizens in the Southern states most prone to conflict. This particular act of government-funded policing galled the Southern Democratic Party profoundly. Southern conservatives chafed under the new and forcibly policed mandates. All they could do was make it too expensive to lay siege to their way of life. The brief trend of racial progress started to crumble under the bureaucratic blockage of Southern Democrat conservatives. Radical Republican control of state and federal legislatures would hold on only until 1871. The Radical Republican Party was fracturing as a Liberal Republican agenda began emerging. Even after trying to legislatively ban the KKK and protect the black vote in Congress, the Radical Republican support eroded.[24]

Aaron Moore, age twelve, was just finishing the curriculum in his Sandy Plain school in 1876 when a Democratic conservative won the governorship and swiftly redrafted the North Carolina Constitution to prohibit interracial marriages and end all integration in public schools. White lawmakers were immediately put back in power throughout the State, and although blacks still had the vote, the lack of representation was a tremendous setback. Many who could not gain enough financial foothold to own property were forced into usurious farming relationships with white landowners, a new kind of slavery.[25] The several generations of landownership in Aaron Moore's family made for a distinct advantage during this period.

The resegregation of schools probably did not affect Aaron personally since his area had already instituted black-run schools for black children, but it may have been discussed at home, in church, or even in the schoolroom. Violent intimidation, lynching, and the burning of churches and property by the KKK was on the rise, and violent retaliation would have been part of the consciousness of those like Israel Moore and John Spaulding who were active in politics. Power in North Carolina quickly concentrated in Raleigh and funneled back into wealthy white hands. Reconstruction was in a downward spiral in North Carolina and throughout the United States.

The Tilden/Hayes election of 1876 was the tipping point for the momentum of Reconstruction at the federal level. Rutherford B. Hayes, the Republican who had chaired the board of the educational fund that granted W. E. B. Du Bois his studies in Berlin, won the popular vote. However, the electoral vote was complicated by violence at the polls in Southern states. After a delegation formed to resolve this issue, the Southern Democrats "granted" Hayes the presidency. He would serve as commander in chief until 1881 in return for removal of all federal troops from the South and an end to Reconstruction. The deal was struck, and with it the Fourteenth and Fifteenth Amendments all but died, along with the new nation imagined by Lincoln and his abolitionist party.[26]

How then did this political landscape in the South roll out a carpet of what could be called opportunity for young Aaron? It was during that precise window of time when hope was highest and progress seemed surest that Aaron attended his first and arguably most formative years of school. His teachers and the older students he looked up to, such as his cousin George Henry White and his own family members, were evidence that there was hope for those who showed themselves able to learn, participate, and strive for status in their world. His unique and self-sufficient farm community upbringing coupled with the engagement of his mentors in the politics of change arguably gave this young mind a new kind of horizon to aim for. The precarious but real security his landowning family enjoyed and their dedication to education enabled Aaron to take the time away from the farm to study.

Aaron's expectations as a teenager and as a young man were higher than those held by anyone in his family before him, and his education was by and large presided over by those, both black and white, who fervently believed in advancing his race to equal status in society. By the time he encountered segregationist policies and the plight of his people in urban life along with the disenfranchisement that was beginning to degrade the hopes of his race, Aaron Moore had acquired the exact tools and resilient attitude he would need to be of assistance. His moorings, rooted firmly in his farming origins, informed by his education, buoyed by his talent for optimism, and, most of all, elevated by his faith, would hold him firmly as he was tested. His fervent mission would become to take the optimism and lofty ideals of his Reconstruction-era education and recreate it for as many generations as he could personally reach.

Those few months of school from October to February were precious, and Moore's gratitude for these first encounters with education and their vital importance to his life would guide him in perpetuity. They made him aspire to dedicate his life to teaching. The normal course would be his next step in accomplishing that goal and would lead the adolescent Aaron Moore to encounter a still more influential mentor: Professor David P. Allen.

NORMAL SCHOOL
Lumberton and Fayetteville

4

Normal school, also called teachers college or teacher-training college,
[is an] institution for the training of teachers. One of the first schools
so named, the École Normale Supérieure ("Normal Superior School"),
was established in Paris in 1794. Based on various German exemplars,
the school was intended to serve as a model for other teacher-training
schools. —Encyclopedia Britannica

After completing the limited curriculum of his school in Columbus
County, and after three years of learning just how much he still didn't
know as a junior country schoolmaster, Aaron McDuffie Moore was at last
on his way to a legitimate teaching certificate.

Professor David P. Allen, who had briefly taught at the Sandy Plain
Rehobeth School in Welches Creek in 1870 before founding the Whittin
Normal School in Lumberton, had carefully mentored Aaron's cousins
George H. White and William Luther Moore. Young Aaron, now a teen-
ager, took his three years of wages from teaching and farmwork and pre-
pared to follow in his cousins' footsteps with Allen at Whittin Normal
School.[1]

Lumberton was only about thirty-five miles from the Moore family
farm, but it might as well have been an ocean away.[2] He was, for the first
time, to live on his own, far from his cocoon of farm labor, watchful eyes,
and familiar faces. He may have been apprehensive, but a boy who had
studied as hard as he had and who loved learning must have also been
elated. Lumberton was a significantly more cosmopolitan environment
than the farm. Aaron would need to acquire city manners and dress every
day like a young man of learning and not of toil.

We know from both George H. White's and W. L. Moore's documented
experiences that Professor Allen boarded a large number of young men
in his own home. Allen had nine children of his own and was able to
accommodate at least an additional dozen students at a time, so either
the house must have been massive or the living quarters very close. The

quality of education that Allen offered was commended by the U.S. Bureau of Education, but it also came at a price.[3] Aaron Moore had been making a teacher's wages in Sandy Plain for a few years prior and could still do so in the summer, along with farmwork, to support his own education. The Moore family likely also contributed. Families could pay for schooling with cash but also with produce, grain, and meat (sometimes starting years before the student would attend), so it is likely that the Moore family sent along various contributions to supplement what young Aaron could himself provide.[4]

Mary Ellen Moore Dial, in a 1969 interview, remembered her father, William Luther Moore, talking about his time under Allen's tutelage in the 1870s, possibly at the same time or just after George H. White's experience. (The interviewer was her son, Dr. Adolph L. Dial, and he designated her responses with an *N* for Mrs. N. H. Dial.)

D: Will you tell me about this teacher, D. P. Allen, in Lumberton? Moore's teacher?

N: Well, he was an intelligent and nice man. They boarded at his home.

D: They boarded at his home and he taught them there?

N: Yes, that's right. Had to do that paying his education.

D: You told me a little anecdote about how he would read the newspaper at the table when it was mealtime. Tell me about that.

N: Well he'd say, "Boys listen now, this is important." And it would be important.... They got a newspaper, *Robesonian*, and he would draw their attention. He was an intelligent man ...

D: Why was he trying to draw their attention at mealtime?

N: ... I reckon one thing is it was a good way to get them together at the table.

D: So they wouldn't eat too much you told me. That was a good way of conserving food.[5]

This pleasant scene speaks to the wit and presence of mind it must have taken to inspire and educate this house full of young minds even while at dinner, still with a wily eye on the budget and the portion sizes.

North Carolina's educational systems, especially where people of color were concerned, were certainly in flux. After the effort initially put forth by the Freedmen's Aid Societies and various Northern philanthropists, educators, and charities, the enormity of the black school-age population began to exhaust both their resources and their enthusiasm. Resentment was growing toward Radical Republicans in general by this time, and white lawmakers accused Northern white teachers of indoctrinating black children in the schools. The black population was simultaneously becoming weary and distrustful of answering to any kind of white guidance, even in the classroom. An unlikely agreement ensued between Southern whites and Southern blacks that it was time for the "Yankee schoolmarms" to go on home and for black teachers to educate black children in their own separate schools. Normal schools—to train a new generation of black teachers and carefully shape their curriculum—gained the support of state government and private and religious philanthropy.[6]

A few committed Northern men and women stayed and founded universities such as Fisk University, Shaw University, Pembroke University, and Fayetteville State University. Some of these institutions began as normal schools.

Normal schools had existed for white teachers in the United States and abroad since before the Civil War. The newly imagined normal schools for aspiring black educators during Reconstruction, however, were to be at the mercy of their own evolution. Institutions created, argued over, and discarded curriculums according to the politics of the region in which each was based. This conflict played out in funding or the lack thereof. Many normal schools were in session only in the summer months and used the facilities of existing college campuses. Some used churches and schoolhouses or any large meeting structure whenever allowed. A few fortunate normal schools had their own dedicated buildings, often built by the students themselves. All of the schools depended heavily on their communities for housing students from out of town and for food, maintenance, and operating costs. Chief among the philanthropic organizations responsible for educational infrastructure in North Carolina and the South was the ubiquitous American National Baptist Convention. Wherever funds could be found, a huge part of a black educational institution's job was fund-raising to maintain these far-from-luxurious facilities.

The fund-raising entreaties of Professor Allen, addressed to a gathering of New England teachers on July 9, 1879, directly illustrate the black educator's experience:

> Ladies and Gentlemen,
> It affords me great pleasure to present my case before you. I graduated from the State Normal School at Westfield, Mass., in the class of '71 [this puts him in Welches Creek on his first school

assignment and for one term]. In '72 I went to Lumberton, N.C., where I opened that year a public school. I found the attainment of the teachers of both races in our community so low that the Superintendent of Public Instruction had ordered a higher grade of certificates throughout the state. This deprived our county of every colored teacher and of nearly half the whites, so that after two years work in the county there was not a colored person in the county that could teach the people, and not more than three hundred children out of a school population of 3,000 were receiving any instruction whatever. In the years '74 and '75 I was moving from district to district in the county, teaching in public schools. A few young men followed me from district to district and thus prepared themselves for teaching. In the year '76 I organized a Normal class of half a dozen, all of whom received certificates to teach. In the year '77 this number reached a dozen, and in '78 it reached nineteen. This year the number has reached twenty-six. Last year the report of the County Board of Education shows twenty-two teachers in the county, all of whom have been sent out from the school in which I teach; and instead of the 300 children taught the first year, I found on going through last year that there were about 2,000 children taught. This Normal School has been regularly organized this summer with classes formed and a course of study the same as that pursued at Westfield.... We have no schoolhouse in our county. Most of the schools are taught in the churches, which are all poorly built. In the town where I live I have taught for seven years in churches.... I suppose none of you have taught where there was no place to teach in; I suppose none of you have taught where the people thought only a spelling book was necessary to teach everything. That is where I have taught—where there is no good comfortable house, and no good books.[7]

From Professor Allen's timeline above, we can guess that he met young Aaron Moore in 1870 in Sandy Plain along with George H. White and W. L. Moore. George must have been one of the "young men" who followed him "from district to district" to gain teaching experience, and then perhaps they were joined by W. L. Moore. As we know from Mary Dial's account, W. L. joined the normal school class in 1877, when the class numbered a dozen. Aaron would most likely have attended Whittin the year this address was made and would have been part of that class of twenty-six students in 1879.

Doubtless, Aaron spent many hours in those early weeks hungry, as only a growing teenage boy can be in a school that hasn't much to feed him, and perhaps a bit lonely in his brand-new surroundings. He had been raised, however, to apply himself, to keep moving in the direction of the work at hand, and to be cheerful and helpful whenever possible. His faith, good manners, and work ethic would have to be his guide.

Aaron did not finish his entire normal school course with Professor D. P. Allen. He transferred to Fayetteville Normal School after one year.[8] It is possible that this transfer was inspired, either directly or indirectly, by Aaron's cousin George H. White, who had just passed the North Carolina State Bar Exam in 1879 and had been advocating for black education as a school principal in New Bern. White had also decided to enter into politics at the state level. In 1880 White was elected as a Republican to the North Carolina State House of Representatives. His first major act in this capacity was to advocate for state funding for normal schools such as Fayetteville in order to address the pressing need for (particularly male) black teachers in the state. Fayetteville Normal School provided a three-year course, with a mandate of three years of teaching upon graduation. This state-sponsored black normal school offered students transportation money and some other scholarship assistance but, as with all black schools, suffered for funds. White is credited with getting additional funding allocated for black normal schools, including Fayetteville, by 1881.

We know that White stayed in regular touch with Allen. Perhaps White alerted Allen to Fayetteville's desire to recruit more black male students and Aaron Moore seemed a good candidate. Regardless, even if White was not directly involved in Moore's transfer, he certainly influenced the funding of Aaron's education from the halls of government, proving that political representation indeed matters and has both direct and lasting effect.[9]

Many normal schools were built around the study of school administration as well as the attainment of as much knowledge as possible to impart once certified. Teachers at this time were looked up to as leaders in their community. Many teachers would, in fact, go on to become pastors or politicians. Society required teachers often to be even more effective parents than parents themselves. They were expected to be purveyors of hope, better dressed, more morally impeccable, and harder working than most other adults one could point to. He or she must do this on little to no salary, often boarding with other families, and while taking side jobs or donations from benefactors in order to make ends meet. The black teacher, in particular, shouldered a tremendous responsibility, and the black normal school education was built to support and encourage bearing that burden with skill and grace.

It is interesting to note that normal school sessions for white students were only one month long and were held at locations convenient to those attending, usually during the summer breaks of larger educational institutions. Normal school sessions for black students, on the other hand, were held at irregular intervals but at fixed locations and usually lasted eight or nine months.[10] The curriculum, especially in the black normal schools, varied greatly and depended on the wishes of the primary donors. Some schools were more academic; others were trade-oriented. Some were narrowly aimed at hygiene and housekeeping and not much formal education at all. For example, Inspector S. G. Atkins, in his observations of the black normal schools of the state, said,

> It might be remarked that the industrial departments of the colleges are doing an important work and are proving themselves admirably adapted to the needs of the lately emancipated race. These departments cover a wide field of operations, including carpentry, printing, cabinet making, needlework, shoemaking, tailoring, blacksmithing, and cooking.
>
> ... It is the opinion of those most interested in and nearly connected with the work of education among the colored people that there can be no permanent advancement of the race on aesthetic and literary lines without improving and perfecting the home life.[11]

Many normal schools were schools within a school. Model schools existed alongside the normal school curriculum, so that no sooner had you learned a subject than you were expected to teach it. Often, what held the normal schools together was the sheer charisma of a principal educator or president, a guru of sorts, who would inspire, admonish, and uplift students so as to instruct them on how to be the same source of light and energy for their pupils. School attendance depended heavily on the social appeal and disciplinary ability of the teachers, who had to rigorously inspire but not crush the spirits of their pupils.

D. P. Allen was a teacher and mentor of this type. George H. White clearly revered him, W. L. Moore spent his career trying to emulate him at the Croatan Normal School, and Aaron Moore, as a token of his respect and gratitude, would send a donation to his memorial fund, along with his colleague C. C. Spaulding, when the esteemed professor passed away in 1917. The announcement of this fund to raise a monument to David P. Allen and his memorial gathering was printed in the *The Robesonian*, the same newspaper he had used to distract his hungry students at the dinner table.[12]

Aaron Moore was sure he was going to be a teacher like Allen when he went to Whittin and then Fayetteville. After all, he came from a family full of schoolteachers. Many of his mother's brothers and sisters had become teachers, and several of Aaron's own siblings were also working toward this goal. The presence of inspiring mentors and like-minded fellow students during his normal school years must have been electrifying and the intense need for education in the students he taught galvanizing. No matter what the schedule, meals, or facilities, normal school was surely preferable to a one-room schoolhouse with lessons being shouted from every corner, barely any books, and no room to breathe.

The days were no doubt challenging in ways Aaron had never encountered before. His characteristic quiet manner and ability to lose himself inside his thoughts and studies must have served him well in making this transition into scholarly life. Was it at Fayetteville that he met Shakespeare for the first time? Was it there that he first encountered classical history or current discoveries in science? Was it through D. P. Allen and his newspaper readings that he learned civic engagement? What was it like for him to receive and process this new level of beauty and cultural variety? It must have felt like his world was expanding with the speed of a runaway train.

We do not know precisely why Aaron was called home from his term at Fayetteville Normal School. We do know that he spent four more years on the farm before he could continue his education and that his older brother Israel Moore Jr. was attending Howard University Normal School in Washington, D.C., at this time. It would have been expensive for a family to support the education of two able-bodied young men when there was a farm to run. Regardless of cause, duty to family was first. Aaron would simply have to wait his turn.[13]

OUT OF EDEN
Shaw University Beckons

5

In the fall of 1885, as the harvest season was drawing to a close, Aaron Moore rode out of town in his father's wagon wearing his Sunday suit on a Friday.[1] Now twenty-two years old, he was taking the first steps on a journey that would pick up the pieces of an education interrupted. He had, at the urgent request of his family, given nearly four years back to the farm. It had been his duty, and he had been glad to labor for those he loved. Today, however, was the day his future was going to become irrevocably his own.

The road to the train station would have taken him past the Sandy Plain Missionary Baptist Church, the central gathering place of Aaron's life thus far. He had spent so many hours there, in prayer and in Sunday school, as both pupil and teacher. Those days had led him to the reward of this one. Aaron was still focused at this moment in his life on bringing knowledge back to the children of his home, which would make their lives better.

At nearly seventy, Israel Moore, his father, was slowing down. A widely respected yet taciturn man, Israel Moore was proud of his youngest son and may have offered some favorite adage or Bible verses over breakfast that morning: "Whatsoever a man sows, that shall he also reap."[2]

Aaron would have taken the train from the station at Whiteville. His ticket to Raleigh would have been for the wooden Negro car, or possibly second class in the white car. Aaron would come to love trains and travel in his later adulthood, and perhaps there was a kernel of wanderlust present in him as that particular train clattered off toward his long-awaited education.

In the modest valise under his feet were his living essentials: sixty dollars cash for his tuition and a little more for food and particulars; clean shirts and underthings; a shaving kit.[3] All of his pay for the four years on the farm and from the produce he had cultivated and sold on his own, his meager teacher's wages, and the dollars given generously by church and family were likely in that bag.[4] In his personal Bible were letters of reference from teachers and pastors affirming his moral character and good citizenship plus written proofs of his educational achievements thus far.[5]

Aaron must have looked forward to beginning this next chapter, to immersing himself in a scholarly environment surrounded by minds as eager as his to learn. University would be nothing like the pleasant chaos of normal school with Professor Allen or at Fayetteville. This would be a gentleman's campus in a town more refined and respectable than Aaron had ever inhabited. There would be lectures and concerts, a library for study, a chapel for prayer, new friends and teachers, cultured young ladies, strict rules of comportment, and a whole new level of challenges to be met. In short, his adult life was about to burst into bloom.

PART TWO *Shaw University and Leonard Medical School*

6

LIKE A TREE PLANTED
BY STREAMS OF WATER

What eventually became known as Shaw University was founded in Raleigh, North Carolina, in 1865, just two years after Aaron Moore's birth. In December 1865, Dr. Henry Martin Tupper (1831–93) formed a theology class that began to meet at the Guion Hotel in Raleigh. Tupper, a native of Massachusetts and graduate of Amherst College, had served as a soldier and chaplain in the Union army. In his ministrations as chaplain, Tupper had seen the very worst of the misery wrought by the Civil War, especially among the emancipated masses who had followed the Union troops across the Southern states. The death rate, disease, poverty, and stoic bravery of the emancipated slaves under his care made Tupper a man on fire with the need to help. He and his young wife asked the Baptist Home Mission Society of New York to place them in Raleigh after the war ended. Together the Tuppers dedicated the rest of their lives to promoting education and equality in the higher professions for the black race.[1]

Martin Tupper's initial theology class inspired such large attendance and the quality of the instruction such praise that he quickly invested all his personal savings, including his wartime pension of $500, to buy a plot of land. There he and his dedicated student body, as well as local black laborers, felled trees, laid bricks, and constructed a two-story building by hand. They called it the Raleigh Theological Institute. The act of erecting their own educational structure must have ignited a unique sense of ownership and pride in the hearts of those pioneering students.[2]

Oddly enough, John Henry Merrick, who would later become Aaron McDuffie Moore's best friend, most trusted business collaborator, and father-in-law to Aaron's daughter Lyda, laid many of those bricks in the institute's buildings. As a young laborer for hire, Merrick actually helped to build the foundations of the university that would launch Moore's entire adult and professional life. Merrick would later be involved in constructing much of Durham's Hayti community, including Dr. Moore's own family home. Even before they knew each other (and years before Aaron arrived on campus), John the builder and Aaron the healer/educator were working in collaboration. Merrick's biographer, R. McCants Andrews, states rather poetically, "On Shaw's shapeless campus and in the making of its first building this lad [Merrick] became, first, hod-carrier and then brick mason, helping to erect a great institution that would mold the lives and character of boys and girls like himself."[3]

Martin Tupper, however, was much more ambitious in his vision, and in 1870, through the generosity of Elijah Shaw, a wool merchant of Massachusetts, he purchased General Barringer's former estate in Raleigh, moved the Raleigh Theological Institute there, and renamed it the Shaw Collegiate Institute. The school grew steadily for the next five years and was finally chartered and incorporated by the state of North Carolina in 1875 as Shaw University, an "Institute of Higher Learning for Negroes."[4]

By the time Aaron was on that train from Whiteville to Shaw University in October 1885, Henry Martin Tupper had achieved yet another long-held dream for his university: a medical school. Leonard Medical School was the first black medical school in North Carolina and would be credited as the first four-year medical school in the nation in the year of Aaron McDuffie Moore's matriculation. The initial grant to add a medical school to Shaw's campus came from Tupper's brother-in-law Judson Wade Leonard, hence the naming of the school in his honor.[5]

Aaron Moore had no idea of being anything but a professor and educator when he arrived at Shaw. Nonetheless, "the leading educators at Shaw at that time ... saw brilliance in this thin, soft-spoken, student from the flat farmlands of the southeast portion of the state.... Moore's decision was irrevocable, almost prophetic, and he, as the psalmist puts it, became 'like a tree planted by streams of water, That bringeth forth its fruit in its season, And whose leaf doth not wither.'"[6] Martin Tupper was, in fact, looking for young men exactly like Aaron McDuffie Moore.

An address titled "A Few Words to Young Men Who Are Thinking of Entering upon the Study of Medicine," by Tupper's successor Charles F. Meserve, is included in the 1909 edition of the Leonard Medical School annual bulletin. It states the mission of the institution as eloquently as any speech that may have been made to inspire the young Aaron Moore to join its ranks. It also very clearly states the "brand" that Leonard would become known for and the kind of atmosphere of rigid expectation that Aaron would be entering:

The race is greatly in need of consecrated, skilled physicians and surgeons, and the Leonard Medical School has been established to meet this want. No one can do more to improve the daily life of the masses than the consecrated, skillful, Christian physician. The young man who aspires to become a physician should not think of what he may be able to do for himself but of the great good he may do for suffering humanity, and that too without receiving, in many cases, a penny for his professional services. Not **self**, but the race, must ever be his motto, and this requires not ability alone but the most rugged and strongest character. The Leonard Medical School has no denominational or religious test for admission. Its students represent nearly all of the denominations while a few have no church connections whatever. Young men of clean pure lives, honest and reliable, and total abstainers from the use of spirituous and malt liquors, who will refrain from the use of tobacco in any form in the rooms and about the grounds of the institution; such young men as these, and these only, need apply for admission. We want the **best** young men and only those who will cheerfully comply with our rules and regulations, and we are determined to make the conditions as favorable as possible for obtaining a thorough education.[7]

This stirring invitation to dedicate his life to the art and science of healing may have felt like an initiation of sorts for twenty-two-year-old Aaron Moore. The dream of being a man whom his race could look up to and count on had already been a big part of his aspiration to be an educator. This sudden shift of his horizon line may have been somewhat dizzying but required no less of his original resolve. The dedication that had kept him working toward a university education during the years he had given back to the family farm already qualified him as the "best" of young men. If that phrase was code for his freedman's family background, then he was certainly qualified there as well. Moore could easily have gone on with his life as a landowning farmer, married and settled among his family, and been a sought-after teacher with what he had already learned from his normal course. He had, nevertheless, kept studying and saving his wages and hoping for the opportunity to do more. Moore's sober and religious upbringing further enhanced his eligibility for the role of a "consecrated" physician. His academic and character references were from the likes of D. P. Allen and the Fayetteville Normal School, so he had already flourished in a learning environment. It is not surprising, then, that

Martin Tupper and his associates saw Aaron McDuffie Moore as an ideal candidate for their second matriculating class of future black physicians.

Did Aaron himself wrestle with this decision? Whom did he consult, if anyone, for advice? A letter might have taken weeks to get answered. Telephone exchanges had just been established in Raleigh in 1882, and even if Aaron had had access to a telephone, whom could he have called with similar access?[8] We can only look at Aaron's patterns of behavior leading up to that life-changing decision. They thus far indicated a relentlessly curious person with a stubborn will to propel him forward toward learning and service. Indeed, what pioneering mind could have turned down this challenge to join some of the most talented men of his race at the forefront of a newly available and fascinating profession? No matter what was said or what he did afterward, we know that Aaron McDuffie Moore walked right in and said yes to this adventure.

There was a massive need during these Reconstruction years for physicians in general and for black physicians in particular. The rampant mistrust of white doctors among black populations was easy to comprehend in light of their medical complicity that had often been a dark part of the slave trade. White doctors had vetted slaves, kept them working, used painful treatments to discourage them from declaring illness, pronounced them worthless, and sold them away from their families.[9] Root doctors and herbalists, ill-informed midwives, and dangerous quacks were the only available options in many black communities. Infectious diseases, birth complications, and malnutrition ravaged the working population. Now, more than ever, as the chaotic South was putting itself back together, it was to everyone's advantage to keep the labor force in the struggling new Southern economies healthy. This was especially true when it came to the more skilled factory labor needed for Southern industry. Whites begrudgingly admitted the need for black doctors to care for black workers, though few in white medical circles believed that the black medical student could be taught.[10]

Just two years before Aaron Moore's matriculation at Leonard, the Illinois State Board of Health published a two-hundred-page report outlining the requirements and laws pertaining to medical education and practice in the United States and Canada, including a census-based ratio of physicians to the population by state. The ratio in North Carolina of physicians to residents was estimated at 1 physician to 1,029 residents.[11] The need, evidently, across all demographics was clear. Notwithstanding, Leonard Medical School was still looked upon by many in the existing white medical establishment as suspicious and even dangerous. The *North Carolina Medical Journal* of 1883, edited by Thomas Fanning Wood (secretary-treasurer of the North Carolina Board of Health), expressed alarm at Leonard's proposed course of study, only backhandedly supported it, and stated that if blacks could learn medicine at all they should have extra instruction due to their race's inferior learning capability: "Admitting the necessity of having Negro and colored physicians, it ought not follow that they should be of lower standard ... because they have a humbler class to deal with. In fact a much larger course should be prescribed for them, as they have more difficulties to overcome. ... Launching into a profession requiring the highest degree of inborn quickness of perception of which the higher races are remarkable ... will almost surely debar them from future success."[12]

The practice of medicine in general up until the mid- to late nineteenth century had been largely an unregulated amalgam of bloodletting practices, expectorants and diuretics, herbal remedies, and the luck of the draw. However, in the age of discoveries such as Louis Pasteur's and Robert Koch's clinical applications for germ theory and Joseph Lister's use of antiseptic in surgical procedures, it must have seemed that the sky was the limit when it came to honing the ability to heal. Pasteur had just famously inoculated and cured the first human case of rabies the July before Aaron Moore made his way to Shaw.[13] Fictional figures like Sherlock Holmes emerged with the excitement and fascination generated by advances in science and forensics being made abroad, particularly in England and France. It was a wild yet important time to be a student of medicine and the human body.

While many in the white medical establishment simply felt it was time blacks took care of their own, Shaw president Martin Tupper believed in the untapped potential of black doctors, a belief rooted in his knowledge of his students' demonstrated abilities at Shaw and his firsthand wartime understanding of the need for physicians who understood and cared for a black patient's plight. Yet even in the face of Tupper's passion for this cause, there was a marked reluctance by the usual sources of philanthropy to finance this kind of education for blacks, even from Shaw's main benefactor, the American Baptist Home Mission Society. Tupper found himself having to promise that if the organization would support the larger institution of Shaw University, Leonard Medical School would remain under the Shaw umbrella but somehow pay for itself. It never did.[14]

Martin Tupper had to innovate in all kinds of ways to get the money he needed to run his medical school without making funders balk. For instance, he might encourage a donor to fund a janitorial position at the university, which would then double as a medical school scholarship for said "janitor."[15] He knew donors would pay for a janitor but not for the education of a black doctor. Most of the medical school students had jobs that paid at least some of their way, although the school expressly forbade them from taking farm labor, as it would exhaust them and interfere with their studies and the ability to keep a steady hand. The most prevalent work available was assisting in the surgeries of white physicians who were their professors and tutoring incoming classmates who may have had uneven levels of schooling before their matriculation. Leonard Medical School provided a comprehensive medical education for rarely more than $100 per year. This was, on average, one-half to one-third of what most medical colleges cost then.[16]

Another major challenge developed during this time that would galvanize Leonard's student body and their study habits: a burgeoning movement among existing white physicians to regulate the practice of medicine at the state level and to form fraternal organizations that would weed out "quackery" but also keep competition for patients to a minimum. The State Board of Medical Examiners was thus formed, and all graduating medical students, black and white, would be required to be board-certified. In the years Aaron attended medical school, there were more obstacles to entering the medical field than had ever existed before in North Carolina for both blacks and whites. As usual, Aaron would be only a year or so behind the leading edge of progress.[17]

The course catalog for Leonard Medical School reads less like a to-do list and more like the guide to a grand adventure. Pride leaps off the page in poetic prose, as do majestic engravings of the medical dormitory and new classroom building. The small faculty of practicing white physicians, surgeons, and specialists from Raleigh and the surrounding area had grown by a few members in 1885.[18]

It bears remarking that these white physicians who made up the faculty of Tupper's fledgling enterprise in medical education were not representatives of the majority opinion of their peers on the matter. They were, in fact, activists in their own right—willing to draw the ire and vitriol of their own institutions, patients, and colleagues and teach a totally untested student population to enter their own profession as peers. There was no great number of practicing black physician educators available at this time in history to staff a medical school on behalf of their own race, and even if there had been and they had been willing to teach at Leonard, it is likely Tupper would not have gotten the school funded. The concept of white doctors supervising, teaching, and "improving" the minds of young black men in order to serve their own race was only barely palatable to white philanthropy, as the end result was considered useful in preventing the kinds of disease that could affect all populations. Thomas Fanning Wood in the aforementioned *North Carolina Medical Journal* article concerning Leonard Medical School went so far as to suggest outright that the white Leonard faculty was substandard: "To achieve a high success in teaching such people, a very high degree of teaching talent would have to be engaged. . . . But everyone knows that such conditions are far from being likely for many a year in Raleigh."[19] The editor's disdain for "such people" as well as his own medical colleagues (and likely readers of his journal) is palpable.

If such a "high degree of teaching talent" was indeed needed to instruct the black medical student, the question then follows (if all such professors must necessarily be white), why have a black medical school at all? Could the black students not simply benefit from existing white university medical programs and get the "high degree" of instruction from the same teaching "talent" as their white peers? A very few black medical students, if they had the means, did leave the South to pursue their studies in white Northern universities. They found, however, that critical aspects of their training would suffer even if they were able, however unwelcome, to enter the classroom portion: "The personal contact that clinical training required brought objections from many patients, and even some school administrators when it required black medical students to administer care to white patients."[20]

It became clear to those white philanthropists who were willing to fund black medical education at all, and in particular institutions in the South where the poor black patient populations were massive and the need was greatest, that funding black medical schools was a way to control not only the curriculum but also the quality of instruction. In their view, having separate black medical schools under white supervision kept blacks out of white universities, and black teaching clinics and hospitals would also keep black physicians away from white patients.

Keeping the black medical schools starved of funds was also a way to make sure they didn't get above themselves and that only a small number of black graduates could afford to finish the training and join the profession. According to scholar Thomas J. Ward Jr., "The message was clear—if black medical students and schools wanted funding from white philanthropies, they needed to concentrate on basic medical skills ... so that they could serve the impoverished African American communities of the rural south."[21] The combination of low societal opinions of black students' ability to learn medicine with the resulting stringency of black medical schools' standards for admission (both in "character" and in academic capability) left schools like Leonard caught between offering extra "remedial" coursework, needing to find tuition assistance for those who would take it on, and keeping a faculty employed of high enough caliber to overcome all those barriers and produce successful physicians. It was a dance on very thin ice, and it seems to have been by design. This precarious position cannot have escaped those white professors willing to enter into this experiment at Leonard Medical School, even if their salaries did make up the majority of the cost of running it.[22] Martin Tupper himself quite literally gave his life to the cause of these students and to the future of medicine in black America. Leonard and black medical schools like it were made a necessity by a society that both needed and abhorred them, and the gift of that semi-isolation became the fraternity and collegial network that was formed among those who would dedicate themselves to the mission of public health and dignity for all.

These Shaw University/Leonard Medical School years would be the crucible and foundation of Aaron Moore's adult life and work. He would learn not only the practice of medicine but also the politics of it and the grit and ingenuity needed to keep such institutions open that would serve his race. He would learn from and spend time with white men in the study of science and do so among black peers who were also taking on this adventure. The world was changing rapidly and so were the post-Reconstruction South, higher education, and the science of the field he was entering. These would be heady times for a country youth from a turpentine farm, four years of the hardest study he had ever experienced. Well, perhaps it could be done in three.

THE FIRST YEAR
Meeting Professors and Starting Classes

7

When Aaron Moore began his studies at Shaw University on Monday, November 2, 1885, the Leonard campus consisted of "two large brick buildings for the especial accommodation of the Medical School[:] ... The Leonard Medical Building ... [containing] lecture rooms, amphitheater, laboratory, dissecting rooms ... [and] the Medical Dormitory ... [with] rooms to accommodate sixty students."[1] Both of these buildings are depicted in the annual announcement for the year 1885.

The medical dormitory that would be Moore's home for the next several years was a large four-story building with tall windows and a gabled attic. It was a requirement that all medical students live in this dorm, and strict rules were in place regarding study hours; all spirits and tobacco were prohibited.[2] An engraving appearing each year in Leonard's early annual announcements shows a rectangular building with a center entrance—no doubt opening onto a small foyer containing the staircase. On each floor, hallways extended to the left and right of the stairs, and eight rooms (each with a window) flanked each hallway. There were sixteen rooms each on the first three floors and twelve rooms in the top-floor attic for a total student occupancy of sixty. All rooms were singles. This dorm was all business, with not so much as a porch or a stoop for leisure. No late-night conviviality was allowed on campus, and the school generally didn't invite those who had such habits to attend. Two tall chimneys rose up on the right side of the dorm and must have served coal- or wood-burning heaters, and a small turret was centered on the roof. Which floor and room would Aaron Moore call home? It seems that wherever his room was, he had a window of his own to look out of and to let the light in. For a young man who had spent so much of his early life outdoors, that window could have meant a great deal.

Leonard Hall, "an imposing structure of beautiful architectural proportions,"[3] was where these young men would learn the academic portion of doctoring. The building is still in use on Shaw's campus in Raleigh. Two stalwart, conical towers rise castle-like on the building's facade, one on each side of the arched entry. The deep red bricks give the building regional style and gravitas. Each of the three stories displays an increasingly rounded and elongated window style, drawing the eye upward. Brick accents surround each window in sunburst patterns, and even more fancy brickwork becomes apparent on closer inspection. It is a deliberately elegant place in which to learn. Ten steps from the sidewalk lead up to the high arched entryway and into the first-floor hall. Tall wooden columns flank the long hall, vaguely Grecian in style and decorated with carved brackets like the branches of trees or wings. Classrooms open to the left and right through tall doors. The floors are warm wood, and the walls are plastered in blinding white. Toward the far southeastern corner, a dark wooden staircase sweeps up to a second similar floor of classrooms and then finally up to the lecture hall and amphitheater. The handrail of the stairs is smooth and rounded and looks like mahogany. The stairs are deep and wide and probably creak grandly. In the amphitheater, rows of wooden benches with high, double-slatted backs are arranged like pews. The light pours into the room through rows of tall windows with deep sills. Candid Leonard classroom photos from the 1880s show that at the front of the amphitheater sat a large desk and an enormous, multilevel chalkboard (complete with a ladder to reach the upper areas) and a human skeleton, dangling upright on a display rack.[4]

The days were full and started early but probably not "farm" early. The habit of waking up before dawn might have afforded Aaron and young men with a similar background a few hours of study before class convened. A printed example of the "schedule of lectures" from later years at Leonard shows that classes took place between 9:00 A.M. and 5:00 P.M. with lectures in the earlier half of the day and labs in the latter half.[5] Students attended meals as regularly and promptly as classes. The dining hall was in the chapel building on campus.[6] Chapel services were held regularly during the week as well as on Sundays. Medical students could worship on campus at the Baptist church or off campus at the church of their choice. In 1886 President Martin Tupper remarked in a Baptist publication that "no class of pupils is more regular in their attendance upon religious services than our medical students."[7] It is likely that Tupper emphasized this image of his students for fund-raising reasons, but Aaron Moore would certainly have participated in religious activities willingly and with easy regularity.

Many of these young men, including Aaron, had come to Leonard having only recently exchanged coveralls and country shoes for the well-shined boots, daily suits, and sober stiff collars expected of a medical student. Because Leonard's medical students were held in such high regard on the Shaw campus and even in Raleigh itself, codes of conduct and dress were imposed on them immediately and for the duration of their education. Photographs taken during this time in Aaron's life show the personal style of his adulthood in development. His small, well-trimmed mustache, close-cropped hair, and neat bow tie are correct, sensible, and plain. These photographs also show his still-strong farmer's hands and robust physique; his shoulders are fuller and larger than the slighter version they would become in his life as a physician.

According to the "Fifth Annual Announcement" of the Leonard Medical School, Aaron McDuffie Moore's first year of study would include anatomy, physiology, general chemistry, and materia medica (now called pharmacology). Since Aaron had not planned to study medicine when he arrived at Shaw, he may have also taken some placement exams or taken advantage of some of the "Preliminary Courses" offered to those young men whose educational backgrounds did not include "Latin, Botany, Physics, Zoology, Chemistry, Physiology and the use of the microscope."[8]

Dr. C. S. Pratt, a recent graduate of Columbia Medical School in New York City, would preside over the anatomy and general chemistry classrooms. The annual announcement admits to a lack of a physiology chair for this session, so it is likely Dr. Pratt also taught physiology. During this session he would also serve as dean and resident physician of the medical school. This being an early post in his career, it seems likely that Pratt was a man close to Aaron's age, although white and Northern-educated. The bulk of this first year of learning would be under Pratt's tutelage. Dr. K. P. Battle would take over the physiology course by the 1886–87 term. A surgeon and resident physician at the North Carolina Deaf, Dumb and Blind Asylum (as well as consulting physician to Dr. Pratt in the Leonard Medical School Hospital), Dr. R. B. Haywood would teach Aaron's first course in materia medica, which would cover substances and medicines, preventive and curative therapies, and the theories of diagnosis and practical presentations designed to give the students practice in diagnosis. These classes may have represented Aaron's first encounters with actual patients in a clinical setting.[9] Leonard Medical School would open its hospital—a twenty-five-bed facility serving the black community of Raleigh—in January of Aaron's first term.[10]

The Leonard course in anatomy used a version of *Gray's Anatomy* (as all medical students to this day do), which at that time was a relatively new text. Developed originally by Sir Henry Gray with illustrations by Henry Vandyke Carter and first published by the Royal College of Surgeons, London, in 1858, it is likely that the version utilized by Leonard in 1885 was the tenth edition, edited by T. Pickering Pick in 1883, or perhaps the eleventh edition (the first one in color), released in 1887.[11] Other textbooks include Quain's *Elements of Anatomy* and Holden's *Manual of Dissection* (for cadaver lab). For physiology, students would study texts by Flint and Dalton, and for general chemistry, the Fownes and Attfield texts. The text for materia medica would be *The National Dispensary* by Biddle and Bartholow.[12]

The annual announcement of 1885 describes with great excitement a new chemistry lab with equipment for the study of electricity and its effects on the body, a microscope, a Magic Lantern (an early form of slide projector), and "almost the complete set of Auzoux and Boch Steiger Anatomical Models, which have been imported from Paris especially for us."[13] These models were a truly miraculous addition to medical education during this time period because they were extraordinarily detailed and could be dissected and reassembled many times. The Auzoux models, for instance, were made only in France and of a secret blend of papier-mâché with the additives of cork and clay to strengthen the paper and glue. They are like works of art and are in many museum collections today, but they might have also been quite startling to a farm boy like Aaron Moore. These models were an effective, practical, and much less expensive way of preparing students for their first encounters with a cadaver.[14]

Titles of the texts used at Leonard were listed in a rather cursory fashion, perhaps because there were so few texts at this time and they needed little introduction to any bookseller or medical librarian. It is unclear whether students were to purchase or acquire the books themselves, but they are not on the supplies list or listed in the costs of admission for the year. It is stated in the annual announcement that medical students will enjoy full use of the Shaw University Library, so perhaps some texts were kept there. Later announcements declare, however, that it is the student's responsibility to acquire the necessary references. It can be safely assumed that a young physician would wish to own the books by which he honed his craft for use as references in practice. Aaron Moore was known for his love of books and later in life accumulated a large and prized collection, so it stands to reason that he would want to own his textbooks eventually, if not immediately.

Whether or not Moore had to buy his medical books, there was still a substantial amount of money due before he could start this unplanned-for adventure. Matriculating costs for Leonard Medical School are listed in the annual announcement for 1885 as follows:

Matriculation (paid annually): $5.00

The five-months' course of lectures: $60.00

Tickets for any one of the different branches of medicine (this must be for larger lectures or labs): $15.00

Graduation fee: $20.00

Incidentals per session: $3.00

The General Assembly of the State of North Carolina have legalized dissection by special act, so material for dissection will be supplied at cost during the winter months, and there will be no extra charge for the Demonstrator of Anatomy's ticket. All fees must be paid invariably in advance. The other expenses will be per month as follows:

Room, rent, lights and fuel: $2.00

Board: $6.00[15]

Students were to pay all costs, other than monthly ones, in advance. In many cases, if a student showed extreme aptitude but also extreme poverty, the Leonard Medical Scholarship was available for at least five recipients to cover the entire sixty-dollar cost of the course of lectures. It is possible that Aaron Moore was offered one of these scholarships since he had not planned to attend medical school when he arrived at Shaw, but we have no record of his receiving scholarship assistance. He would certainly have been a qualified candidate for a scholarship since we know the academic and character requirements for assistance were already in evidence based on the school's desire to recruit him in the first place. Regardless of any such assistance, however, Aaron would still have had to manage the monthly costs of room, board, extra tickets for labs, and incidentals. Leonard students were advised to find ways to do this either with part-time employment deemed suitable by the administration or with summer work. It is probable that Aaron's family could pay a portion of any extra costs and that his personal savings would have been enough to get started. Summer work would surely be available to him as his aptitude as a student became clear.

The assistance Aaron Moore received during the years he spent at Leonard and Shaw, whether monetary or purely educational, made a profound impact on him. As soon as his practice made it possible, Dr. Moore donated generously to his alma mater. This continued throughout his career, and he also gave of his time and expertise on several advisory boards. Financial records of some of these donations still exist. Most notable among them is a final bequest from Aaron's posthumous estate in 1923 to Shaw University (Leonard was closed by this time) for $5,000. This was an extraordinary sum for a man of any color and is the equivalent of over $70,000 in present-day U.S. currency.[16] Leonard Medical School and Shaw University offered the young Aaron McDuffie Moore an opportunity in the years 1885–88 that he never forgot or ceased trying to repay.

The young men of the second class to enter Leonard Medical School would have to be driven souls indeed to capitalize on this opportunity. His classmates came from as far away as Virginia and South Carolina, Georgia and West Virginia, Rhode Island and Alabama. "Mr. A. M. Moore" is the only one from his region of North Carolina, which is listed as "Rosindale,[17] N.C." Two of his classmates came from Tarboro, North Carolina, the town from which a certain young lady who would become Aaron's future bride hailed.[18]

Moore had come to Shaw and now Leonard Medical School from that turpentine farm in Columbus County, however, to finally focus his entire heart and mind on his education. There was so much to take in, discover, and master. All manner of people, especially his own family, depended on it.

8

THE SECOND YEAR
Colleagues and Cadavers

Whether Aaron Moore went home to Farmers Union to work for his summer wages or whether he stayed employed in Raleigh, Monday, November 1, 1886, arrived, and the start of his second medical school term was
upon him.[1]

Leonard Medical School had just graduated its very first class of six
black physicians at the end of the 1885–86 term. Two of those men would
become the first black physicians to take and pass the North Carolina
Medical Board examinations and be licensed by the state: Dr. Monassa
Thomas Pope and Dr. John Taylor Williams. Leonard's educational capa-
bilities and the very fitness of black men to be practitioners of medicine
had been tested and deemed worthy. President Martin Tupper was beside
himself with pride at the success of Leonard's candidates. He had hailed
the commencement exercises of March 31, 1886, as an "unprecedented"
event that had brought more attention to the Shaw campus than ever in
its history. He also relayed to his trustees and benefactors the report of a
faculty member (who was part of the North Carolina examining board)
describing the reactions of his colleagues to the aptitude of Leonard's
candidates as "intensely interesting and exceedingly gratifying."[2] Tupper's faith was vindicated, and a certain triumph must have partnered
with relief that this venture was at last gaining real traction.

Because of all of the anticipation surrounding Leonard's first group
of graduates and the vital importance of their subsequent success at the
North Carolina Medical Boards to the future of Leonard as an institution, the year leading up to this landmark commencement was no doubt
tense and rigorous for all. The 1886–87 term, however, must have taken
on a new and far more celebratory tone. Historic and tangible advances
had now been made, and those who were following closely must have felt
reassured and more confident of their own success.

A rather grand photograph was taken of the Leonard student body:
the first six graduates and the twenty underclassmen. They are all posed

in rows, from seated to standing, in front of a large draped American flag. Aaron Moore, sophomore, is standing in the uppermost row, third from the viewer's right. Many of his fellow classmates are placing one hand in their double-breasted suit jackets, Napoleon style, which was a popular trend of the era, an indication of status and historic importance. Because of the long exposure photographs of the day, which were notoriously difficult to sit for, this "hand in jacket" pose was also a way of keeping the subject's hand still so as not to blur the finished product.[3] It is frankly very touching to see this company of black men dressed in their best and posing in this overtly important way. Aaron himself is not "hand in jacket," although he is grasping the collar of his more modest, single-breasted jacket with his left hand, and his vest pocket is complete with watch chain. He looks serious but also extremely young. There is an intensity and fun in his eyes and in the eyes of his classmates. All of those hands, placed in jackets or not, would soon be the hands of surgeons and were already the hands of men of science. President Tupper was right to hope and to be proud.[4]

Twenty-three-year-old Aaron Moore had managed to pass not only the requirements of his first year of medical school but also whatever prerequisite coursework he may have had to take in order to be squarely on track for his second year. Summer sessions were not offered at Leonard, although summer reading was encouraged. The Leonard Medical School Hospital was also closed during the summer. Taking extra courses during a term, however, was allowed. It is certain that Aaron Moore took on more than the usual course load and probably did so from day one.

There was no small measure of pressure for undergraduate medical students to succeed at Leonard. Their performance was monitored and fostered at nearly every turn. Leonard was known, in fact, for its controlled environment and rigid codes of respectability. Medical professors kept careful attendance as well as academic records and made copious notes on the progress of each student in their classrooms. Written and oral exams were given on a regular basis. Professors often issued academic honor pledges, which were to be signed before the coursework began. Making a student take an immediate and unexpected oral version of a written test often exposed cheating. A guilty finding meant prompt expulsion and removal from the campus.[5]

Professors assessed the academic progress of each medical student routinely, utilizing all available data. If a young man was falling behind but found to be both serious and capable, he received all possible assistance. If scores on the intermittent exams fell below standards at any point, however, the school could ask a candidate to withdraw from that course. Often the first examinations of the term resulted in a number of such withdrawals and dropouts. The failed course could be repeated until the exam work improved, but many didn't have the funds to repeat courses indefinitely. Final exams were the last word on completing a course, provided that interim examinations were also satisfactory.

This parental style of supervision of everything from academics to meals, appearance, and manners was a vital part of the life and reputation of Leonard Medical School. The philosophy of administrators like Tupper was that they were not only training extraordinary black physicians but also producing fine, upstanding, and morally superlative black men. Perhaps this was a goal entirely based on the ideal that education and religious endeavor ennobled any man. However, it also communicates an ongoing awareness of the discomfort many in the white community felt when having to resolve their accustomed antipathy for black men with the concept of black men practicing medicine. Leonard's strict mores were in place not only to sustain philanthropic support but also to function as a built-in buffer when these young men left Leonard's protective walls. They would need every possible mantle of respectability to assist them when entering the profession. Leonard's professors felt it was a large portion of their duty to make the weight and consequence of these standards clear. An inevitable percentage did not succeed; the weight of Leonard's institutional expectations coupled with financial hardship would prove unbearable.[6]

A Leonard trustee, Dr. Keen of Philadelphia (white), wrote in a medical journal of the time, "If the colored man is to enter medicine, he must expect just what the white man does—a fair fight and no favors. If inferior in education and skill he will go to the bottom; if superior he ought to rise to the top." It is indicative of the school's guiding spirit that Dr. Keen makes no mention of race being a particular impediment to success in the medical field and cites only excellence and preparation as determinants of the level to which a physician of any color could rise. His use of "ought," however, reveals a subtle uncertainty. This Reconstruction-reminiscent assimilationist idealism was at the heart of what Leonard and its white faculty and trustees stood for.[7]

The goals and expectations for graduation from Leonard were clearly stated and kept constantly in view in every successive annual announcement. At graduation, the candidate was to be at least twenty-one years of age (no student was admitted under eighteen) and be thought by all his instructors to be "possessed of a high moral character." He must appear before the faculty, submit a one-time graduation fee of twenty dollars, and defend his medical thesis. He then must dissect an entire cadaver and present evidence of having passed all final exams administered by every professor in every branch of medicine studied. If all of his exams, final and otherwise, averaged above a 75 (out of 100), he earned the title of graduate. If he did not pass, the student would be given a second chance to pass whatever course had given him trouble. Not until that student had passed another year's worth of coursework, however, would the school reconsider him for graduation. If the school did not believe a student able to ultimately succeed, it would direct him to leave campus permanently prior to commencement.[8]

The curriculum at Leonard emphasized "doing" rather than just "sitting" for lectures. As soon as students were deemed capable, they could observe their professors treat patients in the hospital or even observe or assist in surgeries. During Aaron's first year, it is likely he only observed interactions with live patients and studied anatomy through slides and models. In this second year, once the winter months made storage of cadavers possible, practical anatomy would begin and students would begin to dissect cadavers.[9]

Cadaver lab is a rite of passage for every medical student, regardless of era. Many of these young Leonard students had come from poverty or farm life, and the Civil War had surely played a prominent part in many of their early childhood memories. Life expectancy was shorter in the nineteenth century, especially in black communities. These young men had likely already encountered death and disease. The experience of dissection, however, is one of wonder and a unique awakening for participants. Complicating the procedure was the rigid religious upbringing and Victorian mores and values that Aaron Moore and young men like him had imbibed and the fact that the overwhelming majority of cadavers used in medical research during the late nineteenth century were black. During this time at the University of North Carolina Medical School, "it was difficult to procure cadavers for dissection, and medical schools were notorious for using bodies disinterred by grave robbers or 'resurrectionists.'" These men preyed on the graves of poor and marginalized people in the South, primarily African Americans. It is unclear how Leonard obtained cadavers in these earliest days of the medical school, but it would be fair to assume that medical students conducted their cadaver studies almost exclusively on black bodies, some of which may have been acquired from "resurrectionists."[10]

One of Aaron's professors at Leonard, K. P. Battle Jr., was the son of the president of the UNC Medical School during this time period, Kemp Plummer Battle Sr. The senior Dr. Plummer recounts in his history of the university that it was his belief that North Carolina outlawed grave robbing in 1885 precisely because of the medical schools in the area.[11] Cadavers could be bought, they could be collected from insane asylums and prisons, and they could arrive from a procurer—no questions asked. Many medical schools have had to come to terms with this darker chapter in their history and the fact that, in both the North and the South, the majority of medical cadavers were African American.[12]

For a black medical student it must have been extraordinarily affecting in any number of ways to encounter one's own people in a cadaver lab. Nothing exposes the myths of prejudice more succinctly than peeling back the physical layer of racial designation to find an anatomy underneath that is the same as every other person's—even in the face of a portion of the scientific community at that time who would argue otherwise.

The courses Aaron Moore and his class took in their second year, besides practical anatomy, were "Medical Chemistry, Physiology, Pathological Anatomy, Practice of Medicine and Surgery."[13] One of the new professors of physiology during Aaron's second term at Leonard, the aforementioned K. P. Battle Jr., is described in the annual announcement for that term as "at present in Europe perfecting his Medical education." A specialist in eye, ear, nose, and throat medicine, Battle was at that time studying in Paris and London. During that sojourn, Sir Joseph Lister invited Battle to accompany him on his surgical rounds at King's College Hospital and observe some of his antiseptic surgeries. Battle even visited Louis Pasteur's laboratory in France and reviewed the most recent research on rabies vaccination. Dr. Battle returned to Leonard at some point during the 1886–87 terms and assumed his duties as professor of physiology. One hopes he also gave presentations on his travels and adventures in medical science abroad. It is remarkable that there was just one degree of separation between the most renowned pioneers of medicine of the nineteenth century and Aaron McDuffie Moore.[14]

The overarching theme of this second term's curriculum was the application to actual human subjects, both living and cadaver, of what Aaron and his fellow students had learned in their first year of mostly lectures. The new hospital had gained the trust of the community over the last year and now offered medical services at no charge.

Any health-care provider can attest to the gravity of those first few encounters with living, breathing patients. The reality of one's calling can come crashing home, and for a man like Aaron, who was already compassionately focused, the mission of his studies must have taken on new urgency. Just as it had been extraordinary to handle his first cadaver and learn the wonders of the biochemical machine that is the body, looking into the eyes of a living patient must have been equally extraordinary. It must also have been a bit awkward for Aaron and his classmates to enter a women's clinic for the first time. Female patients would require a special delicacy and care from these young men, and female medicine itself was a very new field. Aaron's two closest siblings were sisters, and his mother seems to have been a force in his life. Perhaps this is why he exhibited a lifelong aptitude and concern for the health, education, and ambitions of women. When his own commencement day arrived, Aaron Moore received the coveted McKee Prize for Obstetrics.[15] His excellence with female patients surely found its origins in this second year at Leonard Medical School Hospital and would gain momentum in his third year.

Valedictorian Dr. Lawson Andrews Scruggs delivered a speech at Leonard's momentous commencement on March 31, 1886, titled "Medical Education as a Factor in the Elevation of the Colored Race." With profound pride, Dr. Scruggs presented himself to his colleagues thus: "With the same self-sacrifice, courage, and devotion as has ever characterized the profession, we who stand before you tonight are pioneers of the Medical Profession of our race." He also encouraged each new black physician to "harness himself for the battle" for the future of black health, both in the United States and abroad.[16]

Dr. Scruggs would stay on and become one of Aaron's professors and the resident physician (the first black resident physician) at Leonard Hospital. Scruggs was likely the first black physician that Aaron Moore or any of his fellow students would ever witness in practice. His passionate example had to have made a deep impression.[17]

Aaron Moore clearly made an impression on his older peers in those first years of Leonard, because in 1887 three of them would invite him to collaborate in founding the Old North State Medical Society, initially called the North Carolina Medical, Pharmaceutical and Dental Association, one of the first black medical associations in the nation. They established this organization because they understood the need for connectivity in the black medical community in order to collectively raise the quality of life for black people statewide. Black physicians were banned from the all-white North Carolina Medical Society and the gatherings of the national American Medical Association. From very early on in his education Aaron was recognized as forward-looking, as an important collegial ally, and as a young man focused on planning for his future role as both physician and community leader.[18] These four founding physicians of the Old North State Medical Society would remain active and connected as colleagues throughout their careers, and the organization is still serving the black community today.

This second year of his medical training seems to have cemented Aaron Moore's idea of himself as a physician. The headlong rush to reorganize the goals that marked his first term apparently solidified into a new sense of identity. Now Aaron McDuffie Moore was really a medical student, the most revered group on Shaw's campus, and was already allied with three of the six graduates of that mighty first class of Leonard's finest. He was no doubt involved in religious events, lectures, and concerts on campus, but he was also determined to use every moment of his free time to finish his studies early. Aaron Moore was indeed "harness[ing] himself for the battle."

THE THIRD YEAR
Finishing Early

9

Aaron Moore's third term at Leonard Medical School began on Tuesday, November 1, 1887. It was to be his last and perhaps most intense year of study. Leonard required for most students a four-year course of study. An exception is posited, however, in the description of the "course of study" in the annual announcement for that term: "If a student at the end of three years is able to pass an examination in all the branches of Medicine he will be allowed to graduate and receive his diploma."[1]

Moore's subjects for both the third and fourth year are listed as "Therapeutic Obstetrics, Theory and Practice of Medicine, and Surgery, Ophthalmology, Otology, Laryngology, Dermatology, Syphilis and Diseases of the Nervous System, Diseases of Women, Diseases of Children, Operative Surgery, and Forensic Medicine."[2] For him to graduate early, it stands to reason that Aaron, as we have said before, simply added more coursework all along his journey at Leonard. It is also possible that he did the work of term three and term four all at once. Drs. James McKee, A. W. Knox, K. P. Battle Jr., and R. H. Lewis would now teach the majority of his courses. There would be a very definite focus on surgery and on women and children's medicine.

This was the year that the school would award the McKee Prize for Obstetrics to Aaron Moore, the second recipient of this honor, the first being Dr. M. T. Pope of the first graduating class.[3] Dr. James McKee, once a drill sergeant in the Confederate army, had finished his medical degree at the infamous Bellevue Hospital Medical College in New York in 1869. During Aaron's medical school years, McKee was the superintendent of health for Wake County and so would also lecture on matters of public hygiene. A delegate to the American Medical Association and soon to be superintendent of the State Hospital for the Insane, Dr. McKee was respected, connected, and, above all, concerned for the most underserved populations in medicine.[4]

During this era in medicine, obstetrics in general and particularly in black populations was a new arena for male doctors. Midwives had been almost entirely responsible for matters of childbirth for generations. Women, however, died with horrifying regularity in childbirth or from infections following childbirth. New ideas regarding antiseptic births and the possibility of surgery in the event of complications were revolutionary. Dr. McKee's course was described in the "Seventh Annual Announcement": "His lectures on obstetrics will be illustrated by diagrams, models, the cadaver and other preparations used to illustrate such obstetric operations and procedures as can be so presented. He will also lecture on the Diseases of Women and Children."[5]

Dr. A. W. Knox, who was on the North Carolina Board of Medical Examiners, would be the examiner on obstetrics and the diseases of women and children. Although Knox is listed as the instructor of Principles and Practices of Surgery at Leonard, it is likely he would have occasionally assisted Dr. McKee in preparing the graduates of 1888 for their ultimate examination before the Board of Medical Examiners.

Dr. K. P. Battle Jr. was now a full-time presence on the Leonard campus and considered one of the foremost experts of his time on the eye, ear, nose, and throat. More time under his tutelage would surely be exciting. Dr. R. H. Lewis would also guide Aaron Moore and his class in similar subjects and, interestingly, would deliver a "response" to the welcome address, which opened the Thirty-Fifth Annual Meeting of the North Carolina Board of Medical Examiners on May 8, 1888, in Fayetteville.[6]

There is no mention in the annual announcement of which faculty member would be taking on the lectures in forensics. Perhaps the omission was by design, since this was a new and somewhat unpopular discipline. It was a banner year for forensics however, as *La faune des tombeaux* (Fauna of the tombs) by Jean-Pierre Mégnin, considered the founding work of modern forensic science, was published in 1887.[7] Battle had only recently returned from studying in France; he might have been familiar with this publication. Regardless of guidance, we know that Aaron Moore must have taken in enough of this particular course of study to be persuaded one year later to run for county coroner.[8]

In the midst of all of this study and preparation, Aaron somehow also encountered and began a lifelong friendship with John Henry Merrick. Merrick was part owner of a barbershop in Durham by 1887 but had honed his craft in Raleigh, with clients including Washington Duke and his sons. It is unclear how the two men were introduced. Perhaps it was even in the barbershop, since Merrick still had an associate in business in

Raleigh and might have come back and forth for important clients. Since Moore occupied the highest social strata of medical student on Shaw's campus and attended many church functions, it is possible they also met at a church or campus social event. Another way that their paths could have crossed was during the summer work that medical students often sought in barbershops or as Pullman porters, pursuits the Leonard administration considered respectable. Perhaps Aaron himself or one of Aaron's classmates took a summer job in one of Merrick's shops. Regardless of how, their paths did cross, and their association would prove the most important of Aaron Moore's life.

As outlined in the requirements for Leonard graduates, Aaron delivered final exams on all of his coursework with grades above 75 percent. Then he had to pick a medical thesis to present with his final cadaver dissection and appearance before the faculty. There is no record of his thesis, but it may well have been based in obstetrics, as he was to be rewarded for his skills in that arena at commencement.

Then he would have to wait for that crucial letter inviting him to participate in graduation ceremonies. Aaron Moore started his medical education in a class of twenty; he would be one of only five to graduate in the class of 1888. Two of his fellow graduates were from North Carolina and two from Virginia. Together, these five men made up the second graduating class of black physicians in Leonard Medical School history.[9]

Commencement was an affair both solemn and joyous at Shaw and Leonard. There were soaring speeches and religious services, and formal dress was worn. Aaron's family may have attended, but whether or not they were there in body, surely their pride and congratulations reached him by letter. Martin Tupper describes the commencement exercises of 1888 briefly in a note published by the *Baptist Home Mission Monthly*:

Our Medical Commencement took place Thursday Evening March 29. Five young men were graduated. Dr. H. L. Wayland, of Philadelphia, delivered the address to the graduating class; subject, "The Temptations of the Medical Profession." It was inimitable and greatly enjoyed by the audience, both white and colored.

Robert A. Reynolds, of the graduating class, delivered an oration and valedictory address. The diplomas were presented by Colonel C. H. Banes, of Philadelphia, followed by speeches by Elijah Shaw, of Wales, Mass., Colonel Banes, and Dr. Wayland. . . . The term has closed most auspiciously.[10]

Looming on the horizon after this day of celebration, however, was the graduates' meeting with the ultimate arbiters of Leonard's academic legitimacy and their legal right to practice in their chosen field: the North Carolina Board of Medical Examiners. The board was to convene in May 1888 in Fayetteville, the city in which a much younger Aaron Moore had received his normal school instruction.[11] It must have seemed to Aaron as if his educational journey had come full circle. The month of April would, no doubt, be one of painstaking review and preparation.

The North Carolina Board of Medical Examiners convened in 1859, just four years before Aaron Moore was born. It was a long time in development. Throughout the early 1800s, legislators had introduced rules at the state level to regulate the activities and practices of so-called physicians. During those times nearly anyone could proclaim himself a man of medicine or herself a midwife. Snake oil salesmen, traveling quacks, and remedies that were at best castor oil and at worst cocaine were at their height. The need for a governing board, for reasons of medical ethics alone, was great. Legislation stalled in North Carolina, however, as it did in many states. Doctors were respected and wealthy members of most communities, and regulation could pose a threat to their profits and position. Regulation also invited competition and a standard by which competitors could be measured. With no educational standards required, the medical field was full of every level and moral brand of practitioner. There were, however, compassionate and dedicated healers who did their best for the sick and poor; this brand of healer needed a structure and professional network to support his predominance in the field. Finally, in 1858 a committee of five physicians petitioned the General Assembly of the State of North Carolina to pass a bill authorizing a state board of medical examiners. In 1859 they met with success when the legislature passed a bill calling for the organization of such a board, and on May 12, 1859, the same committee elected seven members to North Carolina's first board of medical examiners. This was a great victory, but there was still much to do. The legislation was weak. No penalties existed for not appearing before the board or for practicing without a license. The board also lacked a specific residence and had to meet and examine in rather haphazard locations.

In 1885, the year Aaron entered Leonard Medical School, legislation finally passed that made any "new" doctor guilty of a misdemeanor if he set up practice without first gaining a license through the North Carolina Board of Medical Examiners. Midwives were exempt, and any doctor who had earned a diploma from a medical college prior to 1880 was also exempt.

This meant that Aaron's professors, all white physicians with reputable practices in the community, were not required to be licensed by the board, although Aaron would be fined or even imprisoned should he set up practice without a license. Medicine, including the business and politics of medicine, was changing quickly as Aaron was preparing to practice. It is important to note that the majority of his professors were listed as approved and licensed by the North Carolina Board of Medical Examiners as of Aaron Moore's graduation.[12]

Aaron Moore sat for his medical boards in 1888, the year before legislation requiring *every* physician, not only "new" physicians, regardless of status or practice or education, to appear before the board for licensure or be charged with misdemeanor or worse. Illegal surgeries were punishable to the highest extent.

Every year, by all accounts from the university and the medical board, the examinations had become more stringent and more difficult to pass. They were specifically aimed at those who tried to cheat or pass without attending any kind of university program. Finally, a medical course of study became a requirement, and by the time Aaron sat for his boards, a grade average higher than a B overall was considered a prerequisite for passing.[13]

Aaron Moore's medical board examinations are described as follows:

REPORT OF THE BOARD OF MEDICAL EXAMINERS OF NORTH CAROLINA, WITH APPENDED RULES OF PROCEDURE
Wilmington, N.C., May 22, 1888.
The Board of Medical Examiners of North Carolina met in Fayetteville May 5, 1888. The following members were present: William R. Wood, M.D., President, Examiner on Chemistry and Pharmacy; Frances Duffy, M.D., Examiner on Surgery and Diseases of the Eye and Ear; A. W. Knox, M.D. [Leonard faculty], Examiner on Obstetrics and Diseases of Women and Children; James A. Reagan, M.D., Examiner on Physiology and Hygiene; P. L. Murphy, M.D., Examiner on Anatomy; Willis Alston, M.D., Examiner on Practice of Medicine; W. J. H. Bellamy, M.D., Secretary, and Examiner on Materia Medica and Therapeutics. The Board continued in session at The Hotel La Fayette until the morning of the 12th inst., after having passed upon the qualifications of fifty-three applicants, thirty-

six of whom were licensed, and the remaining seventeen were either rejected or allowed to withdraw.[14]

These examinations took a full four days, and nearly a third of the applicants were rejected. All of Aaron Moore's examiners were white, and only one—Dr. Knox—was likely to be on his side. The list of newly licensed doctors follows the naming of the examiners in the board's report; only two names on this list are marked "(col)" for "colored": "Aaron M. Moore of Rosindale" and "Robert A. Reynolds of Murfreesborough," Aaron's classmate from Leonard. The list also includes one white woman.[15] These examination results were also published in the *Charlotte Democrat* on Friday, May 18, 1888, under the heading "New Doctors."[16]

Dr. Aaron McDuffie Moore became a licensed physician under more scrutiny and more rigorous regulations than had been required of any of his professors or colleagues, black or white, who had graduated before him in his field. He rose to the challenge of these standards and would continue to uphold them as he participated in the education of his fellow black physicians and nurses for the rest of his career. Once again, Dr. Moore's trajectory was on the leading edge of change.

10

DECIDING ON DURHAM

Ask, and it will be given you; seek, and ye will find; knock,
and it will be opened to you. —Matthew 7:7

On May 23, 1888, immediately after passing his boards in Fayetteville on May 12, the newly minted Dr. Aaron McDuffie Moore attended the Republican State Convention at the Metropolitan Hall in Raleigh. Prominent black politician John Campbell Dancy was elected secretary of the convention and delegate to the upcoming National Republican Convention in Chicago. Aaron Moore, following in his father Israel Moore's footsteps, is listed as an alternate delegate from his original home county of Columbus. Moore was also "recommended as a suitable member" of the Committee on Resolutions and was so elected. One of these resolutions, the third, states, "We look upon the Purity of the ballot box as the best possible security against threatening evils and we demand such reasonable State legislation as will fully protect the elector in the exercise of the elective franchise. Any denial of the free and just exercise of the elective franchise by fraud or violence poisons the springs of power."[1]

This statement reflects the passion of the Republican Party of the day to uphold the progress made during Reconstruction toward equality. The turn of the century, however, would see a tremendous backlash against the participation of blacks in the political process, and this eloquent plea to protect voters' rights is evidence of that danger to the ballot box, which was yearly increasing. There had been a number of impediments placed in the path of the black male voter since that initial Reconstruction-era burst of Radical Republican influence in the region. Therefore it became clear that those who were allowed through the narrow restrictions imposed on voters and civic leadership should take their role even more seriously. Historian Leslie Brown notes, "Richard Fitzgerald, William G. Pearson, John Merrick and Aaron M. Moore were among the Black leaders qualified to vote, and all were resolute about Black Suffrage.... Their property ownership, influence ... and professional ventures represented a potential for Black electoral forces to effect change.... Moving from aspiration to action, their willingness ... invoked the threat of social equality, a challenge to White power."[2]

So it was that "A. M. Moore" (not yet even afforded a "Dr." before his name in the paper) resolutely, if reluctantly, entered the political sphere. It is very possible that his colleagues Monassa T. Pope and Lawson A. Scruggs, with whom he had formed the Old North State Medical Society the year before, had voiced their encouragement of Moore's political participation in light of their own political ambitions and beliefs in black representation. John Merrick likely also influenced his decision, and finally, it is quite possible that noted journalist and Republican leader John C. Dancy himself invited Moore to participate. Dancy was an associate of Moore's cousin George H. White. The two had started their political careers at the same time and in the same area of the state. It seems that White and Dancy had a cordial but not warm relationship and that Dancy was certainly more politically adept while White was more openly passionate and morally religious in his beliefs. Aaron Moore's personality and upbringing may have made him more sympathetic to his cousin George's point of view, especially when it came to the sly maneuverings and double-speak that he himself did not admire in the political arena. Moore, however, was known for his own brand of thoughtful reserve, which seems similar to how Dancy is described by White's biographer: "Dancy was cool, cerebral, and polished, capable of playing two contradictory roles at once: detached observer and highly political player."[3] It seems Aaron Moore's personality sat at a center point between the two men. Dancy, however, had a certain niece from Tarboro who had attended St. Augustine Normal School. It might have mattered a great deal to the young Dr. Moore to participate in the circles in which Sarah McCotta Dancy's uncle was prominent, and do well.

After his participation in the Republican State Convention, it was time for Moore to make a final plan about his future home and practice. Durham businessman John Merrick, his friend since his years at Leonard, had persuaded him to become Durham's first (and only) black physician. Merrick was already a successful and well-connected entrepreneur, and his goal was to attract as many like-minded, ambitious black men as he could to Durham to participate in making a new kind of black community. Undertaking this practice would be no small task for the young physician, but it had all the indicators of great service and opportunity wrapped in its tribulations. It also had all of the earmarks of the kind of work that Leonard Medical School's curriculum and ethos had prepared him for.

Durham was a brand-new town. It was unique in that it had no in-grained pre–Civil War history or social infrastructure to speak of. It had grown up in the late 1860s around a small railway station, created be-cause of North Carolina's biggest postwar cash crop: bright leaf tobacco. The Civil War played an oddly key role in the proliferation of Durham's tobacco. Both Union and Confederate soldiers, camped at the nearby Bennitt farm in April 1865 during the drawn-out surrender negotiations between Johnston and Sherman, raided and enjoyed the contents of a local tobacco warehouse. Upon their return home, soldiers from both armies spread the word about the superior quality of bright leaf tobacco. Long-distance orders and brisk sales followed, resulting in the leading producer's need for a trademark. He came up with it over lunch, the story goes, inspired by the bull pictured on the front of a jar of Colman's mus-tard. Genuine Bull Durham Tobacco was born, and the Bull Durham nickname stuck.[4]

Cotton had lost a lot of its luster as a crop, and prices had fallen con-siderably during the Reconstruction era. Tobacco, however, seemed to have no peak in sight, and all of the warehouses that dried, processed, and shipped tobacco clustered around Durham Station. The Duke family built a massive factory and warehouses and staffed them with the hordes of workers arriving from all over the state. Half a dozen textile mills soon followed, producing the cotton bags for loose tobacco as well as denim fabric and hosiery. Durham's population exploded with workers, and most of them were colored folks. Almost nowhere else in the country did there exist so many opportunities for a black community built from the ground up. Men and women alike had work and wages. Families began to need houses, and so brick and lumber businesses grew. Churches formed, and their congregations increased.[5] "The absence of an Old South heri-tage opened the town's power structure enough to let in a range of mav-ericks, Black and White," observes Brown. "For a short period of time, ambition could overcome racial restrictions and challenge power wielded historically by planters."[6]

Regrettably, this "short period of time" ended when those Old South-ern defaults of wage disparity and racism set in. Large and seemingly limitless fortunes were being made in tobacco, and with progress ma-chine labor had also arrived, replacing enough skill sets that the only remaining work was scarce and deeply segregated. Work conditions in tobacco processing, especially for black women, were positively inhuman. Black men, in turn, were being funneled away from skilled labor and into heavy lifting and menial labor, if not back to the farms. Black women who didn't work in the hideous conditions of the factories were washerwomen or domestics in white homes. Factories were also full of black child workers, whose education and future were in jeopardy. Many of Durham's black educators—in particular Richard Fitzgerald, William G. Pearson, and James Whitted—were gravely concerned. Black education in Durham was constantly being threatened by lack of state funds and increasingly openly targeted by disgruntled white arsonists, vandals, and all methods of intimidation from the Ku Klux Klan. Durham's whites refused to have their tax dollars fund black education, perceiving the danger of an educated black populace and fearing "Negro domination" when any progress was made by blacks in the civic arena or in the professional classes. As a result, something of a mass exodus of the black community started out of Durham in 1888–89 to places like Kansas and other points North and West. There was even talk of immigration to the nation of Liberia. The problem with this exodus, however, was that it both robbed white business owners of their labor force and simultaneously threatened the dreams of black leaders like John Merrick of one day seeing a secure and prosperous black middle class in Durham. Merrick made public entreaties during this time period for Durham's black residents to stay the course and not trade away what could be achieved in their city for the unknown. Notwithstanding his charisma, hundreds of men and women of color boarded trains and headed out of town.[7]

When Aaron Moore was choosing to make Durham the first home of his adult life in the autumn of 1888, it was still a mostly wooded area and looked more like farm country with a small town center and a collection of warehouses and factories near the train yards. The "colored" side of town, named Hayti by its residents, was on the far side of the tracks, away from what was becoming Main Street, where the fine houses of the white residents were being built. According to Durham County historian Jean Bradley Anderson, "The first documented use of the name Hayti in Durham is found in a deed of 1877.... Conjecture has attributed it to Whites as a name for any Black settlement, and to Blacks as an expression of their admiration of and hope of emulating the independent island Nation [of Haiti]."[8] Eventually a trolley service would make it more manageable for people to live farther away from the factories, and thus the little town began to grow.[9] Initially, it contained only a few streets and a network of dirt roads. Dr. Moore would have to figure out how best to navigate those roads at all hours during his first year of practice—but not until he had weathered the long months in the late summer and autumn of 1888, when he sat waiting to be called at all.[10]

Moore's main associate in town, John Merrick, a man of great enthusiasm and charisma by all accounts, was no doubt helpful in keeping Aaron's spirits high in these first months. Merrick was about to become sole owner of his barbershop in 1889 and had already built a fine house on Fayetteville Street in Hayti. It would certainly be more difficult for a young black physician to gain the trust of an unfamiliar population of patients than for a charismatic barber to set up shop, but the alliance of the two men would help that trust to build. Moore had already encountered some of the difficulties of establishing a new practice from his first year at Leonard when they had opened the community clinic. He knew it might even take the introduction or recommendation of a white medical colleague to persuade black patients that Moore was not a "root doctor" but a real physician. Being a pioneer in any profession has its challenges, but wielding a needle, a scalpel, or a stethoscope (still a newfangled invention) could make it even more difficult to gain trust and a good reputation.[11]

John Merrick naturally understood the importance of respectability and the need for relationship building in both the white and black communities. He excelled at it. He himself had ascended through masonry and bricklaying to shoe shining and barbering and finally to owning his own enterprise. His ability to entertain, as well as his dapper and intelligent demeanor, made him the ideal gentleman's barber. To some he was even known as "Gentleman John." He is somewhat rapturously described in his posthumous biography as having "a charm that won men's hearts, a vision that pierced men's souls and a transforming intelligence that absorbed an idea, impregnated it and gave its fruitful offspring for the service of his generation. He was laughter and infinite joy and life itself. No man looked upon him whose heart did not soften with favor, for there was no bitterness in him and all his ways were ways of pleasantness."[12] This is only one such opinion; others were gathered from both white and black associates. He was not only driven and energetic but gifted socially, no matter whom he was with.

John Merrick, however, was no one's servant; he was a businessman through and through and had constructed his own business education out of sharp observances of his clients' business behavior and the advice freely offered to him by those who sat in his chair. He gained the highest respect such individuals had to offer a man of color and even what men of vastly differing levels of privilege could call friendship.[13]

The attainment of a similar level of financial and social success for Dr. Aaron Moore was conjecture at this point, of course, on Merrick's part. Moore's performance on the medical boards seems to indicate that the young doctor didn't feel particularly intimidated or daunted by adverse conditions or expectations. It is true that being among the small percentage of men of color entering a "higher" professional career in medicine gave Moore prospects that were more assured than the average newcomer to Durham. However, it was also a fact that the new crop of black physicians all over the South were experiencing tremendous difficulty building practices that could afford them a living at all, much less financial security.[14] Moore didn't have much of an example of getting past the next hurdle; only one group of six black physicians from Leonard had passed into the profession before him. John Merrick, though, seems to have always had his eyes on the next prize, and his enthusiasm must have been infectious even to the more retiring and earnest Moore.

Merrick's biographer R. McCants Andrews describes Dr. Moore's contrasting personality as follows: "[He is] slower of speech and manner, more calculating in thought and judgment. [Moore] has been systematically trained, and intellect completely dominates impulse. A deep, religious current and conviction draw him away from the shouts and laughter of men into the solace and security of spiritual communion. But this outward undisturbed and unemotional form conceals the deepest of emotional natures—a great heart that aches with every hurt of humanity, that senses and shares every pain and every sorrow and wishes itself able to alleviate the evils and sufferings of human kind."[15] The lifelong collaboration of these very different men suggests that both were grateful to have a friend with such a differing personality with whom to enjoy zealous conversations and big plans, and both had in common tremendous hearts.

Dr. Moore had big plans to make indeed if he was to set up a home and a medical practice all at once. A doctor's home, in those days, was also his hospital and place of surgery. He would have to procure supplies as well as a location, and he would need help making that home. The final piece in the puzzle of his professional life would be the updating of the eligible young Dr. Moore's marital status.

Moore's marital intentions were no doubt a topic of great interest in

Moore's echelon of society from the moment he graduated from Leonard. Young ladies of marriageable age may suddenly have needed his advice on headaches or a touch of the heat after church. Perhaps an unusual number of young lady visitors came to any church he might be attending that summer. Certainly he would not have lacked for dinner invitations at the homes of pretty women of good education. Everyone knew a doctor couldn't heal the sick and keep house at the same time, and while an aunt or cousin could "do" for him for a little while, he really ought to think about his future as a respectable family man. These personal concerns had to be at the back of Aaron's mind as he planned his new life.

Finding a suitable wife for the first black physician in Durham was not an easy task. She would have to be of appropriate age, social class, and, yes, color. Aaron Moore, it would have been widely known, came from a predominantly light-skinned landowning family that had been free since before the birth of the nation. His own family and professional colleagues would never have approved of his marrying a girl without a similar educational background and family.[16]

By 1888, as Aaron Moore was forming these vital foundations of his adult life and work, the experiment of Reconstruction-era black colleges and universities in turning out a generation of classically educated, morally refined blacks was starting to achieve the goal of white Northern philanthropists' assimilationist agenda. It was not, however, remaining as true to the more radical antiracist agenda. In other words, those tenacious few who had been educated by whites in black universities were now deemed palatable as leaders in their community by those whites who would occasionally interface socially or politically with them. However, the more radical goal of true racial equality through excellent education was getting kicked further down the road, as evidenced by the attacks on schools and educational funding at this time in Durham. Furthermore, because of the favor shown to blacks who tended to be lighter-skinned, as they were deemed more "attractive" and therefore more "respectable" by white standards, and their more secure earning status through higher education, division was being sown both within the race and without.[17] Pauli Murray, grandniece of brick maker and banker Richard Fitzgerald, the aforementioned colleague and associate of Aaron Moore, wrote about her experience of color growing up in Durham at the turn of the century: "It seemed as if there were only two kinds of people in the world—*They* and *WE*—*White* and *Colored*. The World revolved on color and variations in color.... I picked it up from grown folks around me. I heard it in the house, on the playground, in the streets, everywhere.... Two shades lighter! Two shades darker! Dead White! Coal Black! High Yaller! ... Good Hair! Bad Hair! Stringy Hair! Nappy Hair! Thin lips! Thick lips! ... Straight nosed! Flat nosed! ... To hear people talk, color, features and hair were the most important things to know about a person.... Being neither very dark or very fair, I was a nobody.... I was a minority within a minority."[18]

In 1903 W. E. B. Du Bois, himself a graduate of Harvard University, would call this small percentage of classically educated blacks the "Talented Tenth."[19] By the turn of the century a trend of mostly lighter-skinned students attending classical black colleges and universities was developing, even though this had not at all been the case (or the goal) when Aaron Moore was attending Whittin or Fayetteville Normal Schools or even Leonard Medical School. A class photograph from Leonard Medical School clearly shows a full range of color shades in Moore's classmates and colleagues.[20] Nevertheless, as new trends became enforced at the turn of the century, norms and funding and patronage of higher education—in fact, any education—for blacks deteriorated. The "Talented Tenth" would be tasked with dispelling racism by themselves through "proving" blacks successful as a race while "improving" their communities from the top down, all to measure up to white standards and all with an attitude of modesty and gratitude.[21] As Pauli Murray so vividly stated, color was never absent as a qualifier at this moment in history—nor, arguably, has it ever been since.

Dr. Moore was now a member of that "Talented Tenth," a black man of a relatively fair complexion and of advanced education. Durham's Hayti, as well as Durham's white philanthropic class, would expect him to be a pillar of his community in order to make his practice both respectable and profitable. A young bride was therefore required of irreproachable manners, religious upbringing, good education, and similar complexion at his side. It was simply what was expected. Furthermore, the future Mrs. Dr. A. M. Moore would have to be made of pretty stern stuff if she was to preside over a household that might at any moment be soaked in blood or invaded by contagious disease or the wails of childbirth. She would also have to be someone who wouldn't need or expect much of his company. His life was to be one of service, and all physicians whom he knew kept odd and irregular hours and were seldom at leisure at home. She would also need to share his deep faith and, if he was truly fortunate, perhaps even his love of books and learning.

Moore did have a young lady in mind. He had noticed her while he was at Shaw and she was a student at St. Augustine's, a young lady from Tarboro. More definite personal plans would have to wait, however, until he could set up a home and a rudimentary living. If John Merrick had it right, and it seemed that he usually did, Durham could be a place where a happy, productive future was possible for Aaron, his practice, and someday even a family of his own.

The new Dr. A. M. Moore packed his clothes, books, and instruments and got on the train to Durham Station.

PART THREE *The Young Physician Settles Down*

II

DOCTORING, DURHAM, AND DEARLY BELOVED

Into the molten new society that was Durham, North Carolina, in 1888 came Dr. Aaron McDuffie Moore. With John Merrick's help, he secured a small farm away from the industrial center. The county line ran through part of the property, and a portion of the Fitzgerald Brickyard, a thriving black-owned business, was also on the property. The first Moore farm in Durham was where the Stanford Warren Library stands today.[1] In the absence of a basement, the house sat off the ground to avoid flooding, and stairs rose steeply up to the wide porch, which would become a kind of outdoor surgery area. The front of the house was on a slope, while the back rested on stilts high enough for a small person—or a tall one bent double—to walk underneath. There were fruit trees and enough land to garden and keep livestock. A housekeeping aunt or cousin was likely sent from the country to "do" for Dr. Moore as he got his practice and his little farm together. He began immediately to attend White Rock Baptist Church and was probably introduced every Sunday for months from the pulpit in order to make his presence and his practice known.[2]

It was in these early days that he began to understand the layers of need that most families exhibited. If they trusted him, the doctor did what he could for an immediate crisis. Then he also did what he could to make sure sustenance, warmth, and shelter were available to give the patient a decent chance to heal. He plied his trade and used his expertise, especially in the area of obstetrics and family medicine, to give his patients a fighting chance, but he longed to do more. He had to do more.

A brief foray into Durham politics—he decided to allow himself to be nominated for Durham County coroner—made Dr. Moore's name part of the public record. He is listed as the "colored" nominee in the *Tobacco Plant* of Friday, October 5, 1888, and the *Durham Recorder* of Wednesday, October 3, gives us an ugly snapshot of how that nomination was received:

Do the white people of Durham County want Dr. Moore, colored, to act as their coroner? Will any republican in Durham County swallow the ticket that was nominated Saturday by 11 Negroes and four Whites? We invite all who cannot "stomach" that ticket to come out to the Democratic Party and vote for the success of the white man's Party. W. G. Pearson, colored, is Chairman of the Republican Executive Committee in Durham County. White men of Durham, those who have any respect for the Anglo-Saxon race, will you fail to do your duty on the 6th of November? Will you allow a Negro rule, or a white man's government? Stand to your colors. Vote for the interest of your homes—your children's homes and education.[3]

This article was doubtless only a small part of the threats, intimidation, and vitriol that Moore encountered. His brush with running for office was an ugly awakening for him. The situation was sufficiently alarming that he withdrew from the race and would never run for office of any kind or even participate in any way but peripherally for the rest of his life. This brand of insidious racism and the politics of the Southern Democratic Party in opposition to the party of Lincoln was not new to him in theory, but it had not yet singled him out directly as its target. He was a new name in a new town, and his practice was at stake, not to mention his life and property. It was a rude and dangerous episode indeed, one he never forgot.[4] Historian Walter B. Weare notes, "Even in the late 1880s, well before North Carolina's white supremacy campaigns, he [Aaron Moore] found the white majority ... hostile to his efforts in direct politics, so he, like other black leaders of the New South, redirected his energies to self-help, racial solidarity, and the formation of all-black institutions."[5]

It was a rugged first year for the young doctor in Durham. At the end of it, however, was the prize he had no doubt been hoping and planning for.

Pastor J. W. Perry joined Dr. Aaron McDuffie Moore and Sarah Mc-Cotta Dancy, called "Cottie," in marriage on Wednesday, December 18, 1889.[6] Aaron was just a few months past his twenty-sixth birthday. The ceremony took place in the old brick structure of White Rock Baptist Church, which had become Aaron's spiritual home during his first year in Durham. The witnesses listed in the marriage record were J. D. Harget, C. D. Howard, and J. H. Dancy. This J. H. Dancy, surely a relative of the bride, is not John C. Dancy, Cottie's illustrious uncle, who at this time was the first black recorder of deeds in Washington. John Merrick would seem an obvious choice for a witness, but since only three witnesses are named in most of the entries in the marriage records of that month, there is nothing to prove or disprove who else might have attended. It is very likely John Merrick and his wife were there to celebrate the new pair.

The bride, "Miss Cottie," is listed in the record as age twenty-two, and both the bride and groom are marked with a *C* for "colored." Lyda Moore Merrick (the older of their two daughters) later described her mother's origins as "growing up in the shadow of slavery" and remarked that Sarah McCotta Dancy's mother, Martha Dancy, had borne both "white" and "colored" children. Cottie's father was probably white. Martha Dancy is listed in the census records as a household dependent in several different households, including those of her grown sons.[7] But Cottie's uncle John C. Dancy, a black Republican activist, had made sure that Cottie got the best education, went to St. Augustine for the normal course, and was placed in the coveted society of those colored people allowed to live in the downtown center of Tarboro. It was a serene and pastoral town known for its fine manners and strict social mores. Nevertheless, Lyda recalled her mother saying that she was "anxious to get away" from that little town and to "get a good husband." Cottie taught school for a short time before she apparently caught the interest of young Dr. Moore while she was sitting in church. He spotted her long braided hair hanging down in a pew ahead of him as the collection plate went around. Lyda remembered her mother saying years later how she had been "just plain happy to find anyone who could look after her, give her a home and be kind to her." Lyda added that her father "did all those things excellently."[8]

It would be remiss not to illuminate the aspects of both classism and racism inherent in this match. The nuances of skin color during this era, especially for women, could determine an individual's level of freedom to move about with any degree of safety in society. (That fact is, frankly, not much different today.) Lighter skin meant life could be marginally easier because of the rewards in both black and white communities that came with being more socially "appealing." Aaron had noticed Cottie's beautiful long hair in church because hair quality was deemed socially important. "Good hair" was a prize to be added to the family gene pool and often came from Native American heritage in a freedman family's background. Lighter eyes were also considered desirable. White European standards of beauty were imposed then, as they are now, and the closer one was to that standard, the more acceptable one was on all sides.

Respectability and religious upbringing were estimable in both men and women. Once again, there was safety inherent in the trappings of moral character and propriety. Women who did not work as domestics or appear in any way servile were in less danger of assault or disrespect in public places. They could uphold the reputation of a professional, middle-class family with more success, or so it was widely felt. This intraracial bias was an uncomfortable but very real aspect of everyday life at the turn of the century in the American South.

Lyda Moore Merrick was herself somewhat dismayed in hindsight by the attitudes of the time, even though she was a product of them. When she addressed these "rules" in her taped interviews, her voice faltered in a way that was not like her usual frankness. She laughed nervously, even though her interviewer was also African American and it was the 1980s. Lyda said of her family roots,

> They had a farm, and they lived comfortably. And among them there were brown people and there were black people, and ... [the nervous laugh] there was prejudice, too. As a result, they intermarried quite a bit among cousins, because they didn't want to marry anybody dark. Now, they never told me that verbatim, you know, but we went down there about every other summer, and you observe ... certain things. Everybody down there was what we called "purty" and had "pretty hair." There is quite a settlement of Lumbee Indians down there, and they intermixed with them, too, and still they were not "black" as a rule. All through the family you see the Indian blood in them. I remember them saying "not to marry anyone from Bladen County" [significant pause] they were too dark over there. I don't know, they sort of felt like, if you had good hair, that helped.

Later, in her memories of her mother, Lyda got very emotional about her mother's looks and especially that legendary hair:

> Mama was a little darker than me and my sister, but she had beautiful hair. [Sighs] She could sit on her braid. I remember her taking it like this in her hand and throwing it back with a thump [laughs]. Papa said he wouldn't let her cut it. He used to joke: "I saw that hair before I saw you." She had beautiful hair. It wasn't straight, it was curly, just as soft ... and beautiful.[9]

It seems Cottie was a kind of Rapunzel for Lyda, and Rapunzel she remained in her memory.

Fortunately for Dr. Moore, his choice of a wife went far beyond more superficial or socially imposed dreams of a mate. His bride proved to have a good brain, an indomitable spirit, and a courageous heart under that beautiful soft, curly hair.

Their small wedding ceremony took place on a Wednesday morning in chilly December. The sanctuary of White Rock Baptist Church must have displayed some hints of the Christmas celebrations that the following week would bring. They would be seeing Aaron's mother and father and his home folks soon enough; still, it may have felt a bit lonely to be entering into this chapter of his life without the grounding and connecting presence of family.

This December morning would mark the official end of Moore's youth. Since he was a child, he had always been part of some larger group—a bustling family unit, a congregation. Then he had joined a student body and been surrounded by the fraternity of his colleagues. This impending union would be so very different. This accomplished, sweet St. Augustine girl, who was diminutive yet also precocious—Cottie of the long brown braid and the warm laugh—would today link her life with his forever. Her safety and prosperity would be his entire responsibility. Together, if they were lucky, they could make a world that none could pull asunder. This kind of family life would be, at least initially, frighteningly intimate—one man looking at one woman, depending on one another, reaching for each other's hand in the darkness. The very food she ate and clothes she wore would depend on his ability to provide and succeed. When Aaron was a single man, the possibility of failure inherent in lofty ambitions had been a threat only to himself. As a married one, all successes and all failures would affect her life and the lives of their children. This girl, her eyes as sweet and dark as summer blackberries, would need to be his partner and his dearest friend.

Placing the small ring on her finger, he repeated the words he had heard before at other weddings. He spoke the vows, and her softer voice repeated hers in return: forsaking all others; in sickness and in health; to love, honor, and cherish. And then the Reverend Perry said "man and wife," and they were.

Dr. and Mrs. Moore spent their honeymoon and first Christmas as a married couple with Aaron's family in Columbus County. When they returned home, Durham's society made much of the pair. The community was ready to receive this new bride. Then Aaron and Cottie began setting up housekeeping together in a life that was dazzlingly new.[10] It was a lonely first winter, and Cottie had a lot of adjusting to do. They would need to make a strong family bond and establish their routines quickly in the midst of the chaos of a doctor's life.

Dr. Moore became a father very soon afterward on November 19, 1890, when Lyda Vivian Moore was born. Cottie delivered her at home, because home *was* the hospital. The young couple enjoyed their one-child household until Lyda was two years old, and then Cottie became pregnant with their second child.

Mattie Louise Moore, Aaron's second daughter, was born on June 6, 1893, ready to take on the world with a studious face like her father's and a spicy personality that would astonish her older sister for years to come. Mattie would always be in a hurry to catch up to Lyda—in school, in all areas of accomplishment, even in piano playing and teaching.

"I was always in the shadow of my sister," the first-born Lyda Moore (Merrick) said as she remembered Mattie Louise. "She was always smarter than I was." When asked why, Lyda replied [her voice full of both admiration and annoyance], "Well, she always had a smart answer. Anything anyone could think of, she had an answer. Whoo! She would get you *told*! She had a sense of humor. She was the life of the house." Lyda continued wistfully, "I was always the quieter child."[11]

If Lyda styled herself as quiet, Mattie Louise must have been like a freight train in white muslin and pigtails.

Dr. Moore adored his two girls, and even as a busy doctor he found time to be involved in their lives and notice their different personalities and talents as they grew up. At the end of his day, if they were awake, they would run to see him after he had washed up and tell him all the things he wanted to know about their playtime or studies. Those early years in Durham were a succession of calls and emergencies. "He frantically answered calls from the destitute," wrote scholar Louis D. Mitchell in an article about Moore for *The Crisis*. "He fed the hungry, delivered babies, comforted the bereaved, and dashed about on horse and bicycle in the black community to visit and bring relief to the miserable."[12] At every turn he was faced with the poverty and struggle of his people who had filled the cigarette factories, sewn cotton bags for grain and flour, and worked the looms in the textile mills—domestics, laborers, washerwomen, field hands, railroad porters.

In 1900, in the handwritten U.S. federal census for Durham, Aaron Moore is listed in the sequence of his neighbors with "Physician" next to his name. (The professions of his neighbors read house servant, teacher, sack stringer, field laborer, cook, preacher, locomotive fireman, laundress, hack driver.) His entry is also the only one with a farm schedule number, which would indicate that he had enough land that he was required to report the level of produce and amount of livestock on it to the government at tax time.[13] That land and the sustenance it provided were invaluable to the young doctor, who charged his patients only a dollar per visit. And if the visit was paid for at all, it was rarely in cash. Often gifts would appear on the porch—a loaf of bread or a bag of seed, grain, or milled flour—or he would come home with some eggs in his pockets. He even sold his own produce to make ends meet.[14]

Lyda Moore Merrick remembered her father pulling teeth and doing minor surgeries on the porch of their first farmhouse. On Sunday he might take them on some of his house calls after church and drive them in the buggy through the surrounding neighborhoods. Sometimes they would visit the Fitzgerald mansion and play under the grape arbor.[15] When Lyda was ten years old and still living in the old farmhouse, her papa found time to build her and sister Mattie a backyard playhouse "big enough for them both to turn around in." Mattie had thirteen different dolls, and most of them were in a constant state of sickness and in need of many operations. Both girls undertook these operations but none more zealously than "Dr." Mattie Louise. One of her sick dolls was named Octagon and another one Priscilla. The sisters used to say they wanted to "sleep out in the playhouse all night," but they always lost their courage as soon as night fell and the real house looked warm and full of light and safety. Lyda never much liked the dark, even as an adult. It stands to reason, since darkness back then was more profound than any light-diluted darkness we experience today. The sisters also loved to create whole worlds and neighborhoods in the crawl space under the back porch using bricks and dirt and all sorts of improvised tools. "We made our fun," Lyda reminisced in her taped interviews, a girlish giggle creeping into her voice. "There was always something to do. The chickens never did learn they didn't belong under there."[16]

Gifts for birthdays and Christmas were simple things like art supplies, books, and one year a blackboard on an easel that Papa Aaron liked Lyda and Mattie to keep full of fresh illustrations. He would always pause and comment on their work, no matter how rushed or tired he was when he came home. Lyda's talent for the visual arts likely began with that blackboard easel and the desire to delight her father's attentive eye for beauty.

Lyda remembered that there were gas streetlights on the street, and the lamplighter came around and lit them one by one at dusk. The front parlor had an organ in it, and Cottie played hymns and sang at bedtime while the candle sconces shed a soft light from the walls. But light was expensive. Dark time meant bedtime for all.[17]

12

NOT A "ROOT DOCTOR"

The first year of Dr. Aaron Moore's career in Durham is documented in a rather remarkable artifact: his daily visiting book. The journal is bound in burgundy-brown leather and stamped with the words "Physician's Visiting List without Dates" along the edge where one's fingers would grasp to open it. The book is now very battered but remarkably intact, and in it are details of the first two years of Aaron's life as Durham's first black physician. The opening pages are a kind of shorthand guide to the kinds of treatments a country doctor might need to perform. These pages are in themselves revealing. They include dental instructions and diagrams of teeth, because the doctor in those days was also the dentist. There is a listing of the most current textbooks on various ailments, so these visiting books must have been like an almanac or yearly medical journal of sorts. Yet there are no notes or indications that Dr. Moore used this portion of the journal much; in fact these opening pages are much more pristine than the rest of the book. The undated daily visiting pages, however, are covered with his notes in pencil. They detail names of patients and where he treated them (such as at home or at the factories). The number of times he returned to see them for a specific malady seems to be indicated with hash marks next to the name in the spaces for the days of the week. The visits seem, by and large, to have cost a dollar each, but many are listed for less. We know also from family accounts that many patients paid in trade or over time. An account looked to be settled when he struck through the patient's record. Occasionally he listed his own expenses and did sums in the margins, so this book was a bookkeeping record as well as a patient record. Often he indicated the medicinal remedy used, but rarely did he give more than a single word to indicate the reason for the visit. These entries include "the [family name] baby," "cough," "shot," "snake," "fever," "cystitis," "factory," "smoke," "spasms," "eyes," "bronchitis," and "riggety [wrecked] toe." The most common entries are for babies, fever, and "smoke," which most likely applied to factory conditions or fire-related injuries.[1] Durham was a town that was expanding at the pace of the tobacco and textile industries that fed it. Working conditions were truly wretched, but living conditions, especially in the black neighborhoods, were unsanitary and hazardous to health. "The town had one main sewer, but there were no provisions for garbage collection or for cleaning the mud- and manure-mired streets," observed a Durham nurse. "Outdoor privies were common, and communicable diseases such as tuberculosis, smallpox, and typhoid fever were rampant throughout the community."[2]

The pages of Dr. Moore's visiting book are dated by hand with just the month and the last number of the year, and the entries start on October 7 in what seems to be 1888 (he often left the year blank) and extend through September 1889. This must have indeed been his very first patient record, since we know he moved to Durham directly following his board examinations. It is clear through these entries that his practice started slowly and became extraordinarily busy over the course of that first year. His initial entries are neat and deliberate; he filled in all of the categories and listed the date. He saw on average ten to twelve patients in a day. In only a few months that number increased, and by January 1889, he was filling both sides of the page with as many as fifty patients per page. His writing got more fragmented and his pencil pressed more deeply into the paper. His shorthand became even shorter, and abbreviations replaced full words. It all looks hurried, yet never chaotic. By the time this first book was filled to capacity, he was about to become a married man.[3]

In many ways those first years in Durham were both a social and professional awakening for Aaron Moore. The time he spent in every type of household situation, trying to stabilize and improve the conditions that would lead to better health, brought into focus the needs that his community must meet in order to be in any way healthy, uplifted, or hopeful. Having grown up in a smaller, more isolated, but much more interdependent environment in Columbus County, he was only now, nearing his fourth decade of life, beginning to grasp the weight and pervasiveness of institutionalized racism and disenfranchisement in the context of urban life. Lyda Moore Merrick remarked on the gravity in her father's voice as he tried to express to a white colleague the plight of himself and his patients and their lack of trust as he started his practice: "I remember when Papa, when I was a little thing, old enough to get the meaning, he told a white man, 'If you woke up colored, you'd commit suicide.' He said, 'You meet it the minute you leave your door. Discrimination hits you on every side.' And when Papa came here, the white people—the white doctors—had to tell our people that he wasn't a quack doctor, wasn't a root doctor. They never heard of black doctors."[4]

Durham's neighborhoods alternated between white and black as one traveled away from the center of town and the railroad station. The lower muddier lands with less navigable roads were the black neighborhoods, called "The Bottoms," and are recalled in Pauli Murray's memoir, *Proud Shoes*: "These little communities ... held together by cow paths or rutted wagon tracks were called The Bottoms ... an odorous conglomeration of trash piles, garbage dumps, cow stalls, pig pens, and crowded humanity."[5] Over these hills and into these valleys went Dr. Moore on his daily odyssey into the homes of black Durham. He was a pioneer of black medicine as well as social work and was also gathering data that would lead to his future branches of entrepreneurship, all in the most challenging of situations. Medical knowledge and higher education are useless when there is no trust. A great portion of his task during those first years had to be comprehensive community building rather than just treating illness. This call to action above and beyond his job description seems to have been a gift in disguise. His success in winning the trust of his patients is reflected in Lyda Moore Merrick's earliest memory that many in Hayti referred to her father not just as "Dr. Moore" but as "Daddy Moore."[6]

Dr. Moore's foundation and regular presence in the church certainly helped. He taught Sunday school as soon as there was one to teach and found that it was an excellent way to check in with the children and families under his care. If he didn't see a child on Sunday or heard from them that a parent was ill, he would get on his horse or into his buggy after church and go check on that person. The Moore family also knew that they were expected to carry themselves with dignity and that their collective compassion was a critical part of the healer's effect on his patients. The new Mrs. Cottie Moore learned very quickly to sterilize instruments and sanitize linens, to make soap and disinfectants, and even to assist in surgery in an emergency. Lyda remembered how hard her mother worked to assist her father and also make their household function: "My mother was behind my father in everything he did. She nursed and tended to him and raised us, the two girls.... She was very smart, artistic; all our clothes were made in our house until we were grown. Mama could sew, crochet, knit, tat, everything, busy all the time. She was a great church worker, and she was a club woman ... anywhere she saw she could lead." As the girls grew up, they too had to adjust to the pace of things in their home. "Saturday night was a busy time for folks coming in cut, bleeding. When I'd see them coming in, I'd run across the street to my cousin's because I didn't want to see the blood."[7]

Lyda also recalled that there were epidemics like smallpox and other contagious diseases in Hayti that made an impression in her childhood memories:

> Papa actually took those with contagious diseases into our house. He would isolate them and put on other clothes to go in there and check them out and tried to keep it all as sanitary as possible. They finally had a "pest house" [short for pestilence house, an isolated building for contagious patients] out where it was just woods, you know. That's where they carried those that had smallpox. We as children would call out, "Here comes the pest house wagon!" and we would run! And they would employ people who had already had smallpox to nurse them. I remember this girl named Lucinda Ray. She was a little older than me, very attractive girl, and it just struck us so, "Lucinda Ray's got the smallpox, they're takin' her to the pest house."[8]

Lyda's voice trailed off as if she could still see the face of this older girl whose beauty did not save her from smallpox.

"Mama says Papa started out going to see patients on a Bicycle. Then he had a little two-seat surrey he drove around in, or he rode his horse," Lyda recalled further. "It was a good thing the horse always knew his way back home. Sometimes the doctor was just too tired to remember."[9] Sometimes the horse wanted to go home before the doctor, as the *Durham Globe* reported on Saturday, March 31, 1894: "Dr. A. M. Moore's horse ran away yesterday afternoon, right down Main Street causing much excitement, but doing little damage."[10] The fact that his runaway horse made the Saturday paper speaks to the doctor's growing visibility and social status in town. Six years of practice seems to have made him a household name.

It was also during this very busy time in Dr. Moore's early practice that the man who had likely persuaded him to become a physician, Shaw University founding father Henry Martin Tupper, died. His funeral was held at the University Chapel at Shaw on November 30, 1893, Thanksgiving Day, and even if Aaron Moore did not personally attend, he would have read nearly every word that was said in Tupper's honor in the *Raleigh Gazette* the following week.[11] A new president was to take up the fate of Leonard Medical School with all of its financial woes and the impending crisis of medical school inspections on the horizon. Tupper was buried on the Shaw campus and is there to this day. Thanksgiving took on a new meaning that year for all who had been touched by Tupper's relentless dedication to education and service.

In the seventh year of his practice in Durham, Dr. Moore made his first strides in a new role in service to his community—he became an entrepreneur, joining a small group of black investors to open a pharmacy. Moore's Old North State Medical Society colleague Dr. Monassa T. Pope had made a success of his Queen City Drug Company just a few years before.[12] Pope likely consulted on this project as he did on others in Durham. The Durham Drug Company opened its doors in 1895 and would employ the town's first black pharmacists, who would serve "the black population of the city ... with dignity and provide ... [them] with good service and lower prices."[13] The Durham Drug Company was meant to stand as an empirical symbol that the health of Durham's black residents was important. Historian Jean Bradley Anderson noted, "Moore had as partners in establishing The Durham Drug Company [William G.] Pearson, [Richard] Fitzgerald, [James E.] Shepard, and J. A. Dodson."[14] This pool of entrepreneurs would be the origination of many ensuing fundraising and community-minded enterprises in Durham's growing population of Hayti. The Durham Drug Company may well have been a first step toward Dr. Moore's larger dream of a black hospital like the one he had practiced and learned in at Leonard Medical School. It was likely also linked to the first discussions of a life insurance company, since Dr. Pope had also established in conjunction with his pharmacy an insurance entity called the People's Benevolent Association.[15] The Durham Drug Company was run by two graduates of Shaw University's School of Pharmacy, J. A. Dodson and Dr. James E. Shepard.

Dr. Shepard's tenure in the pharmacy was short-lived as his success at the ensuing Republican convention of 1896 and his political aspirations would lead him instead to become the recorder of deeds in Washington, D.C., by 1897, a coveted post previously held by Frederick Douglass. Shepard would, however, remain associated with Dr. Moore and this group of entrepreneurs in Durham for decades, and his would become an influential voice, particularly in the service of education for his race.[16]

The Durham Drug Company may have been a kind of entrepreneurial trial balloon for black enterprise in Hayti, but it also seems to have been an effort to recruit these two pharmacists and Shaw alumni to Durham and make them part of its growing black talent pool. John Merrick's biographer, R. McCants Andrews, remarks, "The motive for the formation of this first company seems not to have been so much the making of money by the stockholders as it was to help the young pharmacists in the development of new business for the colored citizens."[17] Moore's dedication to his alma mater, coupled with his firsthand knowledge of people's pharmacy needs, would have made him a natural force behind the Durham Drug Company project.

Aaron Moore's continued passion and commitment to educational sponsorship helped recruit another talent to Durham in 1894—C. C. Spaulding. Dr. Moore traveled regularly in the summers to his homeplace in Sandy Plain to visit family, meet with and encourage students, and do what he could for the sick. Spaulding was not only a promising student but also Aaron's nephew, and so Moore sent for Spaulding to live at the Moore residence and to finish his education in Durham. C. C. Spaulding would turn out to be an extraordinary colleague in the years to come.[18]

Yet another important event in black history occurred on September 18, 1895. Thirty-nine-year-old Booker T. Washington gave a speech at the opening ceremonies of the Cotton States and International Exposition in Atlanta. It was remarkable that Washington was given such a platform, but it was a gesture meant to exhibit goodwill and progress between the races at this very Southern but nationally recognized exposition. His speech has since been dubbed "The Atlanta Compromise" and was delivered to an unprecedented mix of thousands of black and white visitors. The *Atlanta Journal-Constitution* described his speech the following day: "The colored race had a representative on the programme of the opening exercises of whom they have great reason to be proud.... It was the first time a colored orator had even stood upon a platform before such a vast audience with white men and women. It was an event in the history of the race. No one expected such a speech from Washington as he made.... There was not a superfluous word in it.... It made a magnificent impression and was frequently interrupted by applause."[19]

Booker T. Washington, who was billed as president of the Tuskegee Normal and Industrial School, advocated for a society that left his people unhindered legally and politically long enough for them to develop their own culture from the ground up and to form their own social structures, economies, and business centers. "Cast your bucket down where you are," he admonished, basing the quote on a story about a ship's crew dying of thirst until they were told they had sailed into fresh water. His implication in this parable was that both blacks and whites should concentrate on bettering what they already had in the South, both by improving the function of their separate societies and by finding critical resources in one another. His speech is full of gentlemanly olive branches and poetic language and such soaring quotes as "The laws of changeless justice bind oppressor with oppressed; and close as sin and suffering joined we march to fate abreast." It is difficult to imagine the effect that a speech like this had on a South just emerging from federally mandated Reconstruction and trying to conceive what life would be like going forward. His appeal to whites to remember the "loyalty and forbearance" of the recently emancipated, both during and after the Civil War, was an echo of a popular impetus for white philanthropy at the time. Upper-class whites still lived with black domestics and depended on their labor to power their fortunes. They needed to believe that black people were "loyal" and "grateful" and wanted only to work hard for a middle-class yet comfortably separate existence. Washington diplomatically reminded whites in his speech that importing immigrant workforces would dilute traditional ways of Southern living and that this might be less desirable even if those immigrants were Caucasian.

The progressive messages of this speech were certainly sugarcoated in their delivery, hence the "compromise," but the tragic naïveté of Washington's speech lay in his reasoning that the affinity that hard-working and respectable human beings have for one another would naturally precipitate good race relations over time. He appealed to the logic that "nearly sixteen millions of hands will aid you in pulling the load upward, or they will pull against you the load downward," his point being that prosperity, education, and equal participation in society would improve every life in the South, whereas leaving a segment of the population behind and disenfranchised would cost the South in the end. He finished his historic speech by acknowledging that while the progress of Reconstruction had allowed his people to advance in education and improve their contributions to exhibitions like the Cotton States and International Exposition, they were mindful of those who had helped them achieve this level of education and social advancement: "We do not for a moment forget that our part in this exhibition would fall far short of your expectations but for the constant help that has come to our educational life, not only from the Southern states, but especially from Northern philanthropists, who have made their gifts a constant stream of blessing and encouragement."[20] While some may have heard this as a humble note of gratitude, it can also be interpreted to mean "The North has been investing in our skills, and we have still chosen to remain in and contribute to the progress of the South with our accomplishments." He closed with hope and a fervent wish for "a willing obedience among all classes to the mandates of law and a spirit that will tolerate nothing but the highest equity in the enforcement of law. This, coupled with our material prosperity, will bring into our beloved South a new heaven and a new earth."[21] This last statement was certainly a plea to protect the black vote, which had of late been under attack in the South through poll taxes, literacy tests, grandfather clauses, and criminal record disqualification.[22] It also was a plea to protect black communities from educational disenfranchisement and state-sanctioned violence. Whether it was Booker T. Washington's tone, charisma, or content or the very fact that a black man was allowed such a platform, this speech was celebrated in newspapers nationwide.

An emotional wave of support from both sides of the racial divide arose for Washington and his way of thinking. Whites found hope for a future in which black entrepreneurship on its own side of town would politically stabilize the workforce on theirs. Booker T. Washington's philosophy also projected a longer horizon for achieving equal citizenship in the communal sphere since that equality was to be "fairly" won through respectability, hard work, and social orderliness. Reconstruction-educated and enterprising blacks hoped that this "compromise" rhetoric would make it possible for them to concentrate on organizing a dignified and upwardly mobile existence rather than be forced to agitate for basic safety and respect in ways that many had come to find exhausting and dangerous.

In hindsight, and in light of the betrayal of goodwill that the 1896 *Plessy v. Ferguson* decision and the ensuing Jim Crow era were to reveal, it is hard not to see this pivotal speech as a platform that benefited from mutual discomfort and tremendous naïveté. Goodwill seems to have existed in fledgling form, but it was fragile and conditional upon dwindling political participation from black citizens. The positive white response to the Atlanta speech may have seemed at the time a positive signal to enterprising blacks that there would be renewed interest in philanthropically assisting their endeavors. Moreover, the passing of Frederick Douglass on February 20 of the same year may have outlined Booker T. Washington as a new alternative national leader. It is important, especially when telling the story of men like Aaron Moore and his associates, to interpret this event and what Washington represented at the Atlanta Exposition as unique to its moment in time. "History lay heavily upon the times and the man," Washington scholar David H. Jackson Jr. observed, "and its layers formed the framework within which he acted."[23]

John Merrick and Booker T. Washington became friends and associates during this time period, although they had differing opinions, especially when it came to politics. Merrick would have read, if not personally witnessed, this speech, and the growth of black enterprise was certainly on his mind. Merrick had by this time a chain of barbershops: three for white clients and two for the black community. He had begun buying up real estate and was helping black families to purchase and build their own homes, using the lumber and materials from dismantled warehouses as Durham's industrial areas expanded. Merrick's home, his second, now graced Fayetteville Street, the avenue where Hayti's larger homes were starting to be built. Merrick had also developed and successfully marketed "Merrick's Dandruff Cure" since 1890. He had some capital that he was ready to invest in community-building infrastructure.[24]

Some of Merrick's product endorsement business sense must have rubbed off on Moore because the doctor himself began promoting a tonic for "wakefulness" in 1896 called Horsford's Acid Phosphate: "Dr. A. M. Moore, Durham, N.C., says, 'I find it of great value in wakefulness due to digestive disorders, and as a general tonic.'"[25] The doctor was evidently thinking outside the box.

Inspired, perhaps, by the Atlanta Exposition, Moore and Merrick also teamed up in 1896 to bring a "Colored Fair" to Durham October 12–16. They are listed in the *Durham Sun* as president (Merrick) and vice president (Moore) of the Durham County Fair Association. "It is proposed to make this the best colored fair ever held in the State. . . . Several prominent speakers have been invited," announced the *Sun*. Such public exhibitions of racial progress were obviously in fashion and gaining momentum. The same article states, "Contributions are solicited from the white friends in Durham who sympathize with Negro advancement."[26]

One of the above-mentioned "prominent speakers" at the Durham Colored Fair was Booker T. Washington himself. President John C. Kilgo of Trinity College invited Washington to give a guest address during chapel exercises to Trinity's all-white student body. Trinity (what would become Duke University) was the first white university to extend such an invitation in Washington's career. In a further gesture of respect and goodwill, President Kilgo suspended classes early so that Trinity students could attend the Colored Fair.[27] In the spirit of Washington's espoused philosophy that no educated man should be above getting his hands dirty, Aaron Moore, the farmer turned physician, exhibited at the fair his roots and his family's commitment to peaceful and respectable industry: an account of the fair in the *Raleigh Gazette* mentions Dr. A. M. Moore proudly displaying tools and produce from his farm and Mrs. Cottie Moore showing some fine examples of handiwork.[28]

The Colored Fair concept was not a new one, although it was new to Durham. Such fairs had been taking place regularly in the Raleigh area since 1879 and after 1890 on the official North Carolina State Fairgrounds as a follow-up to the white state fair. The Colored Fair was created with the fairly assimilationist goal of promoting the progress and education of blacks while extending diplomacy to whites. The North Carolina Industrial Association and its cofounder Charles Norfleet Hunter spearheaded this concept. There were, as a rule, parades, an address from the governor of North Carolina, and a ball. Black leaders would also be invited to speak, and even Frederick Douglass gave an address at the Colored Fair in 1880.[29]

Hunter may have been introduced to Aaron Moore in Raleigh while he was a medical student at Leonard. Hunter was a Shaw man himself. It is likely that Hunter, as a local dignitary, attended the widely publicized first commencement at Leonard Medical School and commencements thereafter, possibly including Moore's. Their paths may have crossed at one of the Colored Fairs themselves, although no record has been found of Aaron Moore attending. Nonetheless, we do know that Charles N. Hunter was a teacher in the Durham colored graded school in 1888, the year Dr. Moore began his practice there, and that ten years later in 1908 he became a traveling agent of the North Carolina Mutual and Provident Association, during which time we have record of his correspondence with Moore, Merrick, and Spaulding. It follows that Hunter must certainly have been at least consulted if not heavily involved in Durham's version of the Colored Fair.[30]

Efforts were indeed in motion in Durham at this time to engender goodwill and attract white philanthropy in support of black enterprise. John Merrick's white clientele in Durham included all those men who were building fortunes and business on their own side of town: the Dukes, the Watts, the Carrs, and the Fullers. In those days, Durham had no men's clubs or boardrooms in which white men of business could socialize and argue politics, and Merrick's barbershop became their open forum of choice. Merrick participated fully in their discourse. Their camaraderie and business acumen were openly shared with him, and their advice and sponsorship were regularly offered as he strove to continue the same kinds of enterprising activities on his own side of town.[31] Merrick understood through these experiences in his own business life that enterprises that were to the advantage of both races received the most protection and opportunity to prosper. Aaron Moore shared this understanding. Symbiosis was not always equal to friendship, but in many cases, especially when money or property was at stake, it could be a stronger bond.

Networking and partnership clubs in the black community were also needed, and with this in mind, Merrick and a group of investors had already purchased (in 1883) the charter for a fraternal order, the Royal Knights of King David. By 1886 it was still operating only in North Carolina, but, since they had very sensibly bought the entire nationwide charter, it was about to become something much larger and more important. The order was originally religious in nature, being named after the Old Testament story of David and Goliath, but it had another very important feature: insurance.[32]

On Wednesday, October 7, 1896, at the Durham Republican Convention, "a ticket [of candidates] had been arranged and Dr. A. M. Moore, Colored, was requested to read the names, which he did, and the convention nominated the ticket without more ado."[33] Moore himself was not on that ticket, although he had been asked to be. His experiences in 1888 with racial backlash still made him certain that his best work would be in participating as a voter, which was still legally assured because of his education, but not as a candidate. The election of 1896, however, was shaping up to be a pivotal one in the post-Reconstruction South, and he dutifully accepted this place of distinction in the democratic process of his city among his fellow Republicans, black and white. He was still participating, as his own father and uncle had done in Columbus County and as members of his extended family and acquaintances were doing, in the affairs of his party, his race, and his nation.

There was much reason in 1896 to hope. The Radical Republican Party, now mostly comprising blacks and Northern sympathizers, and the more centrist Populist Party, which advocated for poor whites and farmers, found an unlikely alignment in their interests and voted as one body against Southern Democrats, who were the plantation class turned factory owners and anti-union voters. The "fusion" of political interests that Southern Democrats had most feared after federally mandated Reconstruction came to an end was coming to pass. According to a brief history of the Pope family, "For the first time in American political history issues of class took precedence over race, and the fusion of the Republicans and the Populists defeated Democrats across the southeast. In North Carolina fusion candidates were most successful in 1896, when Daniel Russell, a white Republican, was elected governor. In that election several African American men were also elected to public office, including George White [Aaron Moore's cousin] to the United States Congress, and three men to the North Carolina State Legislature (including James H. Young, editor of the *Raleigh Gazette*, who was a former [Shaw] classmate and good friend of [Aaron Moore's colleague] Dr. [Monassa T.] Pope)."[34] The Southern Democratic Party regrouped and began to implement long-term plans for a hostile retaking of political power by any means necessary.

After the election in November 1896, the now annual Colored Industrial Association State Fair took place in Raleigh. The fair presented the usual goods, crafts, and musical offerings; fairgoers heard speeches and enjoyed the widespread goodwill. Trains offered discounted fares so that visitors could come from all over the state.[35] The fair of 1896 was especially popular and much anticipated. The Moore household was full of visitors. Mrs. Cottie Moore's mother, Martha Dancy, and two female cousins traveled from Tarboro to take in the fair.[36] Governor Carr opened the festivities,[37] and Aaron Moore's Old North State Medical Society colleague and Leonard Medical School alumnus Dr. Lawson A. Scruggs gave a welcome address. A. M. Moore was listed in the *Raleigh News and Observer* among notables in attendance, which also included John Merrick, G. H. White, and James E. Shepard.[38] The festive spirit of cooperation was evident in every word of the press coverage.[39]

Dr. A. M. Moore had risen in this near decade of practice from an unknown quantity who had to be introduced to Durham's black population as "not a root doctor" to a man who was referred to in newspapers and public forums as "one of the foremost Colored Doctors in North Carolina" and one who had the "confidence" of his race. This rise to important citizenship in Durham was one that Moore seems to have felt the weight of more than he sought its advantages. By the turn of the century, Durham's Hayti would begin to see real change as a result of the leadership of Moore and Merrick and their entrepreneurial colleagues. These favorable political winds, however, were not as fair or as lasting as they seemed.

Map of Columbus County, N.C., drawn by A. Kirkland, 1882. Courtesy of the North Carolina Maps Collection, State Archives of North Carolina, Raleigh.

This photograph is of Aaron McDuffie Moore's cousin, Benjamin Robert Spaulding (born in 1872, when Moore was about ten years old). Benjamin is the son of Rev. Robert Owen Spaulding, who was the son of Moore's mother's brother Iver Spaulding. It is taken in a wheat field on Benjamin's farm in the Hickory Hill Indian Community. This image captures a precious moment of what farm life was like for a young man in Columbus County, N.C., in the late nineteenth century. Courtesy of Milton Campbell.

Portrait in oils of Dr. Aaron McDuffie Moore, painted by his daughter Lyda Moore Merrick. Courtesy of the North Carolina Collection, Stanford L. Warren Branch of the Durham County Public Library, Durham.

African American students and teacher in front of Professor Jacob's School, early 1900s, Lake Waccamaw, Columbus County. Professor Jacob (1855–1925), seated center front, was likely related by blood and definitely related by marriage to Dr. Aaron McDuffie Moore. Jacob's second wife, Mary Freeman Jacob (1870–1916), was Aaron's first cousin once removed, and they shared common ancestors in Benjamin and Edith Spaulding. Courtesy of the State Archives of North Carolina, Raleigh.

Reverend R. O. Spaulding and Annie Jane Spaulding's house, Columbus County. Both spouses were first cousins to Dr. Aaron McDuffie Moore. From Little and Columbus County Bicentennial Commission, *Columbus County, North Carolina.*

Leonard Medical School graduates and undergraduates, 1886. This photograph was taken on the occasion of the graduation of the first class of physicians from Leonard Medical School. Aaron McDuffie Moore, a member of the second graduating class, is in the top row, third from the right. Courtesy of the Shaw University Archives, Raleigh, N.C.

Leonard Medical School, Shaw University, ca. 1888. The main medical classroom building is on the left; the library is on the right. Courtesy of the Shaw University Archives, Raleigh, N.C.

This portrait of Dr. Aaron McDuffie Moore is likely a commencement photo taken around 1888, when he was a newly minted physician. Courtesy of the C. Eileen Watts Welch and James A. Welch Collection.

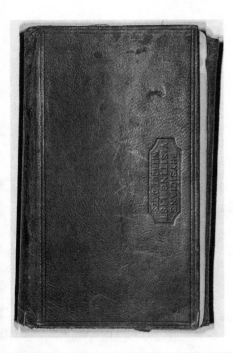

Dr. Aaron McDuffie Moore's "Physician's Visiting List without Dates," an artifact of Moore's first year in practice as Durham's first black physician, 1888–89. The book is full of handwritten notes of various kinds. It is physical evidence of one man's struggle to singlehandedly bring health care to an entire community. Courtesy of the C. C. Spaulding Papers (box #12), David M. Rubenstein Rare Book and Manuscript Library, Duke University, Durham, N.C.

Dr. Aaron McDuffie Moore was clearly very busy, not only documenting patient visits but also doing his accounting in the margins. Courtesy of the C. C. Spaulding Papers (box #12), David M. Rubenstein Rare Book and Manuscript Library, Duke University, Durham, N.C.

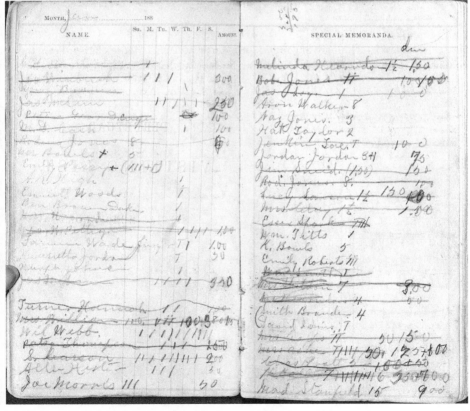

No. 9   To Aron A Moore we have laid off and allotted Eighty two acres in Bogue Township: Beginning at a Stake in the Center of Short and Bear Rail Road in an old line where it crosses said Rail Road A Gum and Oak Pointers and runs with said Old line South 79½° West 14 40/100 chains to a Stake an old Corner, thence North 88½° West 31 63/100 chains to a stake and oak pointers an old Corner, thence North 2½° East 17 4/100 chains to a stake, thence South 88½° East 51½ chains to a stake in the Center of Short and Bear Rail Road an oak a pine and a Gum pointers Henry Spaulding's line thence with said Rail Road South 30½° West 17 60/100 chains to the beginning Corner, and is known and designated as Lot No 9 in this division as appears upon said Plot.

Estate division of Israel Moore Sr. (1817–1898), Aaron McDuffie Moore's father. From the Columbus County Court Minutes, dated March 1889, North Carolina Register of Deeds.

North Carolina Mutual Life Insurance Company founders Dr. Aaron McDuffie Moore and John Merrick. When North Carolina Mutual was re-formed, these two men took on all the risk, buying out all other investors and fighting to keep the company alive. Moore photo courtesy of North Carolina Central University, University Archives, James E. Shepard Memorial Library, Durham; Merrick photo from Andrews, *John Merrick*, 47.

Charles Clinton Spaulding (ca. 1912) was Dr. Aaron McDuffie Moore's nephew. He joined the North Carolina Mutual Life Insurance Company as its first employee after the company re-formed under the sole guidance of John Merrick and Dr. Moore. The youngest member of what became the "Mighty Triumvirate," Spaulding took N.C. Mutual forward as president after the deaths of Merrick and Moore, honoring the ideals of the founders throughout his extraordinary career. Andrews, *John Merrick*, 21.

An early office of the North Carolina Mutual at Kemper's Corner—a back room at Dr. Moore's medical offices, ca. 1913. Seated from left are Aaron McDuffie Moore, who served as medical director and treasurer; N.C. Mutual agent and public relations manager John Moses Avery; N.C. Mutual president John Henry Merrick; Merrick's son Edward Richard Merrick; and C. C. Spaulding. Courtesy of the David M. Rubenstein Rare Book and Manuscript Library, Duke University, Durham, N.C.

Lincoln Hospital's original facility, ca. 1910. The hospital, at Cozart and Proctor Streets, opened in 1901. The Lincoln Hospital School of Nursing can be seen tucked behind the main building. Courtesy of the Durham Historic Photographic Archives (NCC.0055), North Carolina Collection, Durham County Public Library, Durham.

White Rock Baptist Church, ca. 1950. Built in 1890 and renovated and expanded in 1910, White Rock Baptist Church was central to the lives of the entire Moore family. This building was demolished in 1967, and a new building was constructed away from the blighted area left by urban renewal. Courtesy of the Durham Historic Photographic Archives, North Carolina Collection, Durham County Public Library, Durham.

The home of Aaron and Cottie Moore at 606 Fayetteville Street, Durham, ca. 1910. Lyda and Mattie Louise Moore pose on the upper balcony, and White Rock Baptist Church can be seen just next door to the right. Courtesy of Andre D. Vann and the Ruth Spaulding Boyd Collection held at North Carolina Central University, University Archives, James E. Shepard Memorial Library, Durham.

The Merrick home at 506 Fayetteville Street. John and Martha Merrick's home was just a block away from the Moores' home at 606 Fayetteville Street. John Merrick poses on his balcony. Courtesy of the Durham Historic Photographic Archives, North Carolina Collection, Durham County Public Library, Durham.

Sarah McCotta Dancy, ca. 1888. This hand-painted portrait of the young woman who was
to become Dr. Aaron McDuffie Moore's bride is probably a graduation portrait. Her hair
is worn up, but her braid fell below her waist and caught the attention of the young doctor
before he ever saw her face. Courtesy of Blake Hill-Saya.

Sarah McCotta "Cottie" Dancy Moore. Aaron McDuffie Moore chose his bride well.
The niece of political firebrand John C. Dancy, Cottie was educated, warm, industrious,
musical, brave, resourceful, fun, and a true match for the ideals and energy of the young
doctor. An extraordinary woman and a beloved wife and mother, she became a pillar of her
community. After her husband's passing in 1923, she continued her leadership in Hayti.
With Cottie as their model, daughters Lyda and Mattie Louise came to be as informed and
engaged as she was. Courtesy of the C. Eileen Watts Welch and James A. Welch Collection.

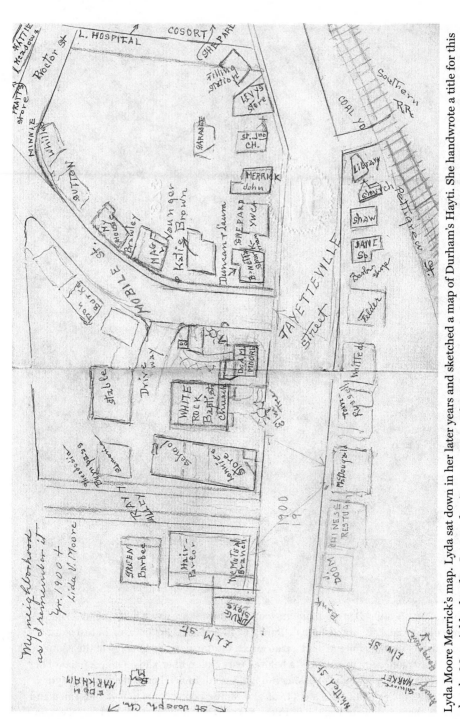

Lyda Moore Merrick's map. Lyda sat down in her later years and sketched a map of Durham's Hayti. She handwrote a title for this sketch: *My neighborhood as I remember it — year 1900+.* The map is not only fairly accurate but also an artifact in and of itself — a loving rendering of the world where Lyda spent her years as a young child. Courtesy of the C. Eileen Watts Welch and James A.

Preschool-aged Lyda and Mattie Louise Moore.
Courtesy of Blake Hill-Saya.

School-aged Lyda Moore.
Courtesy of Blake Hill-Saya.

Wedding of Margaret Spaulding to William J. Kennedy Jr., December 26, 1917, in Durham, N.C. Many of these people were Aaron McDuffie Moore's cousins who migrated to Durham from Columbus County on his invitation. Several of them lived with Aaron and Cottie Moore until they could settle into their own homes. Many worked at N.C. Mutual and attended what was then North Carolina College for Negroes (now North Carolina Central University). Top row (*left to right*): Janie Spaulding, Maggie Moore Lennon, Lyda Vivian Moore Merrick, Aaron McDuffie Moore, Maud Spaulding, Sarah McCotta Dancy Moore, Israel R. Spaulding, Charles Clinton Spaulding, Alonzo G. Spaulding, and G. Wendell White. Third row: Mary Mitchell, Margaret Anne Virginia Moore Spaulding, Benjamin M. Spaulding, and Susannah Spaulding. Second row: John Harrold, Fannie Spaulding (holding Booker Spaulding), William J. Kennedy Jr., and Margaret L. Spaulding. First row: John Spaulding, Lemuel Spaulding, C. C. Spaulding Jr., Margaret S. Shearin, Novella S. Mears, Otelia S. Stewart, Martha S. Dooms, and Mattie Louise Moore McDougald. Courtesy of Marsha Goodwin Kee.

The Durham Colored Library's first freestanding community-based location at 501 Fayetteville Street, where it stood from 1916 to 1940. Standing in the doorway is Hattie B. Wooten, who was the first librarian; she lived on the top floor of the building. This building was donated to the effort by John Merrick when Moore wanted to move the book-loaning service from White Rock Baptist Church for broader community access. Courtesy of the Durham Historic Photographic Archives, North Carolina Collection, Durham County Public Library, Durham.

Librarian Hattie B. Wooten's eyeglass case. Through the generosity of Robyn Davis Sekula, the Durham Colored Library received this very personal item, on the lid of which Wooten wrote the address of the 1919 library because the library building was also her residence. Courtesy of the Durham Colored Library, Inc. Archives, Durham, N.C.

Plaque honoring Dr. Aaron McDuffie Moore for founding the Durham Colored Library. This plaque is in the foyer of the Stanford L. Warren Branch Library, next to Lyda Moore's oil portrait of her father. Courtesy of Blake Hill-Saya.

HONORING THE MEMORY
OF
AARON McDUFFIE MOORE, M.D.

FOUNDER
1864 – 1923

THE DURHAM COLORED LIBRARY WAS ORGANIZED
IN 1913. FOR THE FIRST YEAR OF ITS EXISTENCE,
IT WAS HOUSED IN THE BASEMENT OF WHITE ROCK
BAPTIST CHURCH AND EXTENDED ITS SERVICES
TO THE ENTIRE COMMUNITY. IN 1916 IT WAS MOVED
TO A SMALL TWO-STORY BUILDING ERECTED AT
THE CORNER OF FAYETTEVILLE AND PETTIGREW
STREETS WHERE IT REMAINED UNTIL ITS REMOVAL
TO THE PRESENT SITE IN 1940. . . .

DR. MOORE
WAS A REAL FRIEND AND
FAITHFUL SERVANT TO HIS PEOPLE.

"HE BUILDED WELL
FOR GENERATIONS TO COME."

Portrait of Dr. and Mrs. Aaron McDuffie Moore and family, taken ca. 1915. Lyda and her mother, Cottie, are standing; Aaron and Mattie Louise are seated. Courtesy of the C. Eileen Watts Welch and James A. Welch Collection.

The John H. Merrick family. (*Standing, left to right*) Edward Richard Merrick, Martha Hunter Merrick, and Geneva Merrick (Williams). (*Seated*) Martha "Party" Merrick (Donnell), John H. Merrick, Mimi Violet Merrick (Bruce). John Thene Merrick is on the floor. Courtesy of the C. Eileen Watts Welch and James A. Welch Collection.

Lyda Vivian Moore Merrick in her wedding gown. On November 21, 1916, Aaron McDuffie Moore and Cottie Moore's oldest daughter married John Merrick's oldest son, Edward Richard Merrick. The wedding was the social event of the decade in Durham's Hayti community. Courtesy of the C. Eileen Watts Welch and James A. Welch Collection.

Mr. and Mrs. Richard L. McDougald on their wedding day. The bride, Aaron McDuffie Moore's younger daughter, Mattie Louise, sits as her groom stands lovingly by. Their wedding, on December 25, 1920, was a quieter and more intimate social affair than Lyda and Ed's had been, but it was no less celebrated. R. L. McDougald would become the president of the Mechanics and Farmers Bank. Courtesy of the C. Eileen Watts Welch and James A. Welch Collection.

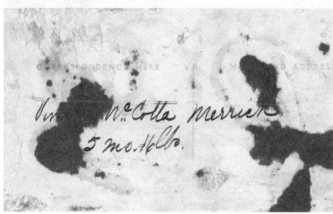

Sarah McCotta "Cottie" Dancy Moore with five-month-old Vivian McCotta Merrick—Aaron McDuffie Moore and Cottie Moore's first grandchild—in February 1918, along with handwritten postcard designation. Courtesy of the C. Eileen Watts Welch and James A. Welch Collection.

Community school plan, Julius Rosenwald Fund. Rosenwald Schools were built through a combination of local fund-raising and matching grants from the Rosenwald Fund. Plans like these helped community members choose a design that was right for them.

Aaron McDuffie Moore's advocacy and persistence resulted in more Rosenwald Schools being built in North Carolina than in any other U.S. state. Courtesy of the Division of Negro Education, Department of Public Instruction Records, State Archives of North Carolina, Raleigh.

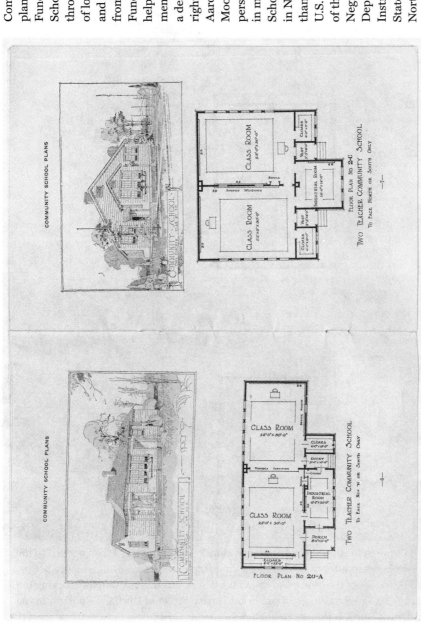

The North Carolina Mutual's second of three home office buildings, which opened to the public in October 1921 after the passing of John Merrick. Aaron McDuffie Moore became the second president of the North Carolina Mutual Life Insurance Company, serving until his death in 1923. This building still stands on Parrish Street in Durham. Courtesy of the State Archives of North Carolina, Raleigh.

Dr. Moore in his declining years. After the death of John Merrick, Moore's workload tripled, and his determination to make N.C. Mutual successful, as well as to tend to his other duties, took a toll on his health. Courtesy of the David M. Rubenstein Rare Book and Manuscript Library, Duke University, Durham, N.C.

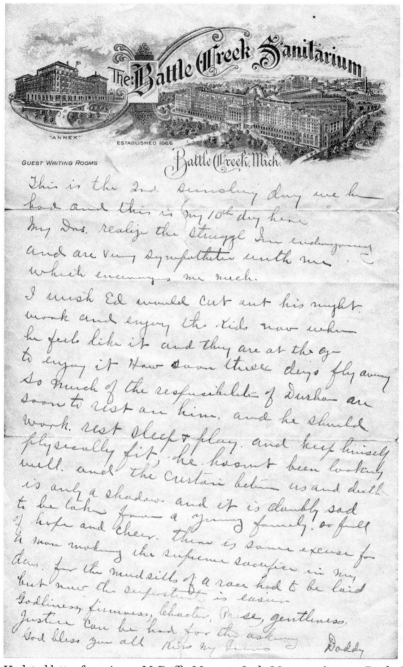

Undated letter from Aaron McDuffie Moore to Lyda Moore, written on Battle Creek Sanitarium letterhead. Aaron spent time in Michigan at the sanitarium in December 1921. Heart disease was wearing him down. Courtesy of the C. Eileen Watts Welch and James A. Welch Collection.

Lincoln Hospital's second facility, 1924. This new hospital at 1301 Fayetteville Street was built after the original hospital was partially destroyed by fire. It was the last dream of Dr. Aaron McDuffie Moore. Moore did not live to see the new Lincoln Hospital completed. He passed away with the plans for this facility spread out on his bed. Courtesy of the Durham Historic Photographic Archives, North Carolina Collection, Durham County Public Library, Durham.

Ed and Lyda Merrick with their daughters, Vivian (seven years old) and Constance (four years old). This portrait was taken ca. 1924, the year after Dr. Aaron McDuffie Moore died. Courtesy of the C. Eileen Watts Welch and James A. Welch Collection.

Mattie Louise Moore McDougald, ca. 1925, posing with her children, Virginia Louise (*center*) and Arona Moore. Arona was named after her grandfather, Aaron McDuffie Moore. Courtesy of Gwendolyn McDougald Parker.

Mrs. Cottie Moore with Ed and Lyda Merrick. This picture was taken during the wedding festivities of Dr. Charles DeWitt Watts and Lyda Constance Merrick (Watts) in the foyer of Ed and Lyda's home on January 5, 1945. Courtesy of the C. Eileen Watts Welch and James A. Welch Collection.

Lyda Moore Merrick, ca. 1950. After the marriage of her daughters in the late 1940s and the death of her mother, Cottie Moore in 1950, Lyda wholeheartedly took on many community, church, and club roles. She cofounded the *Negro Braille Magazine* (now the *Merrick Washington Magazine*) and edited and managed the publication and distribution of it for thirty years. She served as the Durham Colored Library, Inc., board chair and was also a member of the Lincoln Hospital trustee board. She was a valued portraitist whose oil paintings are displayed in public buildings named for her subjects. She also maintained numerous club activities and instilled the same values in her own daughters, Constance and Vivian. Courtesy of the C. Eileen Watts Welch and James A. Welch Collection.

Stanford L. Warren Branch of the Durham County Library system. The present branch was renovated and reopened in 1999. This photograph was taken in 2008. Courtesy of the Durham Historic Photographic Archives, North Carolina Collection, Durham County Public Library, Durham.

A LIVING FAITH

13

Two churches in Durham's Hayti rose to prominence in the 1890s: St. Joseph's AME Church and White Rock Baptist Church. Dr. A. M. Moore was prominent at White Rock, and John Merrick attended St. Joseph's. As Hayti expanded and prospered, the churches grew in size and were renovated to better care for their congregations. Moore was active in raising funds for a renovation of White Rock that was finished in 1896. He would remain a donor of funds, land, and service to his spiritual home of White Rock throughout his life. During this time, larger churches took on the character and tone of universities, prizing higher education in their leadership and encouraging it in their congregations.[1] Other churches then formed to serve those who sought a more charismatic leadership. Regardless of where one attended, however, church remained at the center of black social, political, and spiritual life in Hayti.

The original White Rock Baptist Church—so named because of the large white flint rock that sat in the front yard—stood at the corner of East Pettigrew Street and Coleman Alley. The young Dr. Moore would have attended and married in the original church when he first arrived in Durham. The first brick building to house White Rock took shape on the corner of Fayetteville Street and Mobile Avenue during the ministry of the sixth pastor, Reverend Allen P. Eaton (1886–97). Reverend Augustus Shepard (Dr. James E. Shepard's father) was the eighth pastor of the church, serving from 1901 until his death in 1911.[2] White Rock would be the venue for many conventions, speeches, visiting dignitaries, and historic gatherings. It remains a thriving congregation today.

This first decade of Dr. Aaron Moore's life in Durham tested him in ways that might have cost anyone their faith. Coming face to face with racial hatred when running for county coroner in 1888 in Durham and experiencing firsthand the poverty and hopelessness of those he had come to serve would have been enough to tax the strongest resolve. Add to these experiences the fact that as the only physician available to Hayti, he was not only a surgeon, dentist, and family doctor but also a first responder to terrible crimes, accidents, and human tragedies. It is easy to compare his first decade of practice to being more like a field medic than a "gentleman" doctor. We have his Physician's Visiting List to speak to the volume of his everyday practice, but we also have some newspaper accounts of tragedies he responded to. For example, on July 3, 1896, Dr. Moore attended two young boys badly burned in Hayti: "Yesterday afternoon, on the Guess Road, near Trinity College, two children were severely burned. They were the children of Wilson Collins, colored, about age seven and five years respectively. They were out in the yard trying to kindle a fire and had a can of oil with them. By some means in starting the fire the can of oil exploded and set both of the boys on fire. They were both burned badly by the burning oil. Dr. A. M. Moore was called in and rendered assistance in dressing their burns. The older child was the worse burned of the two. The older one of the children, who was badly burned, died last night. The younger one is doing very well today and will recover."[3] On another occasion in 1898 Dr. Moore attended a serious juvenile stabbing: "The colored boy, who was stabbed in the neck by another colored boy, Wednesday afternoon, is getting along very well today, and will recover. Dr. A. M. Moore, the colored physician, does not apprehend any serious results from the wound."[4]

These are only a few of what must have been fairly regular emergencies that Moore had to respond to. Somehow, however, in the midst of his daily doses of human strife, his faith remained a daily and mindful practice. Moore's core sense of practical yet spiritual morality appeared unshaken even as he daily honed his understanding of science and encountered the grace and failings of the human body. His faith seemed to live and breathe in his interactions with money, commerce, the politics of race, and dealings with those who either had unimaginable wealth or were destitute.

Many great men have become cynical, narcissistic, or isolationist in the face of similar traumas or with the advent of status and personal financial security. Dr. Moore seems to have held firm to his core principles—not in a brittle way but in a warm, direct, and empathetic way. His example illustrates how a sincere and abiding faith can quietly defeat ego and prejudice and successfully unite service with enterprise under the grace of the divine.

White Rock Baptist Church would be Dr. A. M. Moore's regular haven, his incubator of ideas, his classroom, and his springboard for community action. He would build his permanent family home right next door to its new location on Fayetteville Street. The walls of 606 Fayetteville and of White Rock Baptist Church would, over time, become nearly inter-changeable.

Lyda Moore Merrick gave voice to her father's message of faith when she said, "My father passed a torch to me, which I have never let go of: We are blessed to serve."[5] We know this was a mantra instilled in Aaron Moore since his earliest days on the farm, in the schoolroom, and in Sandy Plain's Sunday school. The hands that held him and provided for him, those voices that demanded his attention and obedience and respect, and the hopes that were lifted on his behalf and that propelled him forward had given him a self that was whole and vital. Carefully tended crops had nurtured him and strong backs (including his own) had struggled under heavy burdens to assure their mutual survival. The books that had opened his mind, the professors who had noticed and supported his aspirations, the philanthropists and mentors who carried him away from home and then to Durham—all of these elements, most rooted in faith-based ser-vice, had assisted him so that he could in turn open his own hands, his books, his mind, and his pocketbook for the rest of his adult life in grati-tude. By every account, Moore literally couldn't stop giving back; there would always be one more child to reach and one more life to save, one more need to fill or pain to alleviate.

In that phrase "We are blessed to serve," one can read more than ha-bitual or self-aggrandizing "noblesse oblige." Moore was certainly person-ally aware of (and publicly made aware of) his various gradations of privi-lege, but there is no evidence whatsoever of him acting in any other way than in relentless service. Moore was a man of notable connections and accomplishments, but he was never content with them while suffering could be alleviated and structures could be built to lift the generations to come, as he had himself been lifted. This infinite bargain formed the un-shakable, stoic, and pragmatic foundation of a faith that became deeper with every passing day. This lifelong relationship with faith seems to have kept Moore not only sane amid some of the worst days of racism and po-litical upheaval in our nation's history but also constantly connected to his overarching goals and ideals. All who encountered him also encoun-tered the evidence of this inner life in his outer way of being. He is rarely mentioned without reference to it. The torch of service was indeed passed from his hands and life into the hands and lives of many. "We are blessed to serve," indeed.

PART FOUR *Quiet Enterprise, Personal Loss*

14

1898
A Pivotal Year

The year 1898 must have felt pivotal from its outset for thirty-four-year-old Aaron Moore. Life for the young doctor and family man was at last settling into a rhythm, accommodating his roles as entrepreneur, businessman, and community activist. The new pharmacy in Hayti was progressing well and was laying the groundwork for Moore's arguments regarding the need for local health care for his own people, and there were serious plans developing for the fraternal order of the Royal Knights of King David to take on a new form in Hayti.

Aaron's two daughters, Lyda and Mattie, were seven and four years old, respectively. Both girls were not only healthy and precocious but also ravenous for information and instruction. Lyda had begun to attend school and Mattie was clamoring to keep up. Dr. Moore was proud to determine them both well-behaved enough to travel with their mother to Tarboro over Christmas and New Year's to attend the Dancy-Bridgers wedding, an important social event in black society. The *Raleigh Gazette* mentions their visit in its New Year's edition dated January 1, 1898, which indicates their social status and the pressures that must have accompanied them: "Mrs. Dr. Moore and children, of Durham, are in the 'Boro' on the Tar visiting her Mother and relatives. She was one of the many guests of the Bridgers-Dancy nuptials. The brilliantly lighted church was thronged with friends of the contracting parties, representing 'Elite' of both races. It was the popular and most select affair that has happened in years."[1] At first it might seem odd that Dr. Moore didn't attend such a high-profile event with his family, especially over the holidays. He sent them along without him, however, and with their family's contribution of a gallon of wine to enhance the celebration.

It is a safe assumption, due to the later events of February 1898, that Aaron may have instead traveled alone to his own homeplace over Christmas. Another of life's rites of passage was imminent. The man who had been the iron center of his Columbus County family for over sixty years was about to take his place among the beloved ancestors in Mitchell's Field, near his namesake and the first to die in Aaron's immediate family, Israel Moore Jr., who had passed away seven years earlier.[2]

Israel Moore had lived well beyond the life expectancy for a farmer of his race and generation. He must have always seemed like an "old man" to his youngest son, since he was already forty-six years old when Aaron was born. Israel had been in his late sixties when Aaron finally left Sandy Plain for Shaw University. Aaron's father, however, must have been reaching a critical state of frailty during the Christmas of 1897, and his son, the doctor, would have had a very short window of time to travel home and do what he could for him. What words, if any, would have passed between this father and son? Neither was known for being particularly verbose. There would certainly have been prayer and perhaps some quiet times reading the Bible at his bedside. Then, as any physician knows, it was time to let nature take its course and for Dr. Moore to return to patients whose needs were more urgent than those of his own father.

Israel Moore died on February 18, 1898, just six days before his eighty-second birthday. A telegram may have been an exorbitant expense but was a possible means by which Aaron received this news. Telephones were rare during those times and did not as a rule reach the more rural counties. A letter from home, delivered several days to a week after the event, is the most plausible method.

Regardless of how this difficult news arrived, we know Aaron did not go home for the funeral, nor did his family. Bodies were buried quickly in those days, and travel would have taken a full day each way. Dr. Moore, by all accounts—including his daughter Lyda's—rarely if ever put his own needs or family events before those of his patients. During Moore's adult life, six of his siblings would die, as well as both of his parents.[3] Lyda would have been too young to remember her grandfather Israel passing away, but she recalled that when her grandmother Ann Eliza passed away years later, Dr. Moore did not attend her funeral. She remembered her father taking time daily to sit and read his Bible, and this was the way he customarily dealt with the passing of friends, family, and patients alike. When asked about such things, he would reply simply, "Other sheep have I."[4]

We do know by way of the Columbus County record of deeds that Israel Moore left his son Aaron a parcel of family land; Columbus County court minutes state that the Israel Moore Sr. estate division bequeathed Aaron Moore an eighty-two-acre tract of land.[5] The land was eventually sold in

1917,[6] which seems to indicate that Moore's homeplace had been firmly chosen: Durham.

The passing of the patriarch of the Moore family—a man whom Aaron had looked up to not only for his formidable nature but also because of his status as a Republican community leader—may have brought an even stronger urgency to Moore's own commitment to secure the future of Durham's Hayti. Fresh from their fusionist victory in 1896, Durham's black leaders had been fully engaged in defeating the Dortch Act, an underhanded law that would have essentially wiped out state funding for black education. They now sought funding for black higher education and a possible college while also fighting for the protection of their grade schools, which were being repeatedly destroyed by fire. A similar fusion alliance with white farmers or "Populists" who were concerned about the white concentration of wealth seemed possible in the upcoming election of 1898, which was causing Southern Democrats considerable dismay.[7] They began to plan a coup.

North Carolina in 1898 quickly escalated into a racially charged political battleground. The Southern Democratic Party, under the leadership of Democratic chairman Furnifold Simmons, ran an openly white supremacist campaign. Democrats' list of concerns were designed to appeal to those whites who had become alarmed by the increased presence of blacks in government and by the black population's now obvious power as a voting bloc. "Negro Domination" was their paranoid prediction and rallying cry.[8] One political cartoon at the time depicted a figure labeled "white man" underneath a giant disembodied man's foot in spats marked "The Negro" with the caption "How long will this last?," as if somehow blacks could possibly quash or subjugate the sovereignty of the state and its white citizens.[9]

The political climate in Durham proper was sensitive as well, though not quite as volatile as elsewhere in the state. Jean Bradley Anderson observes in her definitive history of Durham County, "During the very years when racial fires were burning the hottest ... the Black sector of Durham was making strides in business that would shortly give the lie to the White supremacists' argument."[10]

Durham does seem to have avoided some of the more horrific displays of violence during this election period. There is an air of mystery, however, around what may have taken place behind closed doors to secure black Durham's relative safety and trajectory. If such negotiations occurred, Dr. Moore was certainly part of them, as was John Merrick, whose business relationships gave him "white access," and others whose names would become familiar in black Durham's story of progress. Washington Duke, his sons, and Julian Carr were surely also involved. These groups of men shared significant common interests. Leaders of white industry, like tobacco and textiles, needed a reliable labor force to make their fortune, and black leaders needed philanthropy for education and health care and wanted no interference as they built the infrastructure of their own separate society. There is wide speculation that reduced black participation in the political sphere was traded for a "live and let live" policy between the races. Under the very real threat of white supremacist violence, and with Durham's Hayti still at the very beginning of its development, such a policy could be seen as the start of the diplomatic relationship between the races that made that development possible.[11]

The wider schools of more conservative black thought at the time were in general supportive of this kind of thinking. Booker T. Washington's reaction to increased political tension in the South was to preach the currency of cordiality between the races while downplaying any overt call for political participation.[12] Meanwhile, W. E. B. Du Bois, horrified by his own encounters with lynching, continued to voice his deep sociological concerns for the development of the mind, soul, and culture of black people through higher education.[13] The volatility of the political arena around black educational uplift was perhaps what inspired the more focused mobilization of Durham's black leaders on educational protection and funding for community infrastructure.

The Duke family, and Washington Duke in particular, were staunchly Republican, even running a pro–Radical Republican newspaper in Durham in 1896. They had firmly backed the election of Republican governor Daniel L. Russell in 1896 and celebrated it mightily. Their open alliances with black leaders like Merrick and Moore earned them the slur of "scalawag" (a term for a Northern-sympathizing Southerner) in old Southern circles, and as the political tides turned in 1897 they received a large helping of scorn and race-traitor baiting. The majority of the Duke family philanthropy was proudly invested in Trinity College, which would become Duke University, but their philanthropy and efforts in the black community were also a significant source of pride.[14] Julian Carr, however, was a Southern Democrat and vocally opposed to the threat of the educated and mobilized black vote. After the Republican victory in 1896, black leaders had tried to appoint several black justices of the peace, therefore garnering some equality in local law enforcement and voter registration.

This concept of black men sitting in governmental seats where they could erode the dominant position of white people did not sit well with Southern Democrats like Carr. By the 1898 election he was rallying white voters with the notion that North Carolina was the only state in the South in which blacks were in places of power over whites.[15] This kind of rhetoric certainly mobilized educated whites, but to unify the entire white vote, a more insidious brand of fearmongering was needed, the kind that would turn the most educated and well-mannered black man into a monster in the eyes of white society.

The Ku Klux Klan was vital to the success of the Southern Democrats and their goal of voter intimidation in black neighborhoods statewide. A Southern Democratic vigilante group called the "Red Shirts" also blatantly advertised their intention to commit violence against blacks. Lynching was the Klan's primary tool, and the practice had become more frequent with every passing year of black suffrage. Historian Edgar Allan Toppin points out that "in the 1880s lynchings of Blacks averaged 67 a year, and in the 1890s, lynchings occurred on an average of 116 a year.... In 1892 a Black person was murdered by a lynch mob almost every other day."[16]

In the eyes of the Ku Klux Klan and white supremacists, "one drop" of black blood made the carrier inferior and a menace to the natural ascendancy of the white race. Lynching was not their only method; the burning of schools, churches, and homes and every other manner of torture, murder, and humiliation were practiced.[17] Klan members styled themselves in mainstream white society and the media as chivalrous defenders of the Southern way of life, but there is no other term for their acts or their agenda than "terrorism."

In these dangerous times, Dr. A. M. Moore remained engaged in local politics but still preferred to wield his influence from the sidelines. He reasoned publicly that his patients required his time more than politics did, and that was certainly true. He however still found time to campaign for, write letters on behalf of, and speak in churches and gatherings about black education. Merrick and Moore and other black leaders in Durham continued to vote, which, regardless of their position, was a risk and an act of civic engagement against all odds. John C. Dancy, Mrs. Cottie Moore's uncle, was very vocal in his call for black votes, especially on behalf of Dr. Moore's cousin George White, who was up for reelection to Congress.[18]

In Wilmington—the port that had been so influential in the turpentine fortunes of Aaron Moore's ancestors—white supremacist efforts intensified as the election of 1898 approached. Armed red-shirted militias marched down the streets with torches shouting white supremacist slogans in a "White Man's Rally" (and barbecue) the night before the election. Prominent white politician Alfred Moore Waddell, a former congressman, gave a speech at the rally: "You are Anglo-Saxons. You are armed and prepared, and you will do your duty. If you find the Negro out voting, tell him to leave the polls, and if he refuses, kill him, shoot him down in his tracks. We shall win tomorrow if we have to do it with guns."[19]

There had been a considerable escalation in rage on the Southern Democratic side in response to an article by respected black newspaper editor Alex Manly of the *Daily Record* in Wilmington. He had written a dangerously frank rebuttal to a Mrs. Felton from Georgia who had made a public speech in favor of lynching and of the white supremacist Southern Democratic platform, whose slogans and campaigns routinely depicted black men as animalistic brutes who wanted nothing more than to rape white Christian women. Manly, himself the son of a white father (Governor Charles Manly) and an enslaved mother of his household, wrote, "Every Negro lynched is called 'A big, burly black brute,' when in fact many of those who have thus been dealt with had white men for their fathers, and were not only 'black' and 'burly' but were sufficiently attractive for white girls of culture and refinement to fall in love with them. ... Don't ever think that your women will remain pure while you are debauching ours."[20] The pain, truths, and frustrations that these words issued from are palpable in every word of Manly's editorial. The temerity of these widely known truths being published by a black business owner in a public forum was inflammatory to white Southern Democrat sensibilities.

Every manner of obstacle and subterfuge was put into action in favor of the planned Southern Democratic coup. Ballot boxes were stuffed, and votes were openly destroyed.[21] Mrs. Cottie Moore's uncle John C. Dancy spoke publicly at Republican rallies, including in Durham, in defense of black suffrage. Dancy held at this time the position of U.S. Collector of Customs at the Port of Wilmington.[22] Dr. Moore not only must have had grave concerns for Dancy's well-being in Wilmington as the election approached but also likely had access to Dancy's insights and advice. Moore's other close associate and prominent Durham leader James E. Shepard led the Sunday School Convention in an endorsement of Alex Manly's editorial, which was widely distributed by Democrats as evidence that blacks were not backing down and were perhaps even planning a "race war." Fallacious reports of armed groups of black men began circulating, and white fear reached a fever pitch in Durham. A lynching was reported three miles outside city limits.[23]

On the day of the election, Wilmington—a city that had, until that moment, been a symbol of black progress, education, and success in the public and private sectors—was a city under siege. As Waddell had requested the night before, armed Red Shirts patrolled the streets looking for black voters and intimidating any black citizen they encountered. Incredibly, blacks still voted, but their numbers were just not enough to stand up to the violence and widespread voter fraud that the Southern Democrats had mounted in opposition. It was a punishing defeat for the once victorious Republican Party of Lincoln.

On November 9, the day after the election, Waddell publicly proclaimed a "White declaration of Independence," the first article of which read, "The time has passed for the intelligent citizens of the community owning 90% of the property and paying taxes in like proportion, to be ruled by negroes." The final article of this declaration was a call for the banishment of Alexander Manly and the end of his newspaper.[24]

On November 10, 1898, high on Southern Democrats' election success, a large group of armed white men, led by Waddell, marched to the offices of the *Daily Record* to set it on fire and to exact revenge on Alex Manly and his brother, but the two had already narrowly escaped town. The white mob broke down the door of the *Record* and set it on fire; then the rioters posed for a photograph with their guns as the building blazed behind them. But this was not enough to satiate the mob. Into a prosperous middle-class black neighborhood in Wilmington they marched, setting it ablaze and killing whomever they could. They burned black businesses and targeted community leaders and politicians, and women and children were forced out of their homes into the fray. Shots were fired from military-like barricades and formations. There was even a horse-drawn Gatling gun firing 420 rounds per minute and a Hotchkiss gun firing 80–100 rounds per minute at any black body that moved. This was not a riot; this was a calculated and gleeful annihilation. The death tolls that were reported at the time were as downplayed as the event became in American history; eventually numbers reached in excess of 300. Over 1,400 black citizens were documented refugees of the crisis. Many of them fled to Durham. The Republican governor in Raleigh, himself dealing with assassination attempts, called in the infantry to restore the peace, but the damage was done. The final act of the coup was to remove and banish all black leaders from Wilmington.[25] Historian Kenneth Joel Zogry observes, "The Wilmington coup sent chills through black communities across the region. The violence marked not only the end of political fusion, it also brought to a close a period of hope and possibilities not just for African Americans, but of societal progress for all North Carolinians."[26]

John C. Dancy had been right to warn black voters they would lose their suffrage; this election victory would not be enough for the Southern Democrats. The newly empowered white supremacist party desired a long and far-reaching reversal of black civil rights at every level of government. The North Carolina state elections in 1898 saw Southern Democrats regain control of the General Assembly and the election of a Southern Democratic governor to replace Russell. Racist propagandist Furnifold Simmons, for his efforts in North Carolina, would be rewarded in 1900 with a seat in the U.S. Senate that he would hold for the next thirty years. Dr. Moore's cousin George H. White managed to get reelected in 1898 from the Second District of North Carolina to a second term in the U.S. Congress, but his continued vocal opposition to lynching and voter fraud in the South would make his days in that body numbered. Alex Manly resurfaced in White's home in Washington, D.C., and stayed in his employ during his last term. Ironically, he and his brother had been able to escape Wilmington because of the fair complexion that they had inherited from their white slave-owning father.[27] It is very possible that John C. Dancy, with his position at the Port of Wilmington, was instrumental in their escape.

Jim Crow–era disenfranchisement and segregation would settle like a suffocating cloud over the previously held hopes of Reconstruction-reared blacks. It was a sobering time, to say the least, for Durham's Hayti and for those who would build it up and keep it safe.

FOR OUR MUTUAL BENEFIT
Forging the Mighty Triumvirate

15

The *North Carolinian* newspaper of Thursday, December 22, 1898, printed, "This morning, about 3:45 o'clock, fire destroyed a stable belonging to Dr. A. M. Moore, colored, in the negro settlement here. The loss will amount to about $100 with no insurance."[1]

Fire was a dangerous foe in America at the turn of the century. There were many causes, some of which, during these violent times in racial politics, were highly suspect. The cause of the fire at Moore's stable is unknown, but it must have been a fairly severe hardship monetarily, especially if any animals, feed, modes of transport, or equipment were lost. It surely would have been frightening to all concerned, regardless of cause, just a month after the Wilmington coup. Once the barn fire was out and the damage assessed, Dr. Moore and his family would need to either rebuild or relocate. What a nuisance just before Christmas and, as the paper noted, with no insurance.

Insurance was a luxury that was not readily available to black people during this era. For many years during and after Reconstruction, Southern black communities found their only source of stabilizing financial and social infrastructure in the church or in various fraternal orders. Some of these fraternal orders were elaborate, stylized, and secretive; others were practical and recognized forums for community organization, much like a chamber of commerce. As fraternal orders grew, some of them also functioned as banks and loan centers for black customers, and some even had rudimentary insurance benefits for widows' funds and funeral expenses. John Merrick, who had been part of purchasing the national charter of such an order (the Royal Knights of King David) for Durham's Hayti, was also an active member of a larger fraternal order based in Virginia: the Grand United Order of True Reformers. This order was originally founded on the principle of temperance but became much more influential, especially in the 1890s under the guidance of William Washington Brown. Brown died in 1897, but not before he and the True Reformers had influenced a new wave of black entrepreneurs like John Merrick. The establishment of insurance companies that could support black families with more than a one-time death benefit was a popular platform of the True Reformers, as was the establishment of a secure and self-sustaining black middle class.[2] Walter Weare remarks in his book on the history of black businesses in the new South that "what evidence there is suggests that virtually every insurance association founded in the Upper South during the late nineteenth and early twentieth centuries can be traced to ex–True Reformer agents who organized their own societies. . . . Indeed, this is precisely what happened in the case of the North Carolina Mutual."[3]

John Merrick is often apocryphally credited with being tired of people coming to his barbershop to take up collections for widows, fires, and funerals. This characterization may have been true, but his long-standing activity with these influential fraternal orders gives his ideas concerning racial uplift through insurance and infrastructure development a bit more context. Merrick and W. G. Pearson had been members and officers in the Royal Knights of King David for over a decade. That fraternal order had already founded two Industrial Life Insurance companies, in 1893 and 1894.[4] Dr. Moore's firsthand experience with the health and social needs of Durham's black residents would have had particular relevance during the founding of the Durham Drug Company in 1895 and in further business planning throughout the tumultuous years between 1896 and 1898. It is hard to imagine that the electoral drubbing of the party of Lincoln and the accompanying racist atrocities in Wilmington did not also add urgency to the actions of Merrick, Moore, and their colleagues on behalf of the people of Durham's Hayti.

Even while recovering from his own fire losses, Moore put forward capital numerous times to secure this venture and shared his medical office space. He had by this time taken an office at Main and Church Streets in Durham, known as Kemper's Corner, at the site of the old courthouse.[5] Moore and Merrick, along with five other investors—W. G. Pearson, E. A. Johnson, D. T. Watson, J. E. Shepard, and P. W. Dawkins—began meeting at Dr. Moore's office in 1898 to discuss establishing this new pillar in the upward mobility of Hayti: the North Carolina Mutual and Provident Association. Each founder invested $50 for an initial endowment of $300. A large desk and four chairs were purchased and became the nucleus of this new venture: an entirely black-owned, black-run insurance company benefiting black policyholders.[6] The North Carolina Mutual and Provident Association was officially incorporated by the North Carolina General Assembly in 1899, just ten years after Aaron Moore's arrival in Durham.[7]

This fledgling black insurance company opened for business with the start of a new century in view. Unique and community-specific problems immediately presented themselves. For instance, there was little to no actuarial data on black communities. The life expectancy of factory workers and the black community in general was between thirty-five and thirty-nine years, but accidental tragedy was all too common.[8] The early Mutual focused on "industrial insurance," or death benefit insurance. The investors combined Merrick's entrepreneurial business sense with Moore's knowledge of general health statistics. After all, Moore had been the sole health-care provider in black Durham for a decade. They determined that it was easier to find the policyholders, who were often itinerant workers, on a weekly rather than monthly basis to collect premiums, so that schedule adjustment was made. Benefits were also promised within seven days of a policyholder's death for the same reasons. Suitable and dignified funerals were very socially important in this era, not to mention frequent, and quick payouts made those services possible, bringing a great deal of comfort and dignity to both the policyholder and the beneficiary.[9]

A. M. Moore and D. T. Watson created the first accounting system by entering expenses and income in one ledger daily and policy numbers and addresses in a second ledger.[10] Many insurance ventures were trying to gain traction during this time, especially in black communities, and some, of course, were disreputable. There were also some white companies running various scams in black communities. A new company had a lot to prove, and the reputations of both Dr. Moore as medical director and John Merrick as president were instrumental in cementing the Mutual's reputation.

It was a rocky start. Some of the initial investors (Pearson, Johnson, Watson, Shepard, and Dawkins), discouraged by the lack of early sales, left the project. The need arose for either dissolution or reorganization. The remaining investors, Dr. Moore and John Merrick, met privately afterward and resolved to stay the course. Moore pledged to buy out the other five investors (Pearson, Johnson, Watson, Shepard, and Dawkins) by returning their fifty dollars with interest. The Mutual was now in the hands of Merrick and Moore. They reorganized and relaunched.[11]

A new player in the future of that organization and in Durham's "Black

Wall Street" now entered the story: Charles Clinton Spaulding from Columbus County, born August 1, 1874, to Benjamin McIver and Margaret Ann Virginia Moore Spaulding, Aaron Moore's sister. Moore was little more than ten years older than C. C. Spaulding and probably influenced the young man much as George Henry White had inspired Aaron in his early education. In 1894 Spaulding made his way to Durham to stay with his Uncle Aaron and Aunt Cottie Moore and attend Whitted School, finishing at the age of twenty-three. He worked every job he could find. He washed dishes, carried luggage, delivered office supplies, and, in 1898, the year that North Carolina Mutual was founded, graduated and briefly became the manager of a grocery store. At the turn of the century, when the Mutual decided it needed a permanent employee, Charles Clinton Spaulding became the best decision the company ever made for its future. Spaulding took on the title of general manager, which included everything from sales to bookkeeping to mopping the floors. Neither Moore nor Merrick took a salary, and Spaulding worked on commission.[12] Spaulding related his early experience traveling to Raleigh as the sole agent and salesman for the North Carolina Mutual and Provident Association: "My friends and others whom I tried to interest were sympathetic and appreciative of the effort to establish an insurance company, but they did not believe it could be done. Some flatly ridiculed the idea of a Negro insurance company. I returned to Durham thoroughly disgusted and quite willing to resign. I would have quit at this time had it not been for the encouragement of Mr. Merrick and Dr. Moore."[13]

The very first death benefit claim submitted to the Mutual was nearly the demise of this new insurance venture. It was imperative that it be paid in full and promptly, or the credibility of the entire company would be shattered. An emergency meeting was called in the back room of Merrick's barbershop, and forty dollars was raised to complete the payment out of the pockets of the founders themselves. Not only did the company survive, but word also spread of the quick and complete payout. No more effective advertising could have been purchased. This act of integrity, commitment, and professionalism was to be another defining moment.[14]

From 1900 to 1910 the company went from an income of less than $1,000 to $250,000 in revenue. Its workplace, which began in Dr. Moore's medical office, was soon housed in a freestanding building. Its agents went from one—C. C. Spaulding—to hundreds. The North Carolina Mutual and Provident Association expanded to offer service nearly nationwide in the coming years. But the company's influence encompassed much more than the service it offered. Mutual president John Merrick, in a letter to the representatives of the association, warmly proclaimed, "I know I am the Proudest Negro today that lives, because I can say with pride that all over North Carolina the North Carolina Mutual and Provident Association is planted on a firm basis. We are not waiting for this to come to us. We are buying real estate, and taking mortgages on real estate, lending money, and depositing the earnings of the company to the credit of the company.... Every one who holds a policy in this company owns a share in that reserve fund. We have no stockholders ... and we have no fancy salaried men to bankrupt the company.... We pay men according to the work they do. With honest dealing, push and energy, success is ours."[15]

North Carolina Mutual agents and employees had a sense of ownership and purpose because their work served their people directly. The dollars made flowed not into the hands of a few but traveled back into the community in investments, property acquisitions, seed money for more organizations, and stability for the new economy they were working toward together. The company became a symbol of what could be achieved, and for a while it was the place where many new enterprises were nurtured.[16]

A similarly encouraging and personal public statement released by Secretary-Treasurer Dr. A. M. Moore stated, "I am proud of the record the North Carolina Mutual and Provident Association has made; with five years active work, with 10,000 claims paid, and with never a suit presented for negligence or a failure to pay a claim when due. As one of the Directors and as Treasurer I shall never allow one to go unpaid. Not that I am better than anyone else, but it is simply business and to our advantage to have a record of punctuality.... This is my resolve which is as fixed as the principles of godliness implanted within me. That justice be done and every obligation met, and to build the grandest Insurance Company in the country. Our past success tells us we can if we will, and by God's help we will."[17]

None of the company's officers took a salary for a long period of time. On November 23, 1906, at the board of directors meeting, a final accounting was made for all of the personal cash advances made to the company by John Merrick, A. M. Moore, and C. C. Spaulding. They totaled over $1,500 but were paid back in full with interest over that time, with a final payment being disbursed that day. They had patiently fed and tended their venture, and it had finally begun to produce and sustain itself.

The Mutual provided the springboard and the backdrop for multitudes of black achievements. Asa Spaulding, another young cousin from

Farmers Union—who, like C. C. Spaulding, would also come and stay with Aaron and Cottie Moore and go to school in Durham—would achieve high levels of education and certification while working for the Mutual. Asa also became an important part of the growth, prosperity, and trajectory of the North Carolina Mutual and Provident Association.

The three men who took that second chance and made this historic company a reality—Merrick, Moore, and C. C. Spaulding—became affectionately known as the "Mighty Triumvirate."[18]

PART FIVE *Dreams Fulfilled*

16

LINCOLN HOSPITAL AND NURSING SCHOOL

In February 1897, Durham's Hayti nearly lost Dr. Aaron McDuffie Moore to another assignment. He was either recommended or applied to become superintendent of the Eastern Hospital for the Insane in Goldsboro, North Carolina.

Leonard Medical School and Shaw University's new president Charles Meserve wrote the following letter of recommendation on his behalf on February 15, 1897:

> To Whom it may Concern—
> I understand that Dr. A. M. Moore of Durham is a candidate for the position of Superintendent of the Eastern Hospital for the Insane, at Goldsboro. Dr. Moore stands very high as a physician and a citizen, and has the confidence of the Colored people of the State. I believe that if appointed Superintendent of the above institution, he would render good service and conduct the institution in such a way that his race would have it in the utmost confidence.
> Chas. F. Meserve, President[1]

The *Raleigh Gazette* joined its voice with President Meserve's to further endorse Dr. Moore as a candidate for superintendent:

> We see that Dr. A. M. Moore of Durham is being mentioned for the superintendency of the Insane Asylum at Goldsboro under the incoming administration. Dr. Moore is one of the foremost Colored doctors in North Carolina and the administration would do honor to the Colored race by giving him the appointment without any controversy. We think we will voice the sentiment of Eastern North Carolina when we say, "let him be appointed." He is being endorsed by leading Democratic and Republican Newspapers of the State, also the leading white doctors of the State.[2]

The Eastern Hospital for the Insane was a state-funded black hospital, established in 1880. State funding, a rarity, was due to the general discomfort of the white public with black mental patients housed in proximity to white mental patients. It was an overcrowded facility, and what funding it received was sparse, but it was a black hospital, nonetheless, and sat on a vast campus. It was doubtless an institution with a tremendous need for compassion, skill, care, and organization. It is understandable that both the prestige of the post and the requirements would have appealed to Dr. Moore, yet he either did not receive or did not take the job. The Eastern Hospital for the Insane remains in operation today on the same site and is now called Cherry Hospital.[3]

This demonstration of Moore's wish to expand his career prospects and to have a black hospital under his guidance makes it no surprise that in 1898, while also developing their ideas for an insurance company, Dr. Moore and John Merrick began the campaign of social pressure, fundraising and statesmanship that would lead to this wish being realized.

R. McCants Andrews was able to record Dr. Moore's own words as he described the campaign for what became Lincoln Hospital. One can read between the lines of his decorous description a deliberate effort to get autonomous health care for Durham's Hayti:

The movement for a colored hospital was started by me in 1898. I worked hard to arouse the colored and white people in the interest of such an institution for our city, and gradually they began to respond. We were especially endeavoring to win the encouragement of the Duke family. Dr. A. G. Carr, my good friend, was the family doctor for the Dukes, John Merrick was the family barber, W. H. Armstrong was the butler, and Mrs. Addie Evans was the cook. I kept in touch with all these persons, and we had a fairly good opportunity to see that the matter did not grow cold. All these persons helped to win the favor of our friends and benefactors, the Dukes. But I suppose Dr. Carr and Mr. Merrick were more largely responsible for the generous gifts we received. It seemed for a while that we would not have an institution of our own. Mr. George W. Watts had given a hospital for the white people of Durham, and he later announced his intention of adding a colored ward. I took up the matter with Mr. Watts, urging that such provision would lead to practical difficulties, that this plan would not give our Negro physicians sufficient opportunity to develop and that such provision would prove inadequate with the growing Negro population. Mr. Watts decided that he would not open the ward for colored, and the Dukes gave us promise of help. The first gift from the Dukes was $13,000.[4]

In the humid heat of August 1901, Lincoln Hospital opened its doors and its fifty beds to patients in Durham's Hayti. Washington Duke and his sons had indeed endowed the hospital, and it was named for the American president who led his country into a new era of nationhood. A hint of the fraternal element to this structure was inset on the original cornerstone: a square and compass, the symbol of Freemasonry. The inscription read,

Lincoln Hospital
Established 1901
W., B. N. and J. B. Duke, Donors

Two more marble tablets were installed on this original building. One listed the black trustees and officers of the hospital:

A. M. Moore, M.D.
S. L. Warren, M.D.
J. A. Dodson
A. A. Armstrong
A. R. Moore
Geo. W. Stevens
J. W. O'Daniel
D. T. Watson
C. C. Spaulding
M. H. Christmas
J. E. Shepard
John Merrick, President
W. G. Pearson, Secretary
R. B. Fitzgerald, Treasurer

It is interesting to note that Dr. Moore does not list a title after his name other than "M.D." and also that this group includes the "Mighty Triumvirate" of Merrick, Moore, and Spaulding, as well as most of those involved in the insurance enterprise and the pharmacy.

Finally, the tablet that achieved the Duke family's original wish for a "monument" reads,

Memoriam

Lincoln 1901 Hospital

With grateful appreciation and loving remembrance of the fidelity and faithfulness of the Negro slaves to the Mothers and Daughters of the Confederacy, during the Civil War, this institution was founded by one of the Fathers and Sons

B. N. Duke

J. B. Duke

W. Duke

Not one act of disloyalty was recorded against them.

John Merrick, President

A. M. Moore, Founder and Supt.[5]

This dedication expresses that popular sentiment of the post-Reconstruction era in the white community that often accompanied any philanthropy on behalf of the black community. Booker T. Washington reminded his white audience of just such sentiments in his "Atlanta Compromise" speech when he admonished them to return the "fidelity" of Southern blacks with support for their education and uplift. It was certainly fortunate for Durham's black community that Dr. Moore and John Merrick and their advocates were able to concentrate this desire for goodwill into a living hospital instead of a lifeless monument of words on stone.

The original frame building that was Lincoln Hospital stood at the corner of Cozart and Proctor Streets. It had a gracious, homelike feel, with trees and shrubs in the fenced front yard, a porch for visitors to wait on, and deep-set windows all around its two stories. It contained up-to-date facilities for surgery, obstetrics, and infant care, plus an emergency room that was open twenty-four hours a day. Lincoln Hospital was only the second black hospital in the state and the sole one with no religious affiliation.

Lincoln offered medical care free of charge or for whatever a patient could pay. Dr. Moore made it clear to all his staff that every patient was to be treated with the respect and dignity of a family member.[6] Many families paid in produce, volunteer time, or services, but even these payments were not solicited. Moore, Dr. Stanford Warren, and associates made up the hospital's medical staff. Medical residents (many from Leonard Medical School), nurses, and volunteers were responsible for the bulk of the work of running the hospital. Dr. Moore was at last able to give back to Leonard Medical School more than just his financial support; he was providing a teaching hospital where medical graduates could begin their careers. Many of Aaron's professors at Leonard—white physicians— consulted and occasionally taught residents at Lincoln as well. By 1907, Lincoln Hospital had become such a vital part of the growing Durham community that more beds and facilities were needed. The Duke family donated another $20,000, nearly twice their original grant, to add a wing onto the Cozart and Proctor Streets site.[7] Fund-raising and philanthropy within Hayti were also critical to this expansion.

The Lincoln Hospital School of Nursing was officially founded in 1903 and quickly became a vital part of health care in Durham. Dr. Charles Shepard, a graduate of Leonard in 1901, was central in shaping this training facility along with Julia Latta, RN (the first superintendent of nursing from 1903 to 1911), a graduate of Raleigh's St. Agnes Hospital School of Nursing. The indomitable Pattie Hawkins Carter would replace her in 1911. Carter was the daughter of Hawkins W. Carter, who had been a North Carolina representative and a state senator from Warren County during the Reconstruction period. Her early education was at the Warren County school. Later she went to Shaw University, St. Agnes Hospital in Raleigh, and the Lincoln Hospital School of Nursing in New York City. She would shape the Durham school through her intellect, passion, and professionalism for the next thirty-seven years.[8]

Pattie Hawkins Carter became one of Dr. Moore's closest allies at Lincoln Hospital. She was known not only for assisting the superintendent in the running of the hospital but also for cooking hospital meals, mopping floors, doing surgical laundry, and even hand-delivering medications to patients in Durham's Hayti. If the hospital was short-staffed in any capacity, she personally picked up the slack. Dr. Moore, as was widely known, seldom took a salary from the hospital and never when funds were scarce. Carter also refused a salary during lean times but always made sure her nurses were paid in full.[9]

The layout and operation of hospitals at the turn of the century was very different from the hospitals of today. Beds in wards were side by side in long, white-sheeted rows. There was no separation of patients by illness nor partitioning in any way unless for examinations or bathing, when a screen was used. Men and women were in the same wards until 1925, when the new hospital finally had the space to segregate male and female patients and arrange them by ailment to prevent cross-contamination. The ceilings were high to encourage airflow, and windows let in natural light. Physicians then were mostly general practitioners, although some, like Charles Shepard, were beginning to specialize in surgery.

Nurses in their white uniforms, with long aprons and starched white caps, were in constant motion and attendance. Physicians made daily rounds surrounded by residents and nursing students, and Dr. Moore and his colleagues tried not to miss a teachable moment. Doctors worked with nurses and residents daily in addition to carrying out their administrative and business duties. Moore proudly posed with his nursing graduates after their commencement (there are photographs from the very first graduation in 1907[10] and another in 1914, both held at White Rock). A slim and dignified presence in his bow tie and spectacles, he stands among the graduates dressed in their white uniforms, their beribboned diplomas in hand. The nursing school motto, which sounds very much like something Dr. Moore would say, was "Give the best to the world, and the best will come back to you." Moore's signature appears on nursing diplomas as professor as well as hospital superintendent, and an A. M. Moore Prize was awarded at commencement.[11]

Hayti's women's clubs and sororities, such as the Daughters of Dorcas (originally the Busy Women's Club), of which Mrs. Cottie Moore and Maggie Moore Lennon were founding members; the Ladies Board of Lincoln Hospital (both Junior and Senior boards); the Lady Managers and Ladies Auxiliary; the Durham Civic League; Iota Phi Lambda; Alpha Kappa Alpha; and many other church and women's social organizations provided a tremendous amount of support for the hospital. Dr. Moore regularly made time to encourage these organizations in their philanthropic work and to congratulate them on their contributions. They educated the community on hygiene and wellness, raised funds, rolled bandages, led clothing drives, provided meals, sponsored entire rooms in the hospital, and collected and washed blankets and linens. Volunteers were also on hand at Lincoln Hospital to welcome and comfort patients and their families, provide childcare, and ease the fears of those who saw a hospital as a frightening place to die rather than a place to heal. These clubs took on the majority of the work of soliciting charitable donations and community outreach and were greatly responsible for the change in attitude toward modern medicine and Lincoln Hospital itself. Black women's clubs, much like their all-male counterparts, often partnered with white women's clubs to achieve larger fund-raising goals, such as new medical equipment or quarantine quarters. Being a "clubwoman" was an honor and a mark of social grace during this era in black Durham, not to mention a very active calling. Those roots run deep and are still in evidence today.[12]

The Lincoln Hospital School of Nursing benefited both the hospital and community and gave young black women from all parts of the state an opportunity to enter a skilled profession. In a community still disproportionately populated by working black women, this school was a beacon of hope and a tremendous asset to those who could attend. Nursing was becoming a welcome addition to the few professions a woman of color could hope to enter.

As Lincoln Hospital gained its footing in the community, Lincoln nursing students became the primary staff and the mainstay of patient care. Dr. Moore was so proud of his nursing program that he housed and sponsored the education of many nurses himself. Notable among them was Minnie Canarah Lyon, RN, who impressed Dr. Moore with her ambition to become a missionary for White Rock Baptist Church after her graduation. He volunteered to finance her entire education personally, beginning at what is now North Carolina Central University and continuing through seminary at Spelman College in Atlanta and nurses' training at Lincoln Hospital, during which she lived at 606 Fayetteville Street with the Moores. After Lincoln, Lyon became a missionary to Liberia and dedicated her life to bringing compassionate medical care to the people of Africa. Yet again, Dr. Aaron Moore had invested in a mind and a career that would spread the message of health and mutual uplift to black people far beyond the borders of Durham County.[13]

Moore was at long last the superintendent of a freestanding black hospital, and there had been no need to move away from Durham. Lincoln Hospital was not only the realization of a personal dream Moore had held since his earliest days in medicine but also an extraordinary example of what respectful cooperation within the community and between the races could achieve. The alliance of a white tobacco baron's family, a persistent black physician, a group of intrepid black entrepreneurs, and countless women's clubs of both races had yielded a living symbol of community health and mutual respect that would benefit both sides of Durham. This was particularly evident during the flu epidemic of 1918 that would afflict all of Durham County. Lincoln Hospital nursing students were left to manage the main hospital while Lincoln's entire nursing and medical staff traveled to both white and black segments of the community to provide skilled care and preventive hygiene measures. All of Durham would be indebted to the nurses and physicians of Lincoln Hospital during this harrowing ordeal, which took an estimated 675,000 lives across the nation. The experience of some of Lincoln's most skilled black caregivers entering Durham's white households forged an even greater respect for Lincoln Hospital at this critical time. Disease, after all, does not discriminate.[14]

Dr. Moore and his family moved into town from their outlying farm during this busy time. The exact timing is unclear but roughly coincides with the opening of the new hospital. A new and gracious house was completed on Fayetteville Street just a few homes down from John Merrick and next to the newly renovated White Rock Baptist Church. The original Proctor Street location of Lincoln Hospital was a very short walk from the new Moore residence at 606 Fayetteville. The doctor would no longer be rushing out on his horse or bicycle on house calls, pulling teeth on the porch, or taking in bloody Saturday night stabbings. It must have been a real shift in the Moore household routine when the business of doctoring was moved to the new and separate hospital.

For the foreseeable future, Lincoln would be Dr. Moore's default home. The new house became the place he kept his clothes, met with guests, and cared for his family and whatever cousins or protégés he could house. In fact, the new house was scarcely built before Lyda Moore was bundled off to the Scotia Academy for young ladies. She carried a photograph of her home with her, and when her fellow students would ask to look at it, Lyda would gaze in equal disbelief at where she lived. Her sister, Mattie, would follow her to Scotia almost immediately.[15] The girls' rooms at home would be filled in their absence with myriad boarders and guests. The Moore home was now to become the center of Mrs. Cottie Moore's club gatherings as well as church endeavors in support of her and her husband's many community projects. Lyda remembered this of her father during the years he was superintendent at Lincoln Hospital: "He would come home and eat, take a nap, and change his clothes, and he would go right back to the hospital."[16] If Dr. Moore's family wished for more than a glimpse of him, they had to see him in church, at Sunday school, or at Sunday dinner. At least, when she was home during the summer, Lyda would no longer have to run across the street to avoid the blood.

Photographs of Aaron Moore during the years that would be his most fruitful as a physician, community leader, and entrepreneur show him changed from the robust and broad-shouldered young medical student he had been when he arrived in Durham. His face was now thinner and more chiseled, his hairline higher, his cheekbones sharper, and his ears even more prominent. His eyes were warm but heavy-lidded, as if he had not gotten much regular sleep for years, and his mouth was tense, though still sensitive at the corners. He wore spectacles in every photograph now, small ones with a gold nosepiece. His bowtie was always there, neat and plain, although his coats hung looser. His farm boy frame had left him, but his intelligence and the capability of his long fingers were evident in his carriage. He certainly looked like a man whom people would trust with their lives and with their children's lives. His image seemed to project slightly weary, fastidious yet wholly unselfconscious leadership.

606 FAYETTEVILLE STREET 17

Dr. Moore's home was a large, yellow, two-story, attractive frame house, charming with its blue shutters, in a setting of trees with a garden in the back yard and a wide grassy lawn in front with hedges on both ends. This would be my home away from home for the next five years while I attended school. —Asa Spaulding

The Moores' new home, 606 Fayetteville Street, was situated at Fayetteville Street and Ray Alley. John Merrick, now their close neighbor, had been at 506 Fayetteville since 1887 and was instrumental in building most of the houses on northern Fayetteville Street, now collectively called "Sugar Hill."[1] Merrick had in fact quite a talent for real estate and housing development. The North Carolina Mutual and Provident Association was doing well as the new century progressed and was expanding outside of Durham and even into other states. Charles Clinton Spaulding, Aaron's young nephew turned business phenomenon, also built a fine home of his own in 1906 at 1006 Fayetteville after he had been general manager of the Mutual for five years. All of these elegant, but not ostentatious, frame houses likely stood on foundations of Fitzgerald brick from arguably the most thriving black family-owned business in Durham. Richard Fitzgerald's mansion far outpaced the more understated homes of Fayetteville Street and was a real showplace in Durham's West End. "The Maples," as the Fitzgerald home was called, stood at Wilkerson and Gattis Streets and was a fine example of a Queen Anne–style Victorian mansion. Sadly this historic dwelling was entirely lost to fire in 1937.[2] The few photographs still in existence of "The Maples" and other homes in Durham's Hayti reflect a lost world of turrets, gables, columns, shady awnings, sweetheart balconies, and graceful belle epoque style.

R. B. Fitzgerald, whose bricks were an integral part of Durham's rapid expansion, was particularly interested in starting a black-owned-and-operated bank. There was also significant interest, especially from Merrick and Moore, in establishing a building and loan association so that more black families could own their homes in Durham. Dr. Moore himself described these early meetings to R. McCants Andrews, notably mentioning his Old North State Medical Society colleague and fellow Leonard alumnus Monassa T. Pope: "Professor E. A. Johnson and Dr. M. T. Pope, of Raleigh, came to Durham one night in 1907 to work up a building and loan association. We called a meeting of the leading men of the town in order to discuss the matter. It was soon evident that the persons present wanted a bank rather than a building and loan association." A group of stockholders assembled shortly thereafter; the group included John Merrick, A. M. Moore, and C. C. Spaulding as well as R. B. Fitzgerald and most of the co-investors who had started the Mutual and the Durham Drug Company.[3]

On February 15, 1907, the Mechanics and Farmers Bank of Durham was incorporated. The new bank would take its place on Parrish Street along with the Mutual offices and yet another pharmacy, also founded by Merrick, Moore, and Spaulding, called the Bull City Drug Company. The men of the "Mighty Triumvirate" further fulfilled their wish to assist black Durham with home ownership when they later incorporated the Merrick-Moore-Spaulding Real Estate Company in 1910.[4]

In 1912 an important visitor returned to Durham's Hayti: W. E. B. Du Bois, author, activist, and founder of the Niagara Movement and the National Association for the Advancement of Colored People. He published a piece about his visit titled "The Upbuilding of Black Durham: The Success of the Negroes and Their Value to a Tolerant and Helpful Southern City." His observations in this article were key to Durham's black community receiving titles such as "Black Wall Street" and "the Capital of the Black Middle Class." The deeds of Moore, Merrick, and Spaulding, as well as Fitzgerald and Shepard, are referenced by allusion in his account.

There is in this small city a group of five thousand or more colored people, whose social and economic development is perhaps more striking than that of any similar group in the nation.... It is a new "group economy" that characterizes the rise of the Negro American. ... The men who built 200 enterprises are unusual, not because the enterprises in themselves are so remarkable, but because their establishment met peculiar difficulties.... The Negro gathers capital by pennies from people unused to investing; he has no experts whom he may hire and small chance to train experts; and he must literally grope for success through repeated failure.

Three men began the economic building of black Durham: a

minister with college training, a physician with professional training, and a barber who saved his money. These three called to their aid a bright hustling young graduate of the public schools, and with these four, representing vision, knowledge, thrift, and efficiency, the development began.... Others were drawn in—the brickmaker, several teachers, a few college-bred men, and a number of mechanics. As the group began to make money, it expanded and reached out. None of the men are rich—the richest has an income of about $25,000 a year from business investments and eighty tenements; the others of the inner group are making from $5,000 to $15,000— a very modest reward as such rewards go in America.

Quite a number of the colored people have built themselves pretty and well-equipped homes.... There is no evidence of luxury—a horse and carriage and the sending of children off to school is almost the only sign of more than ordinary expenditure.... Today there is a singular group in Durham where a black man may get up in the morning from a mattress made by black men, in a house which a black man built out of lumber which black men cut and planed; he may put on a suit which he bought at a colored haberdashery and socks knit at a colored mill; he may cook victuals from a colored grocery on a stove which black men fashioned; he may earn his living working for colored men, be sick in a colored hospital, and buried from a colored church; and the Negro insurance society will pay his widow enough to keep his children in a colored school. This is surely progress.[5]

The existence of this kind of thriving and prosperous black middle class is a subject that is rarely covered in present-day discussions of American history of this time period. Communities such as Durham's Hayti are often seen as almost mythical and certainly anomalous. One wonders how it might have changed the current social climate if these communities were reanimated and discussed as frequently as the Rockefeller and Roosevelt era and its legacy. As Du Bois remarks above, the fortunes made in Durham's Hayti were by no means commensurate in monetary terms with those made by similar white tycoons of the day, but the entrepreneurship and infrastructure built from less than nothing certainly compares in grit, thrift, and ingenuity. Perhaps another major difference was that men like Merrick, Moore, and Spaulding and their associates were determined to raise the fortunes and better the futures of their *whole* community, not just themselves. Dr. Aaron Moore certainly didn't want to live in a "pretty and well-equipped" home with room for only himself and his family. If anything, all evidence points to his wanting more room in order to take in more guests, more family, more pupils, and more patients.

The house at 606 Fayetteville Street had two gabled roofs, and two chimneys indicated a house heated by wood or coal fires. A wide porch wrapped around nearly the entire house, and a screened porch (possibly still a backup medical treatment area) was on the south side off the kitchen. A prolific fig tree and a kitchen garden grew in the backyard.[6] The windows were wide and tall, and each was shuttered and single-paned with inner drapes that were often drawn to keep it cool inside. In the earliest known photo, circa 1910, the roomy side porch boasts a double-benched glider where no doubt much conversation, companionship, and many cool drinks were enjoyed. The wide front door, with glass panes on either side, is under a peaked roof at the top of two sets of stone steps rising from the sidewalk. White columns surround the porch and a waist-high white railing skirts it all around, making it both shady and private. The most distinctive feature of this two-story house, with attic windows under each gable, is a double-arched second-floor walled balcony that sits directly above the front-door gable. Clearly, the balcony opens at the top of the central staircase and must have afforded a wonderful, breezy, and gracious view of the street. Aaron's two daughters, Lyda and Mattie, appear in this particular photo, both in their early teens and clad in white. Lyda leans back against a pillar on the balcony, and Mattie gazes down at the photographer from the railing with her chin cupped in her hand. Behind them, the spire of White Rock Baptist Church rises above the roof and sits cheek by jowl with the north side of the house. One can imagine the church bells punctuating their hours and days.

Maggie Moore Lennon, Aaron's widowed niece and the daughter of his brother Reverend Daniel James Moore from Columbus County, came to stay and care for the family as housekeeper. Mrs. Cottie Moore and Maggie Moore Lennon reigned supreme in this bustling household. Lyda described her mother as "full of fun" and remembered her playing the accordion and singing, sewing, crocheting, and entertaining a house full of guests nearly constantly. The Moore home became a bridge for many individuals between stages in their lives. Aaron and Cottie were both committed to making 606 Fayetteville Street a place where extended family and promising young people, such as C. C. Spaulding and Asa Spaulding, were welcome to stay while going to school or working for one of Hayti's many enterprises. Census records at this address between 1900 and 1920 document a shifting roster of family, visitors, and boarders, and doubtless there were many more short- and long-term residents.

All long-term boarders were assigned chores and roles in the household. Asa Spaulding, for instance, wrote that he used to get up at five in the morning and light the fireplaces, dust the furniture, and wipe down Dr. Moore's car in the driveway before he walked to school. For this he earned enough to buy a suit that did not show his country origins so plainly in Durham city life. He remembered that his room and chores gave him structure and a sense of belonging in his first months far from home, and he was certainly proud of that suit.[7]

Lyda recalled that her father also often brought ailing family members to the house to convalesce under his watchful eye. In those days, it was also customary for distinguished black travelers who were passing through Durham to stay at houses like 606 Fayetteville that had guest rooms to spare. Travelers reciprocated this kind of hospitality in their own neighborhoods. This kind of social networking in the black community nationwide was vital for safe and comfortable passage across state lines.

North Carolina Mutual, White Rock Baptist Church, and the newly accredited training school (which would later become North Carolina Central University) often hosted receptions and other entertainment for visiting dignitaries. The roster of visitors included W. E. B. Du Bois, Robert Russa Moton, James Weldon Johnson, A. Philip Randolph, Booker T. Washington, and Adam Clayton Powell. It is a pity that the guest books of these gracious homes on Fayetteville Street are not in a museum, but one can certainly imagine the scope and historic nature of those dinners, receptions, and gatherings.[8]

This household must have felt like part library, part conservatory (with Lyda and Mattie both practicing at the piano and Cottie singing), and part Victorian-era hotel with a little health sanitarium thrown in. It likely smelled of books, biscuits, beeswax, disinfectant, wood smoke, lavender soap, and starched linen. The decorative colors of the era were rich and plummy, and patterned wallpaper was fashionable. Lighting by this time was electric, and wall sconces and tall silk-shaded lamps were popular. Some of Cottie's china, silver, and crystal are still in the family. All of the pieces are of fine quality but very understated. The china pattern is not gilded or floral; the silver is not scrolled or ornate; the crystal is beautifully thin with a little gold at the rim but still reserved. A few dining room chairs have also survived. They have high, round backs and are well made, sturdy, and quietly elegant.

How was this enclave allowed to survive, as Jim Crow laws were unleashed and an era of rigid segregation gripped the South? It is logical to conclude that the relationships of mutual tolerance and benefit between the races continued to keep it safe from the violent backlash suffered by other cities with prosperous black communities (such as Wilmington and Tulsa). This relative safety is often further attributed to the fact that Durham's black middle class generally eschewed any outward frippery or ostentatious displays of prosperity. The common ground that religious activity, temperance, and education provided between black leaders and men like Washington Duke and Ben Duke also kept the balance. Most of all, black Durham took care of itself and neither tried to overly interfere in white politics nor asked for too much of the public fund.[9]

Durham's Hayti certainly had its share of struggles, but several generations grew up and benefited from the solid and nurturing environment of this black middle-class oasis. Eventually, time and "urban renewal" programs during the desegregation era wrought the demise of the historic buildings and homes such as 606 Fayetteville Street. A few administrators at White Rock Baptist Church in present day still remember working in the Moore house when it briefly became annexed as church offices before it was eventually torn down. Even then they remember the house felt welcoming, special, and homelike.

All that now remains where we believe the Moore home stood is a partially vacant lot next to the Durham Freeway. A fence runs through the weeds across the center of the lot. It is a lonely sight.[10]

18

THE DURHAM
COLORED LIBRARY

If only my people had something to read!
—A. M. Moore

Aaron Moore had been a book lover all his life. Books had been his wings
and his counselors. The written word had kindled and solidified his faith.
Books had helped him see out and beyond the piney woods of Columbus County. Books had opened the world of science and medicine to him
and given him his profession. Books were ubiquitous in his office and in
his study at home. Lyda Moore Merrick said of her father, "He was a student all his life. He would go to his room nights; we weren't allowed in
there. He had to have quiet, and he would study his books. I see him in
there reading. He was still learning.... You know, you can learn but you'll
die before you get to learn [everything]." Lyda also quoted her father as
saying, "If only my people had something to read!"[1] His personal love of
learning and this often-expressed desire led to the founding of the Durham Colored Library.

The library was born in the basement of White Rock Baptist Church
in 1913 as a Sunday school library. Dr. Moore supported it himself and
solicited donations to expand it. Notable among these early donors was
white hospital benefactor George W. Watts, whom Moore had persuaded
to abandon the idea of a black annex at the white hospital on the way to
founding Lincoln Hospital. The library remained at White Rock until it
outgrew the space in 1916. Dr. Moore was also concerned that those who
attended other churches in the community would not feel as welcome in
a denominationally specific space.[2]

The collection started with 798 volumes and blossomed from there.
Most of the first books were Dr. Moore's and those of his close friend Dr.
James Shepard, but many donations ensued. Soon John Merrick, owner
of a new brick building originally meant for retail purposes, rented the
building to the growing library instead. The Durham Colored Library, one

of only two libraries for blacks in the state, officially opened at the corner of Pettigrew and Fayetteville Streets on August 14, 1916.[3]

The library incorporated as a tax-exempt institution on July 20, 1918.[4] Hattie B. Wooten was its first librarian and lived upstairs in the original building for some years. Dr. Stanford L. Warren, a colleague of Dr. Aaron Moore who was also a community activist and entrepreneur, became a leader in preserving the library and its place in Durham after Aaron Moore's passing. Warren himself donated money to erect another library building, on the corner of Fayetteville and Umstead Streets, which opened in 1940. Dr. Warren's daughter Mrs. Selena Warren Wheeler became the director of the Durham Colored Library System after Hattie Wooten's passing in 1932 and was very active with her father and her husband, John Wheeler, in getting the new building constructed. It included a special children's room and a collection of books by African American authors, bookmobile services to Durham County residents, and several branches within community center settings.

The care of the Durham Colored Library nonprofit and the Durham County Library's Stanford L. Warren Branch has continued to be a family affair for the nearly 100 years since Dr. Aaron Moore made his personal dream come true. His daughter Lyda Moore Merrick became the chair of the board of trustees and in 1949 established a reading room for the blind, inspired by her friendship with John C. Washington. Together they founded and published the *Negro Braille Magazine*, which is no longer in braille but is published in large print as the *Merrick Washington Magazine*. The Stanford L. Warren historic library building was incorporated into the Durham County Library, renovated, and reopened in 1983, due in part to the efforts of a committee headed by Constance Merrick Watts, Aaron's granddaughter. Constance and Charles Watts's daughter C. Eileen Watts Welch, Aaron Moore's great-granddaughter, has since taken up leadership and activist roles with the Durham Colored Library, Inc., as president and board chair for the nonprofit that initiated this book and continues to publish the *Merrick Washington Magazine*.

The Stanford L. Warren historic library building remains part of the Durham County Library System, open and ready to inspire patrons of all ages. A portrait in oils of Dr. A. M. Moore, painted by his daughter Lyda Moore Merrick, hangs in the entrance hall along with her portrait of Stanford L. Warren. Both of these men's faces greet those who enter the building, where there will always be "something for the people to read."

19

THE EXPLORER
Crossing the Nation

Travel in the days of Jim Crow for people of color was a tricky enterprise at best and downright dangerous at worst. At the same time, Americans who were unencumbered by institutionalized racism were able to travel farther and in more comfort than ever before. The phenomenon of increasingly grand world's fairs and exhibitions played into that burgeoning American spirit of adventure. Dr. Aaron Moore's spirit of adventure was certainly piqued by the 1915 World's Fair in San Francisco, all the way on the other side of the nation. His two daughters had finally settled back in Durham's Hayti after having spent the majority of their adolescence and young adulthood getting their education away from home. He had missed them. Lyda recounts that when they returned home from Fisk University, they found that their usually reserved father was in the mood to celebrate their mutual accomplishments with a few surprises. He met them at the train station proudly piloting a new automobile, and Lyda returned home to the thrill of a grand piano in the front parlor. Furthermore, he informed his daughters that they were going to plan a long and incredibly ambitious voyage across the country by train to attend the 1915 World's Fair. Lyda Moore Merrick remembered that trip for the rest of her life. In her reminiscence she made subtle yet constant references to the challenges of traveling and being "colored." She implied that on many occasions they "passed" when in unavoidably segregated areas but always sought out their own people when it came to lodgings or spending any significant time in one town. When she stated that they were "better off" traveling without her mother, she was almost certainly referring to her mother's darker complexion.

> After we finished school. Papa took us [Lyda and Mattie] to the World's Fair in California [in 1915 in San Francisco]. It took us thirteen days to make the trip by train. We went to Salt Lake City, Pike's Peak, and Chicago. We went by the northern route and came

back the southern route by New Orleans. And Mama didn't go—she didn't think Papa was able to do it! I guess we got along better without Mama, too. But that's the way it happened.

My father was fairer than me and my sister. They tried to make us white, you know. But Papa would hunt for the colored people's sections. He'd go to a town and say, "Show me where the colored people live." There's always a colored section, you know. And it became so difficult 'til he just gave up and said, "We'll just go to white hotels." I wouldn't leave my room because I was too brown. Papa would walk around.[1]

They crossed the nation and arrived in San Francisco. A world of wonders awaited the three travelers: hydroplanes, a Palace of Fine Arts with 11,000 artworks, a working model of the new Panama Canal, a 235-foot Aeroscope with a spectacular view of the city, and at the entrance, the Tower of Jewels, the fair's centerpiece, rising hundreds of feet and covered in cut glass that glittered in the sunlight.[2]

Aaron must have felt a thrill of pride in escorting his daughters, now accomplished, educated, and confident young women, a credit to their race and their sex. The three of them had bravely and successfully bisected the nation and arrived to take part in this truly historical pageant of progress in San Francisco, a city newly raised from its own ashes.

How many months of careful planning—writing letters to anyone they knew or could know along their train route and poring over atlases—had finally brought them to this moment? Then there were all of those hours on the train, watching America fly by in greens and grays and blues, seeing faces both friendly and hostile. Every stop along their route must have produced a certain level of anxiety. Diplomacy and social graces were required just to get from the train station to the part of town where black people lived. Then a series of inquiries had to be made as to whom they might know or, if there was no chance of that, who might be open to hosting them on their layover. If they were lucky enough to be warmly received and secure good accommodations—which thankfully most often was the case—they could stay a day and make better acquaintance.

Then there were fellow physicians to meet, hospitals to tour and take notes on, and schools to visit. Lyda recalled at one point begging to have herself admitted at a lying-in hospital in Chicago, saying she was so tired of hospitals she could "lie in" in one herself.[3]

This trip must have been a wonderful reintroduction for Aaron Moore to his two daughters as grown-up and educated young women. It was also a tremendous opportunity to visit other black enterprises across the nation and make new connections for the North Carolina Mutual and Provident Association. Lyda Moore Merrick remembered, "Everywhere we went he would visit hospitals and ask questions and make a mental note of everything that occurred." She recalled most of their stops along the way and their difficulty getting home:

> We stayed in Oakland, I believe. There was no ... [b]ridge then so we had to go by ferry to San Francisco. And the Orientals were there, the Japanese, and Chinatown. We would hang around them. We had never seen Orientals, and they fascinated us. They just wore silk, flowing silks, and diamonds! San Diego, Juarez, then over to New Orleans. Then we were stranded in New Orleans.... A terrible storm, I called it a tidal wave. We were going by train, and we had a drawing room, so we would sleep on the train. He [Dr. Moore] ... was pioneering black travel. So we studied our trip; he taught us geography and we would study all the places we would stop. He would give us a preparatory lesson.... There were some important meetings he went to in the big cities. Then he was interested in Sunday school; he attended the International Sunday School Convention in Chicago. There were many conventions while we were there. It was a learning trip ... he wanted knowledge. The trip lasted all of September 1915. Traveling was so hard then, missing your train and carrying your suitcases. I remember once we stopped at a colored hotel, and I had to sit up all night on the balcony because of the bed bugs. Mostly we stayed with kinfolks wherever we went.[4]

This trip was by any account an enormous undertaking. It was an American odyssey indeed, and to have made it as a man of color with his daughters at this time was downright brave. Earlier that year, on February 8, 1915, D. W. Griffith had opened his epic silent film *The Birth of a Nation* in Los Angeles. Based on the white supremacist novel *The Clansman*, it is credited with being America's first feature film with a three-hour running time. A month later it became the first movie to be shown in the White House, courtesy of President Woodrow Wilson. The film is dripping with racism, demeaning stereotypes, and revisionist history, and "in the film's climax, the Ku Klux Klan rises up to save the South from the Reconstruction Era–prominence of African Americans in Southern public life."[5]

As a prominent African American in Southern public life, Dr. A. M. Moore was exactly the type of person the film identifies as public enemy number one of American white dominance and birthright. D. W. Griffith openly stated that his goals for the film were to make every white person in America feel like a Southern white supremacist and for white women everywhere to be horrified and frightened by black men. The film was wildly successful and is credited with bringing the Klan into vogue all over America. *The Birth of a Nation* also brought lynching back with a vengeance, but now it was out of the shadows. In communities nation-wide it took on a new and festive air; family picnics and press coverage and advanced publicity accompanied these public murders. Meanwhile Woodrow Wilson was starting to use slogans like "America First" and to refer to the identity of a white American as "pure," a code for the "one drop rule" that made a black person (or a non-Anglo-Saxon immigrant) impure and therefore less American.[6]

Nevertheless, the Moores went on their American odyssey, and Lyda and Mattie became experienced travelers along the way with their ever-curious and brave father. The frequency of travel would increase for Dr. Moore in the next decade of his life. His gaze was turned more and more outward to the larger significance of what he and his friends and col-leagues had accomplished in Durham and how those who had spear-headed their enterprises could inform others along a similar path. His daughters were not the only ones who were graduating. Aaron Moore's interests and goals were also evolving to encompass a new level of states-manship on behalf of his race. Perhaps in light of the example of his own daughters and their successful educational development, and with a clear eye toward the sentiments at large in America in 1915, Dr. Moore's inter-est in the plight of black children was reinvigorated.

PART SIX *Building a Legacy*

20

EDUCATION FIRST, LAST, ALWAYS

Youth must recognize individual responsibility to the
race, the nation, and to humanity and prepare themselves
to become a working unit in their development.
—A. M. Moore

Aaron McDuffie Moore had embarked on his college education intent on becoming a teacher. Even as he answered the call to serve his community as a physician, he still managed to spend a great deal of his life teaching. His personal investment in the education of many individuals, both related and unrelated to him, his daily participation in the training of nurses and residents at Lincoln Hospital, and his abiding interest in and attention to the education of his own daughters cumulatively earned him the title of educator. His work in the Sunday school at White Rock punctuated his weeks without fail, and he held a teachers' meeting every Thursday night to support the education, morale, and curriculum planning of local schoolteachers, regardless of denomination.[1]

Moore's ability to learn, to reason, to solve problems, and to implement change is at the very heart of every success in his life story. Moore felt on a visceral level that the pursuit of knowledge opened the world of beauty, complexity, and capability to those who were brave enough to seek it out. If there was a legacy beyond equitable health care that Moore wanted for his community, it was ready access to the power of knowledge and a good education.

Each of the organizations Moore had helped found in Durham gave black people a new level of hope and security. Better health care increased their life expectancy; insurance and the bank allowed them to preserve their equity and to own property; the library provided books, resources, and a dignified space for continued learning; and church renovations made more social services possible. The next logical step was to do everything in his power to enrich and empower healthier and more secure years ahead, the formative years of generations to come. With this in mind, and perhaps spurred by his daughters' interest and ability as classical musicians, Moore organized in 1914 an orchestra called Volkemenia and a Schubert-Shakespeare Club designed to bring theater, concerts, and cultural activities to Hayti.[2]

Starting around the same year, Dr. Moore began to use his accumulated influence as a physician and successful business leader to address educational inequality at the government level. He was no longer a newcomer in Durham's political circles. He was well known and respected, and it was time to put his reputation on the line to advance the idea that all people deserved a chance to do and be their best.

Equality in education was a deeply divisive political discussion at this time, and Dr. Moore was to find that education was a harder sell to white government than black health care had been. Better health care, after all, benefited everyone on both sides of the racial coin. It made white homes safer from communicable disease and white-owned factories more efficient with a healthier and longer-lived workforce. Hygiene and the suppression of infectious disease was an obvious motivator and could win the argument even in the presence of ingrained prejudice.

Education was an entirely different matter, especially when it threatened to raise black people's prospects above the level of the labor trades and domestic service. Talk of educational equality raised the old specter of fusionist political organizations and the upward mobility of the working classes. It also reignited the conflict between poor whites and poor blacks, which had arisen during Reconstruction, when educational funding had been allocated equally albeit briefly. The "separate but equal" rhetoric of Booker T. Washington and his advocacy for technical education over the higher professions had calmed these fears for a while. As long as blacks were striving on their own and not asking for government involvement or funding, whites could turn a blind eye. Any bid for equal funding in the basic services of government, however, sounded an alarm that could be very dangerous for any upwardly mobile black community.[3]

Congressman George Henry White, Aaron Moore's cousin from Columbus County school days, gave a farewell address on January 29, 1901, to the U.S. House of Representatives. He was about to leave office in March, and disenfranchisement, his inability to advance anti-lynching legislation, educational inequality, and equal representation under the law were weighing heavily on his mind. His speech was both historic and visceral and encompassed much of what men like Dr. Aaron Moore and

John Merrick and C. C. Spaulding had accomplished in their lifetimes in Durham and throughout the South. It also, no doubt, spoke to a determination on behalf of future generations. Moore and all his associates would certainly have read, felt, and considered every line:

> I would like to advance the statement that the musty records of 1868, filed away in the archives of Southern capitols, as to what the negro was thirty-two years ago, is not a proper standard by which the negro living on the threshold of the twentieth century should be measured. Since that time we have reduced the illiteracy of the race at least 45 per cent. We have written and published near 500 books. We have nearly 300 newspapers, 3 of which are dailies. We have now in practice over 2,000 lawyers and a corresponding number of doctors. We have accumulated over $12,000,000 worth of school property and about $40,000,000 worth of church property. We have about 140,000 farms and homes, valued in the neighborhood of $750,000,000, and personal property valued at $170,000,000. We have raised about $11,000,000 for educational purposes, and the property per capita for every colored man, woman, and child in the United States is estimated at $75.
>
> We are operating successfully several banks, commercial enterprises among our people in the Southland.... We have 32,000 teachers in the schools of the country; we have built, with the aid of our friends, about 20,000 churches, and support 7 colleges, 17 academies, 50 high schools, 5 law schools, 5 medical schools, and 25 theological seminaries.... All this we have done under the most adverse circumstances. We have done it in the face of lynching, burning at the stake, with the humiliation of "Jim Crow" cars, the disfranchisement of our male citizens, slander and degradation of our Women.... Labor unions ... and those supplying nearly every conceivable avocation for livelihood have banded themselves together to better their condition, but, with few exceptions, the black face has been left out.... With all these odds against us, we are forging our way ahead, slowly, perhaps, but surely. You may tie us and then taunt us for a lack of bravery, but one day we will break the bonds. You may use our labor for two and a half centuries and then taunt us for our poverty, but let me remind you we will not always remain poor. You may withhold even the knowledge of how to read God's word and learn the way from earth to glory and then taunt us for our ignorance,

but we would remind you that there is plenty of room at the top, and we are climbing.[4]

Dr. A. M. Moore wrote the following letter to North Carolina's superintendent of public instruction James Joyner fourteen years later on April 26, 1915, and included a speech Moore intended to give on April 30 of that year. The speech, *Negro Rural School Problem Condition-Remedy: Let Us Reason Together*, would also be produced as a pamphlet or circular, a common practice with many formal addresses during that time.

Dear Sir:

My only reason for presuming to address you this letter is that I believe you to be deeply interested in the future of the colored youth of the state. Doubtless you have often thought of the rising generation and may have put forward tentative plans for their betterment. If so, you will find the subject matter of this letter not entirely discordant with your own views.

As I see it, we are losing valuable opportunities for improving the rural schools and incidentally a majority of the young people of the state. The lack of proper school advantages in the rural districts in North Carolina is responsible in large and increasing measure for the raw and inassimilable material, which is yearly accumulating in our larger towns and cities. You have doubtless observed the timidity with which these recent arrivals in our towns approach any of our urban institutions. It is especially hard to have this element of urban population identify themselves with the churches. Things are so new and strange that they shrink from those things which are designed to aid them.

These people in the main have not had enough schooling either to fit them for the demands of urban life or to make them content in the rural districts. The consequence is that a large percentage of them are recruited to the criminal class in the towns or remain in the rural districts as a discouraged and non-productive contingent. That these conditions are remedial is beyond question, and we can afford to rely on the same agencies, which have always proved their value in all similar circumstances. Schools have always been the instrument used to adjust a backward element of the population to changing conditions, and we cannot afford to discard them in rectifying the conditions, which persist among the colored people of the state. The trouble is that instead of growing more efficient, our rural schools are growing less able to cope with the problems which are arising among colored people.

This failure on the part of the rural schools has become more apparent in recent years. In a rough way, the lessening of interest in the rural school and its problems has been coincident with the disenfranchisement of the colored voter. Before disenfranchisement there were colored men on the school boards, and in consequence they were in position to make demands not only upon the county boards but also upon the local teacher. In this way, more attention was paid to the colored schools, and a relatively larger amount of money was appropriated by the county boards for the maintenance of colored schools. In the matter of appropriation, you are doubtless aware that the county board has final authority. At present, the appropriations by the Durham County board average twice as much for each white child enrolled as for each colored child. Doubtless the same discrimination is a common practice in all the counties of the state in a greater or lesser degree.

This, in outline, is the situation. That it is dark must be admitted; that it can be remedied is not questioned.

In the first place, the colored people themselves are to be aroused by holding popular meetings in the state, counties and school districts. The best method of dealing with local problems will be evolved thereby. It has been in this way that the white people of the state have increased the efficiency of their schools. Where concentrations were thought to be necessary to obtain the best results, it has been recommended by these popular gatherings, and where it was needful to raise money in order to supplement the local school fund, subscriptions have been volunteered in these meetings. Like methods commend themselves in the case of colored schools. As a starter in this direction, the Executive Board of the State Teachers Association has signified its willingness to give a place for a state meeting for this purpose in connection with their annual assemblage to be held this year in Winston-Salem. At this gathering it will be possible to outline, plan and inaugurate movements designed to affect the rural schools of every county in the state.

There is also the possibility of securing the active cooperation of the manager of the Jeanes Fund. [This was an endowment established in 1907 by Quaker Anna T. Jeanes of Philadelphia to fund the training and organization of black teachers and administrators.]

The reason this has not been done hitherto in a general way has been the apathy of the colored people themselves. It would be a good plan to have one hundred public-spirited colored men give ten dollars each, so as to provide a fund of one thousand dollars to be used to supplement the salary or salaries of state, district or county organizers under the Jeanes Fund Managers. In this way a working basis for the whole state could be inaugurated and the main aspects of the problem brought under control.

Mr. Rosenwald, the philanthropist of Chicago, not long since decided to use his good offices in this way around Tuskegee, and so satisfactory and beneficial have been the results that he has judged it beneficial to extend his plans so as to include the State of North Carolina.

These agencies, if given a chance, may be counted on to do much toward the elimination of the faults of our rural schools and introduce a better day for the youth of the state.

I shall be more than pleased to know that the plans as outlined meet your approval and also if we may count on your active cooperation in making the same effective. If you are willing to cooperate with us, drop us a line today conveying such expression and we will communicate with you later, fully stating a plan of work. We are sure you would like to be one of the hundred men forming such an organization. Remember the date of meeting, 6/16/15, in Winston-Salem, N.C. May I hear from you within five days?

Yours for racial uplift,

A. M. Moore, M.D.

Durham, N.C.[5]

The pamphlet and the address must have had a sizable impact because the words reached the attention of E. C. Branson, professor of rural economics and sociology at the University of North Carolina at Chapel Hill. Although Branson's subsequent note reeks of disdain for Moore, whom he calls "this darkey," the pamphlet must have caused Branson to pay enough attention to enclose it in a letter and forward it to Superintendent Joyner himself, via Joyner's clerk, C. E. McIntosh, nearly a month after Aaron Moore published it. He must have also forwarded information on the National Religious Training School and Chautauqua (which would become North Carolina Central University) and its principal founder, James E. Shepard. His description of the school is dismissive and especially ugly in light of his use of UNC–Chapel Hill letterhead printed with his own name and department. He ends with a conspiratorial statement that indicates he wouldn't like his more public persona to appear racist:

May 27, 1915

Mr. C. E. McIntosh,
Raleigh, N.C.
    Dear Mr. McIntosh:
    Please glance over the enclosures. Do you know this darkey? What is he up to? What about him anyway?
    And James E. Shepard of Durham, president of the National Religious Training School? What kind of a thingamabob is that anyway?
    Anything you write me will be in confidence of course.
    With best wishes I am,
    Yours Truly,
    E. C. Branson[6]

Superintendent Joyner's clerk, C. E. McIntosh, responded immediately. His reply is dated May 29, 1915, a Saturday, pointing to an urgency that extended beyond the workweek. It should be noted that in the correspondence archive of Superintendent Joyner or his clerk there is no reply to Dr. Moore's eloquent letter, although he had asked for a reply within five days and signed with a polite "Yours for racial uplift." There can be a benefit of the doubt granted here. Perhaps a telephone call was made or a personal visit. What is irrefutable is the disrespect inherent in the following lengthy and very prompt response to Branson:

Prof. E. C. Branson
Chapel Hill, NC
    Dear Sir:
    I have your letter of the 27th enclosing a circular entitled "The Negro Rural School Problem." It seems to be sent out by A. M. Moore, Durham. I do not know what is back of the circular but it appears to be the mere babble of an ignorant negro and worth very little attention. While I was teaching in Durham I heard a good deal of Jas. E. Shepard, President of the so-called Religious Training School, at Durham, and if my information concerning him is correct, I think he is a good man to let alone.
    I presume the difference in the figures quoted in the leaflet is

due to the fact that very few negro districts have a local tax and that nearly all of them employ a very low grade of teachers. I am sure there is no desire on the part of the department here or any of the county superintendents to discriminate against the negro in the matter of apportionment, provided the same grade of teachers is employed. Supt. Joyner has ruled a dozen times that the local tax collected in special tax districts should be apportioned by the local tax committee to each district so that each race would get an equitable share of the special tax. I am exceedingly busy today and do not have time to examine the report carefully, but as I have said above, I do not think the figures cited in the leaflet will tend to show that the colored race is discriminated against in the slightest degree. If you would like me to look up anything in this line for you, I shall be glad to do so as soon as I get the opportunity.

Very Truly Yours,

Chief Clerk.[7]

The leaflet referred to above is the printed version of Dr. Moore's address that he made in multiple venues in the coming months. It follows in its entirety:

NEGRO RURAL SCHOOL PROBLEM

CONDITION-REMEDY

LET US REASON TOGETHER

The problem of the education of the colored youth in the rural districts of North Carolina is, more or less, at the present time, a serious one, owing to the difficulties and handicaps surrounding and confronting the situation, such as poorly equipped school houses, inadequate teaching facilities, short school terms, low general average attendance, inefficiency of most of the teachers and lack of funds to properly carry on the work.

In addition to the above-mentioned serious aspects of the case, we would call your attention to the following facts and figures bearing upon Negro Education in our own state, which we find in the "Biennial Report of the Superintendent of Public Instruction of North Carolina for The Scholastic Years, 1911–12, 1913–14."

The colored rural school population in 1913–14 was 198,737; the enrollment was 157,684; 41,053 less than the school population. The average attendance was 90,185, one-half of the school population and just a little over one-half of the general enrollment. The average length of the school term was about four months, that of the whites nearly six months. The number of schoolhouses 2,263; the average value of a colored schoolhouse, $247.38. The total number of schoolhouses for whites was 7,619 and the average value of each $851.55. Of course, there should be taken into consideration the fact that the white school population was at the same period 429,399. The number of colored schoolteachers was 2,654, while the whites numbered 8,344. The total amount of money paid the colored teachers was $340,319.42, while the white teachers received $1,963,098.10. The average paid each colored teacher: $128.42 [per year], the white teacher receiving $235.27. Furthermore, the white child received per capita for his or her education $4.57, while the colored got only $1.71.

To infer that it costs less to educate a colored child than it does a white one is paying too great a compliment to the intellect of the former, which we are unwilling to acknowledge. But to the unsuspicious and uninformed, looking at the respective figures in the case, such a conclusion might be drawn. It is a fact that the facilities for Negro education in the rural districts are pitifully inadequate. Although Negroes constituted about 33 percent of the population, less than 15 percent of the money collected and spent for rural education is expended on them. Now, the above are some data for your serious attention and consideration. What are you going to do about it? Nothing is to be gained by whining and complaining and saying that if we had in addition to our usual appropriation all the moneys that went into the general school fund as a result of Negro criminality, which unfortunately furnishes, at least, three fourths of such fund in the state, and also, that which goes into the school fund from the taxation of corporations, such as railroads, banks, building and loan associations, and others, to which we indirectly contribute by thousands of dollars, we would have, perhaps, available twice as much for school purposes as we do actually have now. For do not Negroes ride on the railroads in the state by the tens of thousands annually, and have they not over hundreds of thousands in the white and colored banks, in the building and loan associations in the state, and in other corporations controlled by white and colored men respectively, upon which taxes are assessed according to their earnings; but when it comes to dividing up the taxes pro rata, accordingly as each race has contributed its quota to the profits of these various business enterprises, we get little or nothing from these sources?

All of this is doubtless true, but we must remember that the other man collects the taxes, keeps the books, and divides and appropriates the school funds as, in his opinion, he deems proper and equitable, so there you are. In the meantime, let us be patient but not contented. Rather let us be up and doing. We cannot easily evade this all important and vital question by saying: "I am not particularly interested," nor "Am I my brother's keeper?" Our white fellow citizens are aroused on this subject of rural education at the present as never before, and they are putting into operation every means and every agency they can command to bring about an improved, enlightened, social and physical rural community. While in a few isolated quarters in the state, some of our people, realizing the gravity of the situation, have succeeded in improving the school conditions in their own districts; on the other hand, we fear the great majority of our people are too indifferent and too negligent regarding those matters affecting their intellectual, moral and social welfare. There are doubtless many causes for his apathy and state of mind on the part of the masses. But the chief reason, we believe, is that there is not sufficient agitation on this subject and not enough persistent and insistent reminding of our people of their duty and obligation in the premise. There are already agencies in the state, such as the Jeanes Fund supervisors and employees of the Department of Public Instruction, and there may be others, who are doing the best they can to arouse our people to do their duty. But these agencies are more or less handicapped.

To come down to "brass tacks," so to speak, what we want and need is to put a man in the field ourselves, who, while acting in co-operation with the other forces for the improvement of the rural school communities, will feel absolutely free and untrammeled in his judgment and in his activities along this line, as the conditions and his duty in each case may reveal itself to him from time to time. "The gods help those who first help themselves." For this work we need and must have money to push it. This movement, it is true, is an experiment, but we are encouraged to believe it will be successful, if we can obtain a few hundred faithful, interested, race-loving men and women behind it. What think ye of the proposition? Are you ready and willing to help, and how much?

Our weakness has been that we spend too much time and money in preparation for dying and expensive funerals and too little preparing for living, which is equally important. We give ten dollars for church building for every one dollar given for schoolhouse improvement. In the past quarter of a century, we have remodeled each church an average of three times, while our children remain in the same dingy, half-heated schoolhouses in which we attended school ourselves. The biggest thing we can do, and this seems to me to be our mission, is to empty our lives and character into our children, thereby making them better and wiser citizens than we are or had an opportunity to be.

Racial evolution or involution is absolutely inevitable and constant and the child is either the exponent of progress or the index of physical, moral, or intellectual degeneracy. If we are to ascend the ladder of civilization we must follow the lead of our white neighbors, whose watchword is and has been SELF HELP. There is much we can and must do for ourselves, and we call upon every teacher, preacher, farmer and businessman to arouse himself, and "Let us Reason Together."

OUR PLAN

In Winston, N.C., June 16, in connection with the State Teachers Association, you are invited to the organization of a State and Rural School Association.

OBJECT

Improvement of rural schools

WANTS

100 men who will give $10.00 per year for expenses
100 women who will give $5.00 per year for expenses

OUR AIM

Employ an efficient state organizer full time who shall organize in every county a Board of Education, who shall work under the present legal boards and county superintendents, and who shall organize township boards and county superintendents, and who shall hold school rallies, encourage school attendance, raise funds by private subscription or local taxation, one for improving school buildings, lengthening school terms and improving the teaching corps by augmenting present salaries of teachers.

The appeal is personal to YOU and URGENT. We are in dead earnest. Something must be done. We send this appeal to you, because we know you to be a man of influence and successful in your field of labor. Let us have your pledge within 7 days or check dated June 1, 1915. Act today. Tomorrow won't do.

Address all communications to:

A. M. Moore, MD. Durham, NC

April 30, 1915[8]

With this published leaflet and address, Moore not only indicted the state school board by using its own published numbers but also admonished his own people for spending more on their churches and funeral expenses than on the minds and future prospects of their children. This must have resonated deeply coming from an insurance man as well as a man who had himself participated in fund-raising for the newly renovated White Rock Baptist Church in 1910. The target of his admonishments included himself, and his urgency was never more real than at this point in his life. He had a plan, he had a map to success, and he was not complaining. He was "up and doing."

The momentum of his efforts is reflected in the *Wilmington Morning Star* of Saturday, June 26, 1915, just two months later, as he is indeed reported to have met with leaders (mentioned in the first letter to Joyner) in Winston-Salem to "launch" the Movement to Improve the Negro Rural Schools in North Carolina.

Winston, N.C. June 23—In response to a call sent out by Dr. A. M. Moore of Durham, N.C., quite a number of the leading business men of the Negro race met with the State Teachers Association, colored, convened at the Slater State Normal School, Winston Salem, June 16, and organized for the purpose of improving the negro rural schools of the state. Dr. A. M. Moore, in a strong and earnest address, outlined the object of the meeting as follows: to lengthen the school term, erect better buildings, secure better teachers, provide better salaries, and arouse deeper interest in the uplift of the youth of the race; and to do this in cooperation with the school authorities of the State. Professor Newbold and Professor Sams, representatives of the State Department of Education, being present, made addresses heartily commending the movement and predicted that great good would result from the effort.

The plan contemplates the employment of a State agent whose business it will be to travel throughout the State, ascertain the actual conditions existing in the rural districts, organize in every county and school district improvement clubs, and to urge in every legitimate way the interests of the public schools. A committee of control composed of seven prominent colored men was appointed to supervise this work.... Fully six hundred dollars was secured to aid in starting the movement, and the committee will endeavor to get one hundred colored men who will guarantee the money to meet the necessary expenses of the movement.

In order to secure the cordial support of the white people of the State, Professor Newbold and Professor Sams, of Raleigh, and Professor Coon, of Wilson, were chosen and invited to serve as honorary members of the committee of control. Dr. A. M. Moore was elected Secretary-Treasurer of the committee, and given free hand to develop the undertaking.[9]

As the newly appointed secretary-treasurer of the Movement to Improve the Negro Rural Schools in North Carolina, Dr. Moore's next task was to engage the state agent referred to above and with this person's labor and expertise develop the data needed to present to "the white people of the State." Those "honorary members of the committee," (white) Professors N. C. Newbold and E. E. Sams, would be smoothing the way politically in the meantime.

Charles Henry Moore, native son of Wilmington and a graduate of Amherst College (and no relation to Dr. A. M. Moore), was the man selected as state agent. C. H. Moore had already distinguished himself as an educator in serving as the first colored principal of a "negro graded school" in North Carolina and in helping to found the Negro North Carolina Teachers Association.[10] In July 1915 C. H. Moore was working for the National Negro Business League. He agreed that after his work concluded in Boston that summer, he would return to North Carolina and take up this new and important task.[11]

On September 1, 1915, C. H Moore, Dr. A. M. Moore, and Professors Newbold and Sams met with State Superintendent Joyner, the same man to whom Dr. Moore's letter and leaflet had been addressed the previous April, to apprise him of their plan and try to enlist his support. In less than six months, Dr. Moore had achieved everything he had told Joyner he would do. C. H. Moore describes this initial meeting in his report:

In company with Dr. A. M. Moore ... I went to Raleigh to have a conference with the State Superintendent, Hon. J. H. Joyner, and Professors N. C. Newbold and E. E. Sams of the Department [of]

Rural Elementary and Colored Schools, respectively. After Dr. Moore … had satisfactorily explained what the projectors[,] viz.: The State Teachers' Association, of this new movement intended to accomplish, Dr. Joyner then expressed his approval and, furthermore his willingness not only to cooperate with us, but also to give the State Board's endorsement of this movement by requesting Prof. Newbold to outline and plan the work to be tentatively done in the different counties, to which I would be sent.[12]

This address made after the fact and to a mixed audience still was able to convey that, although the committee now had Joyner's attention, the superintendent still needed a white intermediary (Newbold) to give the state agent direction on his travels through North Carolina.

And what a journey it was. C. H. Moore traveled through thirty-five counties and a total of 12,050 miles by train, streetcar, wagon, boat, and automobile. He addressed every kind of gathering, wrote articles raising awareness for the movement in both white and black newspapers, and delivered three monthly progress reports to Dr. Moore, to Newbold (and through him presumably to Joyner), and to the committee of control. Not only were C. H. Moore's findings definitive in proving that tax dollars were not being spent in black schools in a manner that was remotely equitable, but he was also able, per Newbold's instruction, to encourage and coach communities through the application for Rosenwald matching funds. A community able to raise three-fourths of the funds for a new schoolhouse and then to apply for the grant would receive the other fourth (a maximum of $350) from the Rosenwald Fund, recently established by the philanthropist Julius Rosenwald, who supported black education. In just one summer C. H. Moore was able to get twenty-five to thirty new schoolhouses funded and twelve completed.[13]

During the first two months of C. H. Moore's travels through North Carolina, Booker T. Washington, his friend and colleague in the National Negro Business League,[14] succumbed to high blood pressure and passed away on November 15, 1915, at the age of fifty-nine.[15] The following January, twenty-five applications for Rosenwald School grants were brought before the board in Tuskegee but suffered delays due to Washington's death. C. H. Moore himself was scheduled to appear on their behalf but fell ill himself. By February, however, C. H. Moore received word of twenty accepted applications for Rosenwald funding and encouragement to continue raising awareness and schoolhouse funds.[16]

On June 23, 1916, a little over a year from the inception of Dr. Aaron Moore's initiative, State Inspector of the Negro Schools C. H. Moore delivered his comprehensive address and report before the North Carolina Association of Educators in Greensboro. In this address he presented hard data concerning the fate of schools that had received an inequitable portion of the special taxes for education paid by blacks. He also relayed many anecdotes of community awakening, entrepreneurship, and engagement and included some of the correspondence he received concerning the movement. One such letter is from the aforementioned E. C. Branson, who had earlier written to State Superintendent Joyner's clerk asking, "Do you know this darkey?" and "What about him anyway?" Branson's letter to C. H. Moore is considerably more cordial and certainly exhibits curiosity about his work. Perhaps the rapid unfolding of the plan put forward by Dr. A. M. Moore in that leaflet a year before and the subsequent participation of Superintendent Joyner in the plan was serving to make it less "incoherent."

The University of North Carolina, Rural Economics and Sociology, Chapel Hill, N.C., March 27, 1916
Mr. C. H. Moore, Weldon, N.C.
Dear Mr. Moore:
Please let me have the accounts of your visits to the various counties; it gives me an intimate look into the condition and the progress of Negro school education in the State. You understand, of course, that I am tremendously interested in that.
With Best Wishes, I am, yours truly,
E. C. Branson[17]

In November 1916 a Commission to Study Negro Education gathered in Durham in the Avery Auditorium. Dr. A. M. Moore's friend and fellow world traveler James E. Shepard delivered the welcome. Black educators "from more than twenty states" attended.[18] W. E. B. Du Bois also addressed the gathering, and at the end of the afternoon, Dr. Moore invited all the attendees to the wedding of his daughter Lyda Vivian Moore to John Merrick's son Edward Richard Merrick at White Rock Baptist Church.[19]

The Moore-Merrick wedding was described in the *New York Age* newspaper as

the most brilliant event of the season, and the most beautiful ever witnessed in Durham. The ceremony was performed at White Rock

Baptist Church at 8 o'clock.... The color scheme of the church was white and green.... The Maid of Honor was Miss Mattie Louise Moore, the bride's sister.... The bride was escorted to the altar by her father. Her wedding gown was of white duchesse satin, with pearl and white fur trimmings and an elaborate court train. The white tulle veil was held in place by orange blossoms and she carried white bride's roses.... A reception was tendered the bride and groom at the home of the bride's father from 8:30 to 11 o'clock. Mr. and Mrs. will live at 906 Fayetteville Street in a handsome house designed and presented to the groom by his father as a wedding present.[20]

The following morning, Dr. A. M. Moore was back on the job and delivered his own address concerning the progress of the black school movement to the commission. Not even the morning after his daughter's remarkable wedding was off limits when it came to moving the cause of education forward.[21] Dr. Moore, never one to let luxurious habits take hold, was quoted in the *Durham Reformer* earlier that year, "I fear that our leaders are too much absorbed in money-making and looking after their own selfish interests to make themselves felt in the community life, and this is a fatal mistake in any community. We provide beautiful churches and comfortable pews for our own enjoyment for two hours on Sunday, but our children are forced to dangle their feet from uncomfortable seats in cold and poorly ventilated rooms for five days in the week. This is not right."[22] Even as a man able to escort his daughter in satin and pearls to her wedding vows in the presence of the press, the community, and race leaders such as W. E. B. Du Bois and John C. Dancy, Dr. Moore was aware enough of the suffering in his community to make it a constant part of his work and awareness. Prosperity was good, but prosperity at the cost of empathy for the plight of future generations was disastrously shortsighted.

Dr. Moore's commitment to education at every level became his most pressing concern from this point forward. He remained on the board of directors at Shaw University throughout his life. He fought vigorously against the dissolution of his beloved Leonard Medical School, a loss caused by the racial bias of the controversial Flexner Report, which recommended the closing of all but two black medical schools in the nation. During his lifetime, Dr. Moore was one of Shaw University's most generous donors. He even remembered, as previously mentioned, his alma mater in his will with a $5,000 bequest.[23] When all else was counted,

Aaron Moore knew that education was among his greatest treasures. He never hesitated to remind others of this fact or to invest what treasure he had in the service of that lifelong benefit for others.

The most intimate portrait we have of Aaron McDuffie Moore comes from the daughter whom he walked down the aisle in November 1916. Lyda's recollections of life with her father and of her own education and upbringing are the most personal reflection and evidence we have of what Dr. Moore stood for. It seems fitting to hear in her own words the account of her and her sister Mattie's education. It is important to note that even at its highest levels, education for young black women at the turn of the twentieth century was a luxury but hardly luxurious. Having a father and mother who actively cared for their success was a driving force, one that Lyda referred to again and again. It is not difficult to imagine that all those whose education Dr. Moore supported and advocated for experienced this same strong encouragement.

> Papa sacrificed to give us every advantage he could, kept us in books. We had our own library [at home]. Papa taught us at home. My sister and I could already read when we went to school, so they put us in second grade. I was six years old and always the youngest in the class. I also had piano lessons from the time I was six. I played for Sunday school, and I just pulled myself up by having to get ready for that.

> Papa was my best teacher; he taught me geography and problems and would see that I did my homework. He was a good teacher. One year Papa got me a book on Morocco, and I read it so many times it about fell apart. It was the first time I had ever heard of Africa. When we got big enough to read adult books, Papa would even let us read medical books at the Mutual offices. I remember seeing preserved organs and an embryo in formaldehyde and asking about them. Papa gave me a book to read about them. He also gave me books to read called "Damaged Goods" and "The Scarlet Letter." So that was my education sexually; the rest the dirty-mouthed girls at school told me [she laughs mischievously].

> I went to Whitted School in Durham through the ninth grade and graduated valedictorian, undeserved I think. My daddy always saw that I got my lessons. Others did not have that kind of support. Then I went to Scotia [Seminary] and stayed four years.

> Scotia was a Freedmen's School and mostly full of poor students supported by scholarships. We had to scrub floors and do our laundry

in a steam laundry. We had an outdoor privy. We had a cook, but all the girls did the work. We were all work students. I was just 13 when I went, and I wasn't mature, I had been sheltered so. I had a cousin who taught there, and because I was small in stature I was given the job of answering the front door bell. Boy, I could fly down those steps! I did very well in music, and I played for chapel and marches. Not to be braggadocios, but I was a little bit special there, so I was allowed to practice my piano in the teachers' parlor and study.

The food was so poor I had indigestion and every sort of thing. Papa said when we went there, "You're not going to find it like home, but don't complain," so we were all treated fair and in the same way. We all stole food from the kitchen. I had a roommate who could steal a loaf of bread in her blouse!

It took a lot of my time getting my schoolwork done. But we did a lot of talking just girl-to-girl, and I had never had any of that at home. We talked about everything. It was crowded, five girls to a room, and rats and roaches, yeah! They just didn't have the money to have things like they should be. But they gave me a good foundation. The classes were small; the teachers were all white and colored people. We had study period, and we would all go to chapel. We had monitors and we couldn't say anything. We were supposed to study and were given quiet time to get our lessons done. Then we often had examinations, and we didn't wait for the end of the year. I was trying to make good marks and trying to keep up with my sister [Mattie]. You know she was smarter than me. I went to Scotia two years, and then she came and there was an entrance examination, and she got placed only a year behind me. Then we both went to Fisk [University].

When I went to Fisk, everything was so different, a different atmosphere altogether. Scotia was like high school. I was eighteen when I went to Fisk. Fisk had more money, and it showed in every way. We had good food. I used to sit by my music teacher. She liked me because … well, she just asked that I sit by her. All the time I was there I sat next to a teacher. I had good home training, good manners. Sometimes they would have special things for the teachers, and she would share hers with me. The teachers were into the real art of living and not just frivolity. I just enjoy that kind of conversation.

At Fisk my "major" was the Normal Course. At that time most girls took Normal work [teacher training], because there was nothing to do but teach or do secretarial work, and you didn't need calculus or chemistry to do that, so most of us took the Normal Course. I pursued music and composition, harmony-related courses. When I got to Fisk, I realized I hadn't had very good instruction on the piano, and I just cried. I can read music very fast, sight-reading. It has just always been part of my educational career. When I finished there, my teacher was anxious that I come back and finish a degree in music, but I had been away [a long time] ... and Papa hadn't seen enough of us, so I said no to that.

I stayed very busy at Fisk. I appreciated an opportunity to have those excellent teachers. I didn't waste my time. Mattie moved up another year on me! She dropped the music, you see, and doubled up her class schedule. She just maneuvered her way up and came out right along with me. We were roommates, always together. We were very close.

Mattie and me, we were both *magna cum laude* and both spoke at our commencement.

We spent the summer in New York and Boston after Fisk, and I studied music at the New York Conservatory and art at Columbia. I have been drawing all my life. I just took to arts.

Then I came home to teach.

I had a music class. It was the first real music class. My sister also began the first Kindergarten, and all that we did was church-related. We had Tuesday night choir practice, and I played for that; Wednesday prayer meeting, I had to go to that; Thursday night teachers meeting; Friday night they had a business school and an orchestra, I played the violin in the orchestra [Volkemenia]. Saturday was free. During the afternoons I taught from three until six or until dark. My studio was the pastor's study. They fixed it up nice.

Papa had two girls come to me [boarders] when they were 13 and stayed until they finished college. Papa did the same thing, even C. C. Spaulding stayed at our house, Asa too, all the Spaulding cousins, six girls, four of them stayed through college.

I had a journal, every night I would write down what had happened that day. I wish I knew where that book was. Somebody should write a book about the way it was, and about Papa.[24]

Lyda Moore Merrick finished this series of taped interviews with an impromptu performance of Claude Debussy's *Claire de Lune* on the piano. She remarked that her father always particularly liked when she played Debussy. Even in the year 1983 she played the famous piece with authority, humor, and grace. Lyda never rested on her educational advantages or talent; she used them as her father would have wished, in the service, advocacy, and education of others.

THE GREAT WAR AT
HOME AND ABROAD

21

As Dr. Aaron Moore was waging the battle for black education in North Carolina and fighting segregationist attitudes and policies, the First World War was scorching battlefields abroad between 1914 and 1918. Volunteering to fight overseas was, for many men of color, a way to a better measure of honor at home. Military author Jami L. Bryan writes, "When the United States declared war against Germany in April of 1917, War Department planners quickly realized that the standing Army of 126,000 men would not be enough to ensure victory overseas.... On 18 May 1917 Congress passed the Selective Service Act requiring all male citizens between the ages of 21 and 31 to register for the draft. Even before the act was passed, African American males from all over the country eagerly joined the war effort. They viewed the conflict as an opportunity to prove their loyalty, patriotism, and worthiness for equal treatment in the United States."[1]

Not only were black soldiers needed to swell troop numbers abroad, but African American labor was vital to the workforce at home, also. The retention and management of the black labor force became urgent and of great interest, especially to Southern states like North Carolina. Many black people were choosing to leave the South and segregation for a better chance at citizenship in the North and West. Farming and industry suddenly woke up to the value of their black workforce.

The Department of Labor needed advice on how to proceed, and Dr. A. M. Moore would once again find himself on the front lines of economic and social development. The department chose North Carolina to be the first state for implementation of a program to promote the success of "Negro wage earners." It is very likely that North Carolina was selected for this experiment because of the example of Durham's Hayti and "Black Wall Street." It is also likely that Moore's effective activism for education and rapport with white leaders in the state made him an obvious choice to lead the effort. The job the department asked of him would be similar to the one he had given Charles H. Moore: community organizer, data collector, and intercessor.

The U.S. Employment Service appointed Dr. A. M. Moore "Supervisor of Negro Economics" and special agent of the Employment Service for the entire duration of World War I (and for seven months after the war) as a "dollar-a-year man."[2] This dollar-a-year invitation was one generally extended to owners of banks, franchises, and the ruling class—those whose fortunes were made. It is interesting that the government saw Dr. Moore as someone available for this category of service; that being said, the government certainly got its dollar's worth.[3] Moore was also assigned an assistant supervisor in this work, R. McCants Andrews,[4] who would subsequently write the definitive biography of John Merrick. Together these two men traveled to twenty-three or more counties, not only gathering data but also encouraging the formation of local counsels for black labor. In many cases, they also successfully mediated between white bosses and black workers. They became the representatives of an African American workforce too often labeled by white employers as "shiftless" rather than a valuable resource, one worth making an effort to cultivate and hear. Dr. Moore summarized these travels, observations, and activities in an address before a meeting that included the governor and other state officials on June 1, 1919.[5] In the key excerpts that follow, note how Dr. Moore never loses an opportunity to stress the importance of education:

> How to keep the Negro workers and make them satisfied with their lot is the problem now presented to the South.... Some planters and industrial establishments are already demonstrating by means of better pay and greater care for their employees what such considerations will do ... and the more efficient Negro schools have for years been pointing the way.
>
> ... The improvement of race relations is a matter of time, and rests largely on the satisfactory solution of the economic problems of farm life. Several noteworthy tendencies were, however, noticeably strengthened by the loss of Negro labor. The first of these was the tendency of the leaders of the two races to draw closer together.... Until more interest is taken in these meetings by the white leaders, and until they are followed by constructive programs for better law enforcement and education they can not measurably influence the tendency of the Negro to move....
>
> On May 1, 1918, The Secretary of Labor, Hon. William B. Wilson,

realizing that the Negro constitutes about one-seventh of the total working population of the country, appointed a Negro, Dr. George E. Haynes, as advisory to the Secretary with the title Director of Negro Economics....

North Carolina led the way.—On June 19, 1918, Gov. T. W. Bickett ... called a conference in his office which was attended by 17 of the most substantial Negro citizens from all parts of the State and 5 white citizens.... A State Negro workers' committee of leading Negro men and women of North Carolina was appointed and plans were formed for the creation of county and city committees. There were on April 1 of the present year [1919] 25 of these committees actively at work in our State.[6]

Dr. Moore goes into deeper detail in this address on what kinds of changes should be made in each of the most prevalent industries, such as cotton production and farming, guano, cotton oil production, knitting mills, and, of course, tobacco. He advocates for more reasonable hours or workweeks; honesty and fair dealing in initial contracts; cleanliness of living conditions; incentives such as insurance for those who stayed employed for the past six months; bonuses for work that was remote or dangerous, such as lumber production; training for seasonal workers to supplement year-round workforces, so that the lives of those year-round workers could be more stable; locker rooms and washrooms for those workers who did not wish to take the dirt of the factory home with them; and a safer, better lighted, and more respectable workspace for young women in the year-round factories.[7]

Dr. Moore closed his address:

It is urgently hoped that all public spirited citizens of both races who have at heart the agricultural and industrial expansion of our State, and who realize that such expansion and development can only come through the improvement of Negro labor will sustain this far-sighted effort of the Department of Labor and will give active support to the program of work of the Division of Negro Economics, and to the undersigned,

A. M. Moore, M.D.,
Special Agent and Supervisor
of Negro Economics for North Carolina,
Durham, N.C.

The Treaty of Versailles was signed just twenty-seven days after Moore delivered the address. Dr. Moore's friend and fellow activist W. E. B. Du Bois had spent a year in Paris covering the negotiations for *The Crisis* and telling the stories of black soldiers abroad, both the heroism they displayed and the racism they faced. White newspapers in the United States told a different story, with white Southern officers accusing black soldiers of incompetence and cowardice. President Wilson himself rejected the proposal that the newly created League of Nations charter support "equality of all peoples." Black soldiers might return to the United States and expect equality immediately, which could throw the nation into chaos. Once again the invitation to participate equally in the hard work of building and defending the nation did not include the reward of respect, either as a citizen or as a human being. Du Bois wrote a firebrand of an article titled "We Return Fighting" in the May 1919 *Crisis* that the U.S. Postal Service initially refused to deliver. The racist film *The Birth of a Nation* began to tour movie houses, and the term "New Negro" started to be used to describe new black leaders like Marcus Garvey and James Weldon Johnson, who advocated an end to polite negotiation with white leaders and instead urged "fighting back." Johnson actually called the summer of 1919 the "Red Summer" because white-on-black violence was as bloody that summer as it had been when the Klan first rose to power during Reconstruction.[8] What was to become of all of the hard work Dr. Moore and R. McCants Andrews had done on behalf of the black worker?

The worst blow of all to Aaron Moore and Durham's Hayti, however, fell just one month later: the "Mighty Triumvirate" would be broken by the death of John Merrick. His health had been declining steadily for several years, so this was not an unexpected event. It was, however, a shock to the morale of the community, one that would place an unimaginable weight upon Dr. A. M. Moore's shoulders and conscience.

22

A GIANT FALLS

There is nothing sweeter than memories of such a friend.
He loved me in life; I loved him in life and in death.
—A. M. Moore

The twentieth anniversary of the North Carolina Mutual and Provident Association, on June 20, 1919, had been an important day of celebration in Durham's Hayti. More than 250 guests were present, representing at least ten different states. The majority of these visitors were North Carolina Mutual agents joined by other distinguished guests. They congregated in the sanctuary of Dr. Aaron Moore's spiritual home, White Rock Baptist Church.

After brief opening remarks by C. C. Spaulding, Moore addressed the crowd. All present were in a festive mood, and yet all felt the absence of one notable face among the men at the podium. John Merrick, their beloved founder and president, had been unwell, and there was apprehension concerning his ability to appear on this momentous occasion. Moore, no doubt, could feel their eyes searching for Merrick as he stood to welcome them with these words:

> It is no more a question in the minds of the American people as
> to whether or not Negroes can unite and carry on large business
> enterprises involving the handling of dollars into the millions, for
> North Carolina Mutual has answered the question, and I am proud
> to see that you have come up here nearly 300 strong to see for
> yourselves and to go back and tell your people what we are doing.
> I need not tell you that you are welcome, for you know that. We are
> just proud to have you here. This is the greatest city in the country.
> The white people and colored people are too busy to have racial
> differences; each is attending to his own business and hasn't time
> to look after that of the other fellow. We believe in thrift and in
> building up.[1]

C. C. Spaulding followed with his own inspiring account of the "building up" of this now mighty organization. As he was finishing his address, into the aisle at the rear of the sanctuary came the figure they had all hoped to see. John Merrick was barely able, with much assistance from his daughter, to make his way to the front of the church. To encourage his progress, a spontaneous chorus of "Praise God from Whom All Blessings Flow" was sung, all present having risen to attention. What an inspiring moment this must have been for all who witnessed it and for this man who had recently survived a life-saving but agonizing foot amputation. The *Durham Morning Herald* reported that John Merrick reached the podium in tears and had to pause to gather himself. He gave a tenderly authentic greeting:

> I am glad to meet you. Yes, I came here anyway. I could not help from shedding a few tears when I came in. I am not going to talk loud or long, because I am not a loud speaker and my nerves will not allow me to talk long; but I have come in here to look on some of the friends that I haven't seen in two or three years, and some that I have never seen.
>
> I don't want anybody in the house to think that I am shedding a tear because of this figure (pointing to leg). I am not shedding tears for that but I am thanking God that there is this much of me left that I can come in here and see you. I have more to thank God for than everybody put together in this house.
>
> I do want to say a great many things to you, friends, and to speak about the things you have done and the things you are doing and the things you have got to do. That is the chief thing that I have thought of and I have thought of that so often. (Breaks down and cries.) As long as it is God's will, I want this institution to move, for men to support their families; and God will let it live. That is what I am interested about and God knows it. I want this institution to live and she will! God bless you all.[2]

One can imagine that this humble but impassioned speech from their president not only moved those in the audience but also conveyed a new finality and underlying sadness from a man who was looking at his days in a new and numbered way. His dear friend Aaron, who knew the grimness of Merrick's illness from a professional standpoint, must have felt the weight of his own responsibility to see Merrick's legacy survive. They were looking at a monument to the potential of their race that they had created together, brick by brick.

John Merrick's health unraveled painfully over the next two years, and as their friend became less able, Dr. Aaron Moore and C. C. Spaulding re-dedicated their own efforts to fill the roles Merrick had played. It must have been hard on a man who had been so vigorous and busy, a lover of life and good company, to be bedridden. It must have been equally hard for those who had come to depend on his energy and optimism. Merrick's innate talent for friendship, both in and out of business, was precious, and never more so than when it was waning. Throughout his life, those Merrick had encountered in life—black or white, millionaire or pauper, student or widow—spoke of him as the very definition of a gentleman.

Merrick appeared in public rarely as his illness progressed, once to watch a baseball game from his car and once to make a personal dona-tion to the struggling YMCA. After several difficult trips to Baltimore for radium treatments for his infected leg, he withdrew from all but family.[3]

John Merrick left this life with grace on August 6, 1919. Funeral solem-nities were held on Friday, August 8, at 4:00 P.M. at St. Joseph's AME Church. The Reverend W. C. Cleland presided. Flowers and telegrams were sent from "people in all walks of life, and of both races, North and South."[4]

In October 1921, North Carolina Mutual—by now renamed the North Carolina Mutual Life Insurance Company—would open its brand-new state-of-the-art, fireproof office building on Parrish Street. Standing eighty-six feet and six stories high, it gleamed with Tennessee gray marble and was complete with an elevator. Merrick's prayer was answered. His beloved institution lives.

EVEN MIGHTY HEARTS
MUST REST

23

I'm so happy to be so much unafraid.
—*A. M. Moore*

As the year 1919 came to a close, Aaron Moore was asked to replace John
Merrick as president of North Carolina Mutual at one of its most difficult
moments. The end of World War I had triggered an economic recession
that is often overlooked in the shadow of the Great Depression of a decade later.[1] Suddenly Mutual insurance premiums were lapsing because
families had to choose between food and insurance. The Mutual had to
come up with a plan to reinstate these lapsed policyholders and needed
their new president, Dr. Moore, to get out and energize Mutual agents
and communities. The Mutual needed policyholders to stay with the company, or it would surely fail and with it John Merrick's legacy.

We have two handwritten letters from Moore during this period. The
first is a draft to superintendents and agents of the Mutual:

> Dear Supts. and Agents,
> Due to the financial depression through which we have passed
> during the past few months, thousands of our good policyholders
> were forced to allow their policies to lapse against their wills. These
> unfortunates need the protection of our great company, and the
> payment of premiums is evidence of their faith and honest purpose
> to become permanent members with us. We regretted to see them
> lapsed and have yet a great desire to reinstate them into the fold. This
> is official notice to you that as a special inducement we will reinstate
> all who will pay up back premiums due, and we will pay for medical
> examinations for all who will apply within 90 days from May 1, 1922.
> As inducement to Agents, we will allow a flat rate of five percent
> commission for 90 days. Please see every policyholder written on
> your field and explain this proposition. The advantage we offer them
> is manifold.

1) To reinstate they receive a premium rating, which they can never get again in any company
2) They will be entitled to loan values which a new policy class does not grant until 3 years
3) The smaller premium for which they will qualify will more than repay for the payment of back premiums
4) No one can know whether the health of a candidate will warrant acceptance for a new contract
5) This will no doubt be the very last chance to get insurance from any company.

Urge immediate action. Let each agent make a personal cause of each policyholder and report on each individual case. We are writing each one today and telling them you are coming. Make a 90-day canvass. Let this take precedence over everything else. The cost of securing this business and carrying the same on our books has been a loss to the company, and since we have paid for it, we must reinstate every policy possible.

—A. M. Moore[2]

The second letter, also handwritten, is warmer and more informal and is addressed to C. C. Spaulding and the Mutual board. Moore wrote to them as he traveled through Florida on his own goodwill tour for the insurance company:

Dear C. C. and Board,
We are doing well. Going to St. Petersburg today, back tomorrow. To St. Augustine Friday. To Savannah Monday. To St. Aug. will be there a few days. Send anything for that district to me there.
Have E. R. [Merrick, likely] run over them to see we are written fully. I am enclosing a proposed draft to agents [the above letter]. I am sure these lapsed members will hardly pay back dues and medical examination too. I believe as a special inducement and for the protection of the company we had better pay for reexamination. This is subject to the board's action. I am sure with the additional cost for ex and canvass that this business will be cheaper than new business. If you think so, draft a letter along these lines and send to each Supt. and agent a list of lapses for each district.... I am still doing well but this nasty water and hot weather are pulling on me.
Love to all, A. M. M.[3]

The president of the Mutual was obviously tired. His handwriting was limp, and he used every possible abbreviation as if he were overworked and in a hurry. The hot weather of Florida in May and June was obviously hard on him.

We also have a letter from Dr. Moore to W. E. B. Du Bois during this time period, which alludes to a trip he wished to take abroad with Du Bois, likely to advocate for the independence of African nations from European oversight (a major cause for Du Bois and *The Crisis*), and which would include a stop in Liberia. If taken, this would be Dr. Moore's third major trip abroad. It is also the first mention we have on record of Dr. Moore having been in the hospital.

Dr. W. E. B. Du Bois   April 21, 1921
New York, NY.

   Dear Sir,

    It has been over a month since your letter was received, and at that time I was in the hospital and am just getting out.

    I am planning to take the trip with you. On account of other meetings, can the time of sailing be delayed until the second week in September? ... Dr. Graham and myself will want to come back through Liberia. I hope you can find out if the trip can be made and let me know. Please keep me informed as to time and requirements.[4]

Moore never took that September trip. Years of pushing himself past the point of exhaustion and the relentless travel of the last several years had sapped his strength. In December 1921, Dr. Moore instead checked himself into the Battle Creek Sanitarium in Michigan for its famous "rest cure."

This move speaks to the doctor's state of mind and level of exhaustion. Battle Creek was a very popular resort, and in many ways America can trace the origins of fad diets, breakfast cereals, nutritional breakdowns of foods, fitness gyms, and health spas back to the hallowed halls of Battle Creek Sanitarium. Dignitaries, movie stars, authors, and poets alike checked themselves in for ailments as serious as opiate and alcohol abuse and as mundane as weight loss and beautification. The overarching ideas of the place were unusual for the 1920s but not entirely off base. Fiber-rich foods, hydrotherapy, enemas, vigorous exercise, and high-minded discourse delivered in religious, respectable, and gracious surroundings often did make mostly healthy people feel refreshed.

Nutrition, scientific discussion, music, and piety in an environment that encouraged rest might have been extremely attractive to the exhausted Aaron Moore, even if he, as a physician, knew his own prognosis. Heart disease, which would prove fatal for Moore, began exhibiting symptoms, it seems, around 1921. Hypertension, swelling, fatigue, shortness of breath, and all the usual effects of years of little to no rest were conspiring against him. He chose to send himself away to this respectable but somewhat frivolous resort—the "San," as it was widely known—and over Christmas, no less. He had, by this time, three grandchildren he could have spent his holiday near. He must have been willing to try anything to feel better. He wrote the following emotional and introspective letter to his wife, Cottie:

December 20, 1921
Battle Creek Sanitarium
Handwritten letter on Battle Creek Stationery
    My Dear Wife:
    I've just read your sweet letter and can say I have been happy all these 32 years. I know you have been just the girl I needed, and if all Mothers and Wives were like you, the prisons would be vacant and many more homes would be happy. I am so proud of my children who have never given me a moment's trouble in any way, and this I attribute to you and your own Christian piety. God bless you all now. Do not think of me for anything for Xmas, just look after the folks there. I'm so happy to be so much unafraid, let this joy go to others who need your gifts more. Give money to aid suffering, and do not forget yourself. I cannot buy anything here, and I haven't been to town yet. I have been going all day to lectures, and I'm tired and sleepy. So, a sweet good night. Tell Mag, Asa, Lil, Mat, and Lyda I can't write when I'm tired, but I enjoyed this letter.
    Lovingly,
    AMM

[Next page:]

Saturday morning
    I find myself feeling better today. The weather is cloudy and pleasant. I am going for a walk. Yesterday I was tired following examinations. Have not had breakfast as yet. Have two more Dr.s

to face. Folks are exceedingly nice. Dr. Tully is quite cautious and sympathetic.

Love to all, especially the board who have been so kind to me.

AMM[5]

Battle Creek was not all cloistered rooms and napping. There was a schedule of activities and appointments that kept everyone organized and vigorous. In his letter of December 20, Moore enclosed a menu, dated December 2, 1921, which implies the length of his stay. Each item on the menu is listed not only by category but also by nutritional value, acidity or alkalinity, carbohydrates, fats, protein, and weight in ounces. This practice seems normal to us now, but it was a totally new way of looking at food at the time.

Moore also included in his letter a program for a day during his stay. The daily schedule was full of gymnastic exercises or folk dancing, vigorous walks, singing, lectures, an orchestral concert, and twice-daily worship. When Aaron says in his letter that he was tired and also sleepy, one can imagine why he might be, especially considering his malady—and some might wonder whether this time at Battle Creek did more harm than good.

His letter also gives us a window into his very human response to illness, despite his education and expertise. We all want easy answers and comfort when we are ill, especially if we are coming face to face with our mortality. The tone of his letter seems fatalistic and a little sad. For a man who loved to be surrounded by family and community, voluntarily leaving for a strange midwestern town seems a drastic measure. Perhaps he simply needed time and privacy to regroup and plan his steps in light of his state of health.

We have one other letter from Moore's stay at Battle Creek Sanitarium, to his daughter Lyda, that further illustrates his state of mind, length of stay, and knowledge of his condition. There is an unmistakable tone of regret for Dr. Moore's work-filled hours and time away from his own family. It is evident in both of these letters that this "rest cure" forced real perspective upon Moore. Yet he remained serene and even poetic in his prose, and his words are full of hope for his family and his race.

This is the 2nd sunshining day we have had and this is my 10th day here. My Drs. realize the struggle I'm undergoing and are very sympathetic with me which encourages me much....

I wish Ed [Lyda's husband] would cut out his night work and

enjoy the kids now when he feels like it and they are at the age to enjoy it. How soon these days fly away.... The curtain between us and death is only a shadow.... There is some excuse for a man making the supreme sacrifice in my day, for the mud sills[6] of a race had to be laid but now the superstructure is easier. Godliness, firmness, character, poise, gentleness, justice can be had for the asking. God bless you all. Kiss my grands, Daddy[7]

Aaron Moore returned to Durham's Hayti after his retreat, and, having secured John Merrick's legacy of the Mutual with his last burst of energy, he was faced with a setback regarding his own. Lincoln Hospital, with plans already underway for a new facility, suffered significant loss when fire swept through the hospital in early 1922.[8] The final year of Aaron Moore's life would be consumed with plans for a new hospital and managing the fallout of this fire. There is no real mention of his long illness in any posthumous tributes, and even his daughter Lyda spoke rarely of his being ill, although she did occasionally sadly punctuate her memories with statements like, "Daddy was sick by then, you know." It seems that his energy simply faded, and he spent more and more time at home. Perhaps, as he had said of his own parents' passing, he simply "knew he had to die."

Aaron McDuffie Moore's death certificate tells us he died at home, just after midnight on Sunday, April 29, 1923.[9] That shadowy "veil between life and death" was made permeable for him at last. The specificity of the time and the date that the attendant physician stated he had last seen him alive (earlier that day) speaks to a vigil of sorts. Dr. Clyde Donnell, the listed physician, stated that Moore had been in his care since September 1, 1922. A close community like Hayti would have drawn in and around this family and held them close as they nursed "Daddy Moore" through his final days. Care would have been modest and earnest, according to the way the Moore family had always done things, and Aaron's faith and intelligence would have helped him make an exit that was both dignified and serene. As he said in his letter from Battle Creek, he was "glad to be so much unafraid."

How ironic that such a mighty heart could ever fail.

Aaron McDuffie Moore was born on a Sunday in 1863 into a house full of family and community, and he died fifty-nine years later on a Sunday in 1923 in a house equally full of love and grace, if not fuller.

His daughter Lyda recalled that when he died, he had the plans of the new Lincoln Hospital spread out on his bed. She said very little, however, about her father's hour or manner of death, or even anything at all about the day of his funeral. Clearly the years had not diminished the pain of losing him.[10]

Two days later, on Tuesday, May 1, 1923, Dr. Moore was laid to rest. The funeral was held at his beloved White Rock Baptist Church at three o'clock under the guidance of Reverend J. E. Kirkland.

> Over two thousand persons crowded every available space of the church to pay their last tribute to Dr. Moore. Hundreds, unable to secure seats or standing room, stood in the churchyard that they might hear a part of the service and by their presence show their esteem for the man who had lived such a useful and noble life. There were present over one hundred out-of-town visitors.... The ex-Mayor of Durham, M. E. Newsome, and [former Southern Democratic political opponent] General Julian Carr were among the representatives of the White citizens of Durham. One hundred and fifty floral designs from insurance companies, fraternal orders, church organizations, friends and state officials were artistically arranged around the altar and formed a beautiful testimony of the respect with which vast numbers of individuals and organizations held Dr. Moore.
>
> The remains of the deceased were carried into the church at eleven o'clock Tuesday morning. From that time until two o'clock, when the coffin was closed, thousands upon thousands of children, men and women of all races bowed with sad hearts and tearful eyes as they viewed for the last time the man who had been a comforter to the sick of body, mind and soul. One thousand children of the Hillside Park Public High school silently marched in a double line through the streets to the church and passed before the bier of this great man.
>
> The Funeral services began with "The End of a Perfect Day," with Professor W. P. Twadell (White), organist of the Temple Baptist church, at the console. The procession came into the church led by the ministers of Durham followed by the directors of North Carolina Mutual, Mechanics and Farmers Bank Mutual Savings and Loan Association and the Bank and Fire Insurance Company, members of the North Carolina Medical and Dental and Pharmaceutical Society as honorary pallbearers, the family, close friends and business

associates, nurses of Lincoln Hospital, and Home Office and Field Representatives of North Carolina Mutual from eleven states and the District of Columbia.... Thousands ... looked on and joined the procession to Violet Cemetery, where the final rites of the church were administered.[11]

His original burial site, at Violet Park Cemetery, was also called Wolf's Den.[12] North Carolina Mutual later bought plots for the company's founding families at Durham's Beechwood Cemetery and moved Aaron Moore and John Merrick there around 1940. Lyda Moore Merrick rests there beside her father, as do Mrs. Cottie Moore and Mattie Louise Moore McDougald.

Dr. Aaron McDuffie Moore would not return in death to Mitchell Field in Columbus County, where hundreds of his ancestors still hallow the ground. It was his wish to finish his physical journey in Durham, in Hayti, where his life and work had been the most joyful and potent.

No matter how much his beloved Hayti would transform and diminish, at Beechwood he and all those who were dearest to him would be a part of that sacred ground. The earthly remains of these extraordinary souls lie together where they took a stand, where they built a life whose reverberations still touch those of us alert enough to feel them. Even in death their fellowship is intact. For Dr. Aaron McDuffie Moore, this was indeed "The End of a Perfect Day."

Obituaries of Dr. A. M. Moore were featured in publications across the nation. He was most notably eulogized in *Crisis Magazine* by Louis D. Mitchell. A high school was named for both Merrick and Moore in Durham, as was a building on the campus of his beloved alma mater, Shaw University.[13] Lincoln Hospital was rebuilt—of bricks this time—but its founder would not live to see it. "Following the departure of this man, Aaron McDuffie Moore, there was a hushed pause," scholar Louis D. Mitchell wrote. "There descended a choking sense of loss. There was grief everywhere.... Durham lost a pioneer, a philanthropist, a believer in men, a businessman, an educator, and a religious leader.... North Carolina lost a brave man who learned ... the ancient and enduring tensions of racism. He dared to confront that evil element—in his own calm way—with a conviction that there was better on earth for his people.[14]

Aaron McDuffie Moore died as he lived: "unafraid" and wishing, with every beat of his mighty heart, to lift his people up.

AFTERWORD

C. EILEEN WATTS WELCH, *President
and CEO, Durham Colored Library, Inc.*

The idea for this book converged from several avenues. We knew that future generations of both our family members and historians needed well-researched, accurate information about what motivated my maternal great-grandfather, Dr. Aaron McDuffie Moore, to accomplish so much. We were determined to provide an accurate, authoritative reference source. My father, Dr. Charles DeWitt Watts, left a treasure trove of information about Moore, who was his grandfather-in-law. Among the saved material, we found previously unpublished references about Moore's daily struggles and his broad impact on health care during the early 1900s. Dad seemed to be urging me to develop this book because he admired the shoulders on which he'd stood for so long. Four years after Dad's death, my niece Blake Hill-Saya and I could see a space in our lives to dive in, and we began the research and writing that led to the complete manuscript. At the time, we had no idea of the extent of this endeavor; we just knew it had to be done and we were the ones to do it.

While this book has been a labor of love by many, the fortuitous timing of a major funding grant through the Durham Colored Library, Inc. (DCL, Inc.), as well as the ongoing support of the organization's board, is ultimately responsible for its publication. Dr. Aaron McDuffie Moore created the Durham Colored Library to provide books and educational resources to uplift his community's families. He began with a book-lending service in the basement of Durham's old White Rock Baptist Church in 1913, donating numerous personal volumes to stock the first shelves. He was instrumental in securing a dedicated library building in 1916 and chartering the nonprofit Durham Colored Library, Inc., two years later. In turn, DCL, Inc., undertook this biography of its founder.

My father was North Carolina's first board-certified African American surgeon, and he had a lifelong interest in history that led him to maintain extensive records. During what turned out to be Dad's final illness in the fall of 2003, my mother, Constance Merrick Watts, and I decided to begin decluttering the home where she and Dad had lived for sixty years. There, I discovered an abundance of memorabilia relating to the lives, careers, and community work of our family members going back many decades. One of my most important finds was a huge plastic bag stuffed under Dad's desk. Opening it, I was surprised to find his handwritten journal notes and a jumbled collection of various papers, pamphlets, and other materials about the life of Great-grandpapa Moore, whom I knew my Dad had long admired.

As I made my way through the bag's contents, I remembered Dad's passionate discussions about Great-grandpapa Moore's influence on Durham, particularly the city's Hayti community. Included in his papers was information on the closing of the Leonard School of Medicine at Shaw University in Raleigh, where Great-grandpapa Moore received his medical training. There were some details of his unsuccessful fight to keep the school open.

Dad's notes described how he admired Moore for many reasons, but especially for his founding of Durham's Lincoln Hospital, one of the few places where an African American surgeon like himself could practice in a hospital setting in America prior to the 1960s. It was because there was a Lincoln Hospital that my father decided to build his medical practice and career in Durham. It was because of Lincoln Hospital that African American people from Durham, as well as surrounding rural counties, had access to medical care provided by professionals who not only looked like them but also were equipped to care for and about them well beyond their current health crisis. It was because there was a Lincoln Hospital that Durham's African American residents could access physicians, often trained at the historically black medical schools Howard University School of Medicine in Washington, D.C., and Meharry Medical College in Nashville, Tennessee. Many of these physicians held specialties in surgery, pediatrics, obstetrics, gynecology, ophthalmology, and other areas. Because of Lincoln Hospital, many of these African American specialists and nurses settled in Durham to raise their families. As history unfolds, the impact of Lincoln Hospital and the Lincoln School of Nursing on Durham and throughout the state is increasingly impressive.

In 1972, after the Civil Rights Act and its required desegregation of hospitals caused the closing of Lincoln Hospital, Dad followed in Great-grandpapa Moore's footsteps by founding the Lincoln Community Health Center. Both doctors' motives, a half century apart, were the same: to provide access to quality health care for the African American citizens of Durham.

My siblings, our friends, and I grew up in what I think of as the "Hayti Cocoon," which was a safe place for Durham's African American citizens. This cocoon remained in place and, in hindsight, was one of the benefits of segregation through the civil rights movement of the mid-1960s. While living in the Hayti Cocoon, we were surrounded by a community of proud African Americans. Many were part of my Great-grandpapa Moore's extended family. We and other children of that time grew up seeing people of color who held graduate degrees and were successful in many professions. For example, many of our high school teachers held Ph.D.'s and Ed.D.'s, the music director at my church was a professor on the faculty at North Carolina College (now North Carolina Central University), the executives and agent managers at North Carolina Mutual Life Insurance Company and other Black Wall Street businesses lived in Durham, and many of them and their families contributed to North Carolina's political architecture.

I left Durham to attend Spelman College in Atlanta. After graduation, my college sweetheart, James A. Welch, and I married and moved to Northern Virginia, living there for thirty years while raising our two sons. Once our sons were enrolled at Morehouse College, I enrolled at George Mason University, completing an MBA one year after they'd both earned their undergraduate degrees. Jim and I relocated to Durham when Duke University reached out to me and I accepted a position there.

Living in Durham, Jim and I noticed that the old magic had gone out of Hayti. Much of the community had been bulldozed in 1967 to make way for the Durham Freeway (N.C. Highway 147). In the late 1990s, the Durham Colored Library, Inc., which was no longer managing a system of brick-and-mortar facilities, was relatively stagnant, although it had retained its IRS status as a 501(c)3 nonprofit. For about forty years, the organization provided few services other than the continued publication of the *Merrick Washington Magazine*—the successor to the *Negro Braille* magazine, founded by Lyda Moore Merrick in 1952—which was being mailed to a dwindling list of blind braille readers worldwide. At that time, my mother served as the treasurer and board chair of DCL, Inc. Mom, to her credit, realized the organization was not living up to its potential and asked if Jim and I would help by reexamining its mission and finding a way the organization could be of more value to the community.

I began my volunteer involvement with DCL, Inc., on the magazine committee, gained a sense of the organization's overall operations, and began to visualize its potential. After I retired from Duke in 2013, both Jim and I officially joined the board as volunteers. Jim agreed to serve in the financial manager/treasurer's role. Within a year, a nice corps of family members and friends joined us to expand the organization with the intent of adopting projects to continue the original mission. I succeeded my mother as chief executive officer and president of DCL, Inc., in 2013. We enlarged the board and updated the governance and communications infrastructure, and board members agreed on their first new project: a biography of our founder.

Jim and I had noticed that too much erroneous information about Great-grandpapa Moore, my mother's paternal grandfather, John Henry Merrick, and our other extended family members, who were some of Durham's early pioneers, was being repeated year after year, especially during Black History Month. One thing we believed we could accomplish with a well-researched biography was to set the public record straight. Our vision was to portray Great-grandpapa Moore's life by describing the cultural, societal, and family settings in which he was born, lived, and worked. In so doing, we would document his impact on health care and education for African Americans. The origins of his vision for developing what became major African American–owned businesses and an inspired rural education system all are integral parts of Durham's and North Carolina's rich legacy. DCL, Inc., would thus create, very appropriately, an accurate historical resource for future scholars, educators, and civic leaders.

Great-grandpapa Moore died in 1923, but his economic and educational influence is still felt today, not only in Durham but also statewide and nationally. His legacy contributed to Durham's reputation as a strong African American business community often recognized for its "Black Wall Street," so named in the early 1900s by both W. E. B. Du Bois and Booker T. Washington. Durham's African American entrepreneurial environment has continued in large part because of the capital financing and successful models provided by North Carolina Mutual, Mechanics & Farmers Bank, and other financial institutions. According to a recent U.S. Census report, African American–owned firms made up more than a quarter of the companies in Durham in 2012, nearly twice the percentage of African American–owned firms in North Carolina as a whole and higher than figures nationally, where only one in ten businesses is African American owned.

Businesses spawned by Durham's Black Wall Street include not only those in which Moore had a direct role in founding but also newer African American start-ups that are thriving today. A local contemporary example is Piedmont Investment Advisors, LLC (PIA), currently a Durham-headquartered investment management firm for which North Carolina Mutual and Mutual Community Savings Bank, together with PIA's founders, were the key original venture capital investors. PIA is now one of the largest African American money-management firms in America.

In a 2013 report titled "North Carolina Mutual Life Insurance Company—By the Numbers, 1898–2013," Dr. Darryl Banks, then a professor at North Carolina Central University, and Jordan McBride, an NCCU/North Carolina Mutual marketing intern, document the over $40 billion impact of North Carolina Mutual in its more than 100 years of providing for the needs of Americans through employment, mortgages, and insurance premiums collected and circulated, as well as the lives the company has influenced. (A summary of the report appears on page 221 of this book.) Ever since North Carolina Mutual's first employees worked in the back office of Great-grandpapa Moore's medical offices, the company was keenly aware of the importance of partnerships and alliances. Generations of families, organizations, and institutions looked to the North Carolina Mutual for its help and endorsement.

One of the rewards of working on this book has been my increased knowledge of the collective impact of individuals in our family. For instance, I loved learning that the man who wrote Great-grandpapa Moore's obituary for the NAACP's *The Crisis* magazine, Louis D. Mitchell, was a functionally blind cousin who was probably one of my grandmother's inspirations for founding the *Negro Braille Magazine*.

As one of Dr. Aaron McDuffie Moore's great-granddaughters, I have found it a privilege to join Jim, the board of DCL, Inc., and other volunteers in publishing this book and carrying on the work of one of the least-known organizations that Great-grandpapa Moore founded. DCL, Inc., continues to support the African American community's intellectual growth through its mission: *lifting up stories about African Americans, both current and historical, to help create a more comprehensive picture of the American experience.*

Working with so many people who share a belief in the value of this endeavor has been the experience of a lifetime and a reward in itself.

ACKNOWLEDGMENTS

BLAKE HILL-SAYA

As author, I would first like to thank my intrepid partners in this enterprise, C. Eileen Watts Welch, James Welch, and Cindy Gardiner, for their talent, patience, and elegance. I also thank my husband, Cody Saya, for his extraordinary partnership and his love, which is the treasure of my life; my father, Robert Paul Hill, for his wisdom and the DNA of a writer; my stepmother, Louise Hill, for her light; and my brothers, Adam and Ryan. Other family members and friends I'm grateful to are Joy Hill; all of the Wattses, Welches, Merricks, Moores, Sansoms, Stewarts, and Benjamin and Edith Spaulding descendants; John and Roberta Serbia and family; Catherine Scott and family; Gail Gordon and Richard Drapkin; and John and Sheva Rajaee.

I am indebted to those who encouraged me along the way or gave vital assistance: Luke Alexander, Todd Savitt, Edward Boyer, Jean Bradley Anderson, Brooke Chaffin, Michal and Grey Blavin, Zachary Gordin, Victoria Kirsch, Michael Alexander, Celia Tran, Aingal Searchant, Daniel Stessen, Katie Thompson, Kathryn Fauble, Ken Simms, Cati Jean, Bertha Suarez, Melody Akbari, Krislam Chin and Jay Josue, and Todd and Nancy Allan. I treasure loved ones who have departed my life yet remain utterly near: Deborah Chase Watts Hill (Mama), Dr. Charles DeWitt Watts and Constance Merrick Watts, Lyda Moore Merrick, Vivian Merrick Sansom, Roberta Hill, and Mike Hill.

C. EILEEN WATTS WELCH

This book has been six years in the making, a project of Durham Colored Library, Inc., which was founded in 1918 as a nonprofit and continues to operate as one of the oldest nonprofits in Durham, North Carolina. There are many steadfast friends, family, colleagues, and associates to acknowledge here who have supported this project in many ways.

First, my thanks go to my niece Blake Hill-Saya, a talented author. Blake's capability and dedication are evident. She wove into being a well-researched and finely crafted manuscript that is both reliably accurate and enjoyably readable. I respect and admire her ability to create beautiful prose while connecting various historical events to Aaron Moore's life. I also thank her husband, Cody Saya, for his steady support, and her network of close family and friends who stood by and encouraged her creative and inspiring writing.

Cindy Gardiner, our editor, brought a wealth of pertinent experience, a personal commitment, a calming aura, and the ability to provide authentic feedback. She has become a good friend and a great sounding board.

We are grateful to U.S. Representative G. K. Butterfield for his early encouragement and willingness to submit the foreword. I've heard him speak on many occasions, and his passion for accurate North Carolina history is apparent. Thus, he is the perfect contributor to this long-overdue biography.

For this book, I've served as project manager for Durham Colored Library, Inc. (DCL, Inc.), in addition to the organization's chief executive officer. Many thanks to our board members who have worked to bring this project to publication. They were funders, sounding boards, strategic advisers, and awareness builders in the community. Of special help early on was the commitment and dedicated leadership of Ida Daniel Dark, Nathan Garrett, Brandi Sansom Stewart, Mary Ann Black, and JoAnn Sampson Welch. My husband, James A. (Jim) Welch, serves on the DCL, Inc., board as treasurer and is my rock; without his wise advice, solid committed leadership, and financial expertise we would be lost. Newer board members Cecile Chadwick, Leon Herndon, Eugene Tatum, and Babu Guai Welch bring new energy and commitment while generously lending their resources and ideas as we develop future organizational direction.

Special recognition goes to Meredythe Johnson Holmes, my closest friend and confidante, who volunteered to interview my grandmother Lyda Moore Merrick on tape more than thirty years ago, creating a first-person historical narrative and a family treasure. Meredythe often helped both Blake and me stay the course.

Thanks go to all who have given philanthropic support since 2013, particularly those who earmarked their donations for this Aaron Moore Biography Project. We thank them for their trust and patience in waiting to see the outcome of their investment. We wish it could have been faster, too. Early major gift donors included corporate sponsors from companies that Aaron McDuffie Moore worked to found: N.C. Mutual and Mechanics and Farmers Bank.

In addition to board members, our early major gift level donors were made up of a number of corporations, foundations, and friends, including our pivotal first backer, the Lincoln Hospital Foundation Board, led by Larry Suitt, whose career included serving as an administrator to Lincoln Hospital. Before Larry passed, he expressed the kinship he felt while standing on the shoulders of those like Aaron McDuffie Moore. Other contributors included John Atkins, Duke Medicine, the Duke University Office of Durham and Regional Affairs, the Renaissance Group of Durham, and the Charles Dewitt Watts, M.D., Fund of the Triangle Community Foundation (established in 2004 from gifts in his memory). In 2015 many individuals sent memorial gifts to this fund in memory of my mother, and we thank them again for remembering her in this way.

On Blake's first trip to Durham for this project, she and I visited the North Carolina Collection of the Durham County Library and met Joanne Able, a Rosenwald Schools expert, and Lynn Richardson, then director of the collection. We thank both Joanne and Lynn, who lent their expertise and enthusiastic support.

It has been a joy to support Blake with much of the hands-on local research, meeting with the Spaulding, Moore, and McDougald family members and exploring the Shaw University and State of North Carolina Archives, where I found evidence supporting Aaron's work to improve rural schools for North Carolina's African American population. Duke University's David M. Rubenstein Rare Book and Manuscript Library, where the North Carolina Mutual company archives are deposited, was an invaluable resource. I won't forget the day I found Aaron's leather-bound "Physician's Visiting List" there. Holding it in my hands sent chills up my spine. We also owe special gratitude to Andre Vann, North Carolina Central University archivist, who willingly shared materials from both the college and his personal collection.

We were blessed with many friends who served as readers, critics, and encouragers. Included are Mary Champagne, Eddie Davis, Veronica Biggins, Lois DeLoatch, Laurel Chadwick and her family, Wanda Garrett, Lori Jones Gibbs, Boydie Girimont, Margaret Keller, Hilda Pinnix-Ragland, Mickey Michaux, Myka Bailey Sparrow, and Frances Dyer Stewart.

I also gratefully acknowledge the Benjamin and Edith Spaulding descendants, many of whom were key to Blake's and my better understanding of our Spaulding and Moore heritage. Without Milton Campbell showing me around Columbus County and arranging other family guides, we would not have such a clear vision of Aaron Moore's birthplace. Cousin Luke Alexander is a walking database of family history and always willingly shared what he knew and what he could find out with just a little more research. Because of Luke, this book contains more depth about A. M. Moore's origins. Gwendolyn McDougald Parker provided photographs and information connecting us more closely to her grandmother Mattie Louise Moore McDougald and her daughters' families. Sylvia and Fred Black's and Paula and Vincent Spaulding's love and support made a difference as well.

Jim and I appreciate the members of our immediate family, our extended family, and distant relatives for their many acts, both great and small, in support of this project. Thanks go to Sule and Cecily Welch and Cassandra Nash, as well other members of our Welch family tree branch: Arthuryne J. Taylor (matriarch), Reginald Welch, and Melvadeen Welch Bailey. We thank all of our Sansom cousins: James and June Sansom, Beryl and Tony Gilmore, Genevieve and Michael Stewart, and Joseph Merrick and Kate Sansom. Their interest, encouragement, and philanthropic support as we moved toward completion boosted our resolve immeasurably.

Those cited here are joined by others too numerous to mention. I thank them all for making it possible for readers to get to know Aaron McDuffie Moore.

THE $40 BILLION ECONOMIC IMPACT OF NORTH CAROLINA MUTUAL LIFE INSURANCE COMPANY

$3,144,391,262 Premium Income Collected

$276,770,148.20 Sales and Wages Paid

$165,000,000 Assets

$2,900,000,000 Insurance in Force

$40,734,986,986.73 Mortgage Loans and Disbursements
   with Multipliers

In 2013 Professor Darryl Banks of the North Carolina Central University Business School and his student Jordan McBride (who was also an intern at North Carolina Mutual at the time) compiled the numbers above to calculate North Carolina Mutual's cumulative economic impact of more than $40 billion since its founding.

Since its first employees worked in the back office of Dr. Aaron McDuffie Moore, one of its founders, the company has been keenly aware of the importance of partnerships and alliances. Generations of African American families, organizations, and institutions have looked to North Carolina Mutual for its commitment to social uplift.

For a business that often found itself marginalized in terms of economic power and progress, North Carolina Mutual, through its product and service offerings, brought billions of dollars into the economy throughout the country with its district offices and field staff.

TIMELINE OF EVENTS
AND MILESTONES

1773   Benjamin Spaulding (Aaron Moore's [AM] grandfather and
        patriarch of the Spaulding descendants) is born
1786   Edith Delphia Freeman (AM's grandmother and matriarch of
        the Spaulding descendants) is born
1811   Date of issue of the earliest family-owned deeds to land in the
        Farmers Union area of Columbus County, N.C.
1817   Israel Moore Sr., AM's father, is born
1822   Ann Eliza Spaulding, AM's mother, is born
1843   Lewis Moore, AM's oldest brother, is born (grandfather of R. L.
        McDougald)
1845   Calvin B. Moore, AM's second brother, is born
1847   Mary Edith Moore, AM's oldest sister, is born; her husband,
        John White, was George Henry White's brother
1849   Margaret Ann Virginia Moore, AM's second sister and mother
        of C. C. Spaulding, is born
1852   George Henry White, AM's cousin, is born
1853   Caroline Ann Moore, AM's third sister, is born
1856   Daniel James Moore, AM's third brother, is born
1858   Israel Moore Jr., AM's fourth brother, is born
1859   John Henry Merrick is born in Clinton, N.C.
1861   Delphia Ann Moore, AM's fourth and nearest sister, is born
1863   AM is born
1865   What becomes known as Shaw University forms in Raleigh,
        N.C. (where AM will attend medical school)
1866   Ann Elizabeth Moore, AM's youngest sister and the last sibling,
        is born
            Sarah McCotta Dancy (AM's future wife) is born in Tarboro,
        N.C.
1868   Approximate year that AM begins to attend the county school

Howard University Medical School is founded to educate black physicians

1869   AM attends the county school for second grade

The city of Durham, N.C., where AM will live his adult life, is incorporated

1870–74   AM attends the county school for third through seventh grades

1874   Charles Clinton Spaulding is born at Clarkton near Whiteville, N.C.

1875   AM attends the county school for eighth grade

AM turns twelve years old and becomes a teacher at the county school

White Rock Baptist Church in Durham is established

1877   AM begins his years at Whittin Normal School in Lumberton, N.C.

1879–80   AM attends Fayetteville Normal School

1880   John Merrick marries Martha; moves to Durham

1881   AM leaves Fayetteville Normal School and returns to the farm

Durham County is formed

Leonard Medical School is founded at Shaw University

1883   AM continues to work on the family farm

John Merrick and associates purchase the rights to the Royal Knights of King David organization and incorporate it in their own name (it would later evolve into the Mechanics and Farmers Bank and the North Carolina Mutual and Provident Association)

1884   AM plans to attend Shaw University

The National Medical Association of Black Physicians organizes (Atlanta)

1885   AM enrolls at Shaw/Leonard Medical School

1886   AM attends Leonard Medical School

Edward R. Merrick, son of John Merrick (and AM's future son-in-law), is born

1887   AM attends Leonard Medical School; cofounds the Old North State Medical Society, still in operation today

1888   AM comes before the North Carolina Board of Medical Examiners, passes, and is one of only two black candidates among the forty-six applicants to pass the exams and become a licensed doctor

AM moves to Durham and runs for county coroner, meets with significant racial opposition, and withdraws from politics

1889   AM marries Sarah McCotta "Cottie" Dancy, niece of John C. Dancy

1890   AM's first child, Lyda Vivian Moore, is born

1891   AM's nearest brother, Israel Moore Jr., dies

1893   AM's second child, Mattie Louise Moore, is born

Black surgeon Dr. Daniel Hale Williams performs the first successful open heart surgery in America on James Cornish at Provident Hospital in Chicago, a black hospital founded by Dr. Williams

1894   C. C. Spaulding leaves the farm and moves to Durham; stays with AM

1895   The Durham Drug Company opens

1896   George Henry White is elected to the U.S. Congress

Booker T. Washington speaks at Trinity College

1898   AM's father, Israel Moore Sr., dies

The North Carolina Mutual and Provident Association is chartered

George Henry White is reelected to the U.S. Congress

C.C. Spaulding becomes general manager of a grocery store in Hayti

1899   North Carolina Mutual opens doors for business in AM's medical office at Kemper's Corner

1900   North Carolina Mutual is relaunched and moves to larger offices on Main Street

C. C. Spaulding is the Mutual's first employee, soon to be general manager; he marries Fanny Jones, John Merrick's half-sister

George Henry White introduces the first bill in Congress to make lynching a federal crime; chooses not to seek a third term

1901   AM cofounds Lincoln Hospital and begins twenty-two years as its superintendent

Congressman George Henry White gives his "Phoenix" farewell speech to U.S. House of Representatives

Lincoln Hospital opens its doors to all patients regardless of their ability to pay

1902   Mary Edith Moore White (AM's sister and George H. White's sister-in-law) dies

1904   North Carolina Mutual purchases property on Parrish Street to expand offices

AM's oldest brother, Lewis Moore, dies

1905   North Carolina Mutual is able to employ a full-time president, John Merrick, and provide stipends for officers

1906   AM's mother, Ann Eliza Spaulding Moore, dies

1907   Mechanics and Farmers Bank is chartered

1908   AM's brother Reverend Daniel James Moore dies

1909   The Mutual attains legal reserve basis, a huge step forward in stability

AM, John Merrick, and C. C. Spaulding travel to Cuba together

Dr. James Shepard (along with John Merrick, AM, and William G. Pearson) charters the National Religious Training School and Chautauqua (later North Carolina Central University)

1910   White Rock Baptist Church remodeling is completed

The Mutual expands to South Carolina and Georgia

1912   North Carolina Mutual publishes assets of $79,132.60, the largest black enterprise of its kind on record

W. E. B. Du Bois visits Durham

Merrick-Moore-Spaulding Real Estate Company is founded

1913   AM founds the Durham Colored Library in the basement of White Rock Baptist Church

AM's second brother, Calvin B. Moore, dies

The Mutual suffers $9,000 in damages in fire that sweeps adjacent block

1914   AM begins work to bring Rosenwald philanthropy to North Carolina schools

AM organizes an orchestra (Volkemenia) and the Schubert-Shakespeare Club in Durham's Hayti community to provide concerts and cultural activities for all

1915   AM announces plans to improve rural schools with Rosenwald funding

1916   The Durham Colored Library opens a permanent building on Fayetteville Street

The Mutual expands to Virginia, the District of Columbia, Maryland, and Tennessee, making it a seven-state operation

AM's older daughter, Lyda Vivian Moore, marries John Merrick's son Edward R. Merrick; W. E. B. Du Bois and other dignitaries attend the wedding at White Rock Baptist Church

1917 The city of Durham begins making monthly contributions to the Durham County Library

AM, with his wife, Cottie Moore, assist in the re-forming of the Daughters of Dorcas, a women's social service club in Hayti, into a charitable organization

AM's first grandchild, Vivian McCotta Merrick (Sansom), is born to Lyda and Ed Merrick

1918 North Carolina Mutual is called the "largest colored insurance company" in the world by the *Durham Morning Herald*; sells subscriptions for Liberty loan bonds for World War I

Leonard Medical School declares its last session will be 1918–19, although AM fought hard to keep his alma mater open

AM addresses a conference called by Governor Bickett to discuss the promotion of black enterprise in the region and is appointed Supervisor of Negro Economics and Special Agent of the U.S. Employment Service, a post he keeps through World War I

Lincoln Hospital dispatches nurses and takes patients during the Spanish flu epidemic, which cost 14,000 North Carolinians their lives; North Carolina Mutual pays $100,000 in "flu" claims for sickness and death in the community

North Carolina Mutual shows $300,000 sold in thrift stamps and Liberty bonds for the war effort, evidence of remarkable black patriotism, even during segregation

1919 North Carolina Mutual (now renamed the North Carolina Mutual Life Insurance Company) becomes a million-dollar organization

AM presents "How to Keep Negro Labor" report to the Division of Negro Economics

North Carolina Mutual celebrates twentieth anniversary at White Rock Baptist Church, where John Merrick addresses crowd of more than 250 agents from ten states

C. C. Spaulding's wife, Fanny Spaulding (John Merrick's half-sister), dies

John Henry Merrick dies

1920   Durham Colored Library circulation grows and becomes
        arguably the most successful black city library in North Carolina
            AM becomes the second president of the Mutual after John
        Merrick's passing
            AM's sister Margaret Ann Virginia Moore Spaulding (mother
        of C. C. Spaulding) dies
            AM welcomes second granddaughter, Lyda Constance
        Merrick
            AM's younger daughter, Mattie Louise, weds Richard L.
        McDougald
1921   The Durham Commercial and Security Company also opens to
        aid black entrepreneurs; AM is cofounder
            The Mutual Savings and Loan is founded
            Mattie Louise and Richard L. McDougald welcome their first
        child, Virginia Louise McDougald, AM's third granddaughter
            North Carolina Mutual Life Insurance Company new office
        building completed on Parrish Street.
            AM's health begins to fail
            AM writes to Cottie from the famous Battle Creek
        Sanitarium in Michigan
1922   Lincoln Hospital burns
1923   A new Lincoln Hospital building breaks ground
            AM dies at home of heart failure and complications from
        hypertension
1924   Mattie Louise and Richard L. McDougald welcome a
        daughter, Arona Moore McDougald, naming this fourth Moore
        granddaughter after her dearly departed grandfather
            Lincoln hospital opens the new facility
1928   Mattie Louise Moore McDougald dies at age thirty-five of
        complications from tuberculosis
1932   AM's sister Delphia Ann Moore Jacobs Spaulding dies
1935   AM's sister Caroline Anne Moore Spaulding dies
            The Durham Committee on Negro Affairs forms
1943   AM's youngest sister and last living sibling, Ann Elizabeth
        Moore Spaulding, dies
1950   Sarah McCotta "Cottie" Dancy Moore dies
1958   Durham's Hayti community is "renewed"/destroyed by the
        Durham Redevelopment Commission

NOTES

PROLOGUE

1 Based on approximate trip itinerary, passport information, and accounts of similar church events.

2 Hayti (pronounced HAY-tie) was a name often used in the southern states for the African American side of town during segregation and Jim Crow (in the way Chinatown or Little Italy would be used today). Durham adopted the Hayti designation in the 1890s in homage to the nation of Haiti, which had declared its independence from France in 1804 and remains a free black nation.

3 Chairs from Dr. Moore's dining set are still owned by family members.

4 The Moores' home at this time was at 606 Fayetteville Street; photographs exist and family recollections have been used to describe the interior.

5 Based on travel plans from A. M. Moore's U.S. passport, 1916. See Department of State, Passport Applications, 1795–1925, National Archives and Records Administration, Washington, D.C.

6 In taped interviews, A. M. Moore's daughter Mrs. Lyda Moore Merrick remarked that he seldom slept and had seemingly relentless energy. See her interview by Meredythe Holmes, 1983.

7 This furniture piece is still in the family.

8 White Rock Baptist Church was located next door to 606 Fayetteville Street.

9 Public addresses exist on similar topics, and his preference for remaining in the background is widely commented upon in accounts of him.

10 White Rock women raised $300 to build a missionary center in St. Marc, Haiti (Mitchell, "Aaron McDuffie Moore," 248).

CHAPTER ONE

1 Columbus County was established in 1808 from portions of Bladen and Brunswick Counties. The boundaries were tweaked several times until the county's current borders were set in 1877; however, the Sandy Plain (now Farmers Union) neighborhood was firmly within north-central Columbus County adjacent to its border with Bladen County for decades before the birth of Dr. Moore in 1863. When townships were established in 1868, this area made up the eastern portion of Welches Creek Township. See Lewis, "Columbus County, N.C. — 1878–1880" and "Bladen County, N.C. — 1875–1880."

2 "Spaulding Family History," Benjamin and Edith Spaulding Descendants As-

sociation (BESDA) and Benjamin and Edith Spaulding Descendants' Foundation (BESDF), https://www.spauldingfamily.org/history.

3 U.S. Bureau of the Census, *Ninth Census*, Welches Creek, Columbus County, N.C.

4 "Genealogy," BESDA, https://www.spauldingfamily.org/genealogy.

5 The two pecan trees still stand in Columbus County on the site where the house used to be.

6 Map of Columbus County, North Carolina, drawn by A. Kirkland, 1882, courtesy of the North Carolina Maps Collection, State Archives of North Carolina, Raleigh.

7 Justesen, *George Henry White*, 12.

8 Pohanka, "Fort Wagner and the 54th Massachusetts Volunteer Infantry."

9 Nash, "Economic History."

10 Outland, *Tapping the Pines*, 67–70.

11 "Spaulding Family History."

12 Spaulding Family Papers, compiled by Luke Alexander, BESDA Archive.

13 Nash, "Economic History."

14 Official court proceedings log of Swindell's petition for Benjamin Spaulding's manumission (document in author's personal possession).

15 Edith "Eady" Freeman Spaulding (1786–1871), North Carolina Land Deeds Acquired in Her Name, 1811–1823, Spaulding Family Papers, compiled by Luke Alexander, BESDA Archive.

16 J. Moore, *Noble Ancestry and Descendants*, 7.

17 February 8, 1816, Columbus County, North Carolina, Deed Book B, 101, and December 28, 1818, Columbus County, North Carolina, Deed Book C, 278, North Carolina Register of Deeds, Whiteville.

18 She is identified as an Abraham Freeman heir in October 28, 1820, Columbus County, North Carolina, Deed Book D, 195, North Carolina Register of Deeds.

19 "Genealogy," BESDA, https://www.spauldingfamily.org/genealogy.

20 "Reflections of Growing Up on a Farm: 1902–1918," Asa T. Spaulding Papers, David M. Rubenstein Rare Book and Manuscript Library, Duke University.

21 U.S. Bureau of the Census, Agricultural Schedule, 1850 (before Columbus County was scheduled separately), National Archives and Records Administration, Washington, D.C.

22 U.S. Bureau of the Census, *Eighth Census*.

23 U.S. Bureau of the Census, *Eighth Census*, listed as unable to read and write.

24 J. Moore, *Noble Ancestry and Descendants*, 5–6.

25 Ben and Edith rest to this day on family land in Columbus County's Mitchell Field Cemetery, surrounded by their ancestors and more than a hundred years of descendants. They are honored with a monument outlining their immediate family tree. Aaron's mother Ann Eliza's name is there with her brothers.

26 J. Moore, *Noble Ancestry and Descendants*, 5.

27 Justesen, *George Henry White*, 12.

28 Kickler, "N.C. Played Crucial Role at Civil War's End."

29 Kickler, "N.C. Played Crucial Role at Civil War's End."

CHAPTER TWO

1 Whitted, *History of the Negro Baptists of North Carolina*, 79.
2 Crow, Escott, and Hatley, *History of African Americans in North Carolina*, 28.
3 Brooks, "Evolution of the Negro Baptist Church," 15.
4 Whitted, *History of the Negro Baptists of North Carolina*, 18.
5 Brooks, "Evolution of the Negro Baptist Church," 19.
6 The Wilmington and Charlotte Railroad lies a few miles north of Moore's birthplace, crossing southern Bladen County in a line parallel with its border with Columbus County. The railroad was built in 1857 and continues to handle freight traffic today as part of the CSX Railroad System.
7 "Reflections of Growing Up on a Farm: 1902–1918," Asa T. Spaulding Papers.
8 The foundation of that original Rehobeth AME Church site still peeks through the weeds in a lot next to the newer brick church. Rehobeth still welcomes congregations in Farmers Union with its lovely stained glass windows and high arched doors. (The author visited the site in 2015.) Watson and Grill, *Historical Directory of Churches*, 25.
9 Justesen, *George Henry White*, 19.

CHAPTER THREE

1 E. R. Merrick, interview by Meredythe Holmes, 1983.
2 The Farmers Union School existed from 1870 to 1968, when its student body was merged with those of other local schools due to federal desegregation.
3 "Recollections of School," Asa T. Spaulding Papers, 10.
4 Justesen, *George Henry White*, 18–19.
5 Mitchell, "Aaron McDuffie Moore," 248.
6 Justesen, *George Henry White*, 18–19.
7 Locklear, "UNCP's Founders."
8 Kendi, *Stamped from the Beginning*, 232–34.
9 Kendi, 219–21.
10 Crow, Escott, and Hatley, *History of African Americans in North Carolina*, 83–84.
11 "Black Codes."
12 Kendi, *Stamped from the Beginning*, 238–39.
13 "Reconstruction."
14 Toppin, *Biographical History of Blacks in America*, 129–33.
15 Crow, Escott, and Hatley, *History of African Americans in North Carolina*, 84.
16 Crow, Escott, and Hatley, 84.
17 Toppin, *Biographical History of Blacks in America*, 130–33.
18 U.S. Bureau of Refugees, Freedmen, and Abandoned Lands, Records of the Freedmen's Branch of the Adjutant General's Office, 1868, National Archives and Records Administration, Washington, D.C.
19 Israel Moore and J. W. Spaulding, "Columbus County," *Weekly Carolina Era*, April 4, 1872, 3.
20 Moore and Spaulding, 3.
21 Kendi, *Stamped from the Beginning*, 243–44.

22 "Reconstruction."

23 "Reconstruction."

24 "Reconstruction."

25 Crow, Escott, and Hatley, *History of African Americans in North Carolina*, 92.

26 "Reconstruction."

CHAPTER FOUR

1 Mitchell, "Aaron McDuffie Moore," 248.

2 Justesen, *George Henry White*, 21.

3 Justesen, 20.

4 "Recollections of School," Asa T. Spaulding Papers.

5 Dial interviewed his mother for his Lumbee Oral History Project.

6 Fairclough, *Better Day Coming*, 67–70.

7 David P. Allen address to a gathering of New England teachers, July 9, 1879, Annual Meeting of the American Institute of Instruction, 1879 (proceedings, second day, July 9).

8 Mitchell, "Aaron McDuffie Moore," 248.

9 Justesen, *George Henry White*, 63–81.

10 C. Smith, *History of Education in North Carolina*, 174–75.

11 C. Smith, 162.

12 David P. Allen Memorial Association, "D. P. Allen Monument," *The Robesonian*, December 17, 1917, 3.

13 The *1882–83 Catalog of the Officers and Students of Howard University* lists his older brother Israel Jr. as entering in the normal course.

CHAPTER FIVE

1 It was customary to travel in one's best clothes, and it was also safer for a young black man to appear as respectable as possible. Shaw University required that inbound students not travel on the Sabbath, and term would begin on a Monday.

2 Galatians 6:7 (KJV).

3 Cost of tuition, room, and board is listed in the Shaw Bulletin the year of his matriculation. "Fifth Annual Announcement, Session of 1885 and 1886, Shaw University," Shaw University Medical, Pharmacy, and Law Catalogs, Shaw University Archives, Raleigh.

4 We know from both George White's and Asa Spaulding's accounts that these were the ways tuition money could be earned. See Justesen, *George Henry White*; and Asa T. Spaulding Papers.

5 Listed as requirements for entry into Shaw in the bulletin. "Fifth Annual Announcement, Session of 1885 and 1886."

CHAPTER SIX

1 Madden, "December 1865."

2 Savitt, "Training the 'Consecrated, Skillful, Christian Physician.'"

3 Andrews, *John Merrick*, 22–23.

4 Madden, "December 1865."

5 Ward, *Black Physicians in the Jim Crow South*, 8.

6 Mitchell, "Aaron McDuffie Moore," 249.

7 "Ninth Annual Announcement, Session of 1889–1890, Shaw University," Shaw University Medical, Pharmacy, and Law Catalogs.

8 Horton, "Telephones."

9 Washington, *Medical Apartheid*, 43.

10 Savitt, *Race and Medicine*, 156.

11 Illinois State Board of Health, *Annual Report*, 121.

12 Wood, *North Carolina Medical Journal*, 1878.

13 Cohn, "Life and Times of Louis Pasteur."

14 Savitt, *Race and Medicine*, 160.

15 Ward, *Black Physicians in the Jim Crow South*, 16.

16 Savitt, "Education of Black Physicians."

17 Savitt, "Training the 'Consecrated, Skillful, Christian Physician.'"

18 "Fifth Annual Announcement, Session of 1885 and 1886."

19 Wood, *North Carolina Medical Journal*, 220.

20 Ward, *Black Physicians in the Jim Crow South*, 50.

21 Ward, 38.

22 Ward, 9.

CHAPTER SEVEN

1 "Fifth Annual Announcement, Session of 1885 and 1886," 7.

2 Savitt, *Race and Medicine*, 181.

3 "Fifth Annual Announcement, Session of 1885 and 1886," 7.

4 Details ascertained through a personal visit by the author to Shaw University in 2015 and a Raleigh Historic Landmark Designation Application filed June 30, 2011, concerning Leonard Hall, by Cynthia de Miranda, historical consultant for Raleigh Historical Development Commission, Section 10c, Architectural Significance. Photo from Reynolds, *Durham's Lincoln Hospital*, 12.

5 "Twenty-Eighth Annual Catalog of the Officers and Students of the Leonard Medical School," Shaw University Medical, Pharmacy, and Law Catalogs, 16.

6 Photos of the chapel are marked "Chapel" and "Dining Hall." "Twenty-Eighth Annual Catalog of the Officers and Students of the Leonard Medical School," 16.

7 Savitt, *Race and Medicine*, 181.

8 "Fifth Annual Announcement, Session of 1885 and 1886," 10.

9 "Fifth Annual Announcement, Session of 1885 and 1886."

10 Savitt, *Race and Medicine*, 160.

11 "Brief History of Gray's Anatomy."

12 "Fifth Annual Announcement, Session of 1885 and 1886," 13.

13 "Fifth Annual Announcement, Session of 1885 and 1886," 7–8.

14 Maerker, "Dr. Auzoux's Papier-Mâché models."

15 "Fifth Annual Announcement, Session of 1885 and 1886," 11.

16 A. M. Moore, final settlement of estate, E. R. Merrick executor, filed 1923,

James E. Shepard Memorial Library, University Archives, Records, and History Center, North Carolina Central University.

17 After the Civil War, Moore's home in the Farmers Union area of Columbus County was served by the Rosindale post office, across the county line in Bladen County.

18 "Fifth Annual Announcement, Session of 1885–86."

CHAPTER EIGHT

1 "Sixth Annual Announcement, Session of 1886–87," Shaw University Medical, Pharmacy, and Law College.

2 Savitt, "Training the 'Consecrated, Skillful, Christian Physician,'" 169–224.

3 Feldman, *How Does Aspirin Find a Headache?*, 19–23.

4 See the photo in the gallery of illustrations. Courtesy of the Shaw University Archives, Raleigh.

5 Savitt, *Race and Medicine*, 186–87.

6 Savitt, 250–78.

7 "Fifth Annual Announcement, Session of 1885–86," 9.

8 "Fifth Annual Announcement, Session of 1885–86"; "Seventh Annual Announcement, Session of 1887–88," Shaw University Medical, Pharmacy, and Law College.

9 Savitt, *Race and Medicine*, 250–78.

10 Coggins, "Human Dissection."

11 Coggins, "Human Dissection."

12 Stolze, "Bodies in the Basement."

13 "Sixth Annual Announcement, Session of 1886–87," 9.

14 Wells, "Battle, Kemp Plummer, Jr."

15 "Sixth Annual Announcement, Session of 1886–87."

16 *African Expositor*, April 1896, p. 3, North Carolina Collection, Wilson Library, University of North Carolina at Chapel Hill.

17 "Seventh Annual Announcement, Session of 1887–88."

18 Raleigh Historic Development Commission, *Dr. M. T. Pope House Statewide Significance Report*.

CHAPTER NINE

1 "Seventh Annual Announcement, Session of 1887–88," 8.

2 "Seventh Annual Announcement, Session of 1887–88," 9.

3 Zogry, "House That Dr. Pope Built," 46.

4 McKee, "McKee, James."

5 "Seventh Annual Announcement, Session of 1887–88," 6.

6 Medical Society of the State of North Carolina, *Transactions of the Medical Society of the State of North Carolina*.

7 Mégnin, *La faune des tombeaux*.

8 "Fifteen Rads Put Out a Ticket," *Tobacco Plant*, October 5, 1888, 3.

9 "Eighth Annual Announcement, Sessions of 1888–1889," Shaw University Medical, Pharmacy, and Law Catalogs, 10–16.

10 Tupper, "Educational Department."

11 Medical Society of the State of North Carolina, *Transactions of the Medical Society of the State of North Carolina.*

12 Proctor, *One Hundred Year History*, 1–8.

13 Proctor, 1–8.

14 Medical Society of the State of North Carolina, *Transactions of the Medical Society of the State of North Carolina*, 57–59.

15 Medical Society of the State of North Carolina, 57–59.

16 "State News, New Doctors," *Charlotte Democrat*, May 18, 1888, 3.

CHAPTER TEN

1 "Republican State Convention," *Raleigh Signal*, May 31, 1888, 4.

2 Brown, *Upbuilding Black Durham*, 47.

3 Justesen, *George Henry White*, 64.

4 Anderson, *Durham County*, 97–107.

5 Anderson, 108–29.

6 Brown, *Upbuilding Black Durham*, 41.

7 Brown, 46–53.

8 Anderson, *Durham County*, 132.

9 Anderson, 132–34.

10 Merrick interview.

11 Ward, *Black Physicians in the Jim Crow South*, 104–8.

12 Andrews, *John Merrick*, 18.

13 Andrews, 180.

14 Savitt, *Race and Medicine*, 269–71.

15 Andrews, *John Merrick*, 18.

16 Merrick interview.

17 Kendi, *Stamped from the Beginning*, 243–44.

18 P. Murray, *Proud Shoes*, 270–71.

19 Du Bois, "Talented Tenth."

20 Class photograph, Leonard Medical School, 1886, courtesy of Shaw University Archives, Raleigh. See the photo in the gallery of illustrations.

21 Kendi, *Stamped from the Beginning*.

CHAPTER ELEVEN

1 Jones, *End of an Era*, 59.

2 Ward, *Black Physicians in the Jim Crow South*, 106.

3 "Local Matter," *Durham Recorder*, October 3, 1888, 5.

4 Dancy, *Sands against the Wind*, 70.

5 Weare, "Moore, Aaron McDuffie."

6 North Carolina, Marriage Records, 1741–2011, Ancestry.com.

7 U.S. Bureau of the Census, *Ninth Census*, Martha Dancy.

8 Moore Merrick interview.

9 Moore Merrick interview.

10 North Carolina, Marriage Records, 1741–2011, Ancestry.com.

11 Moore Merrick interview.

12 Mitchell, "Aaron McDuffie Moore," 250.

13 U.S. Bureau of the Census, *Twelfth Census*.

14 Moore Merrick interview.

15 Jones, *End of an Era*, 59–60.

16 Moore Merrick interview.

17 Moore Merrick interview.

CHAPTER TWELVE

1 Aaron M. Moore's "Physicians Visiting List," C. C. Spaulding Papers, David M. Rubenstein Rare Book and Manuscript Library, Duke University.

2 Wicker, *Voices*, 9.

3 Aaron M. Moore's "Physicians Visiting List," C. C. Spaulding Papers.

4 Moore Merrick interview.

5 P. Murray, *Proud Shoes*, 26–27.

6 Jones, *End of an Era*, 59.

7 Wilson and Mullally, "In This Dark World and Wide," 70–71.

8 Wilson and Mullally, 70–71.

9 Moore Merrick interview.

10 "Live Local Links," *Durham Globe*, March 31, 1894, 6.

11 "Memorial Service," *Raleigh Gazette*, December 9, 1893, 2.

12 "Historic Context for the Pope Family."

13 Mitchell, "Aaron McDuffie Moore," 252.

14 Anderson, *Durham County*, 190.

15 Anderson, 190.

16 Davis, *Selected Writings and Speeches of James E. Shepard*.

17 Andrews, *John Merrick*, 56–57.

18 Mitchell, "Aaron McDuffie Moore," 252.

19 "A Plea for His Race, Booker T. Washington Tells about the Efforts of the Negro," *Atlanta Journal-Constitution*, September 19, 1895, 4.

20 "Plea for His Race."

21 "Plea for His Race."

22 Toppin, *A Biographical History of Blacks in America*, 145.

23 Jackson, *Booker T. Washington*, 2.

24 Andrews, *John Merrick*, 34–37.

25 E. C. Crawford, "For Wakefulness," *Houston Post*, February 10, 1896, 6. Horsford's Acid Phosphate is actually still sold today by Vintage Bar Suppliers as bitters for cocktails. Extinct Chemical Company lists the ingredients as "a partially neutralized solution made with salts of calcium, magnesium and potassium. The solution has a pH between 2.0 and 2.2, or about the same as fresh squeezed lime juice."

26 "Durham County Fair Association," *Durham Sun*, August 29, 1896, 1.

27 King, "Booker T. Washington Visits Trinity College."

28 W. S. Mitchell, "Durham Colored Fair—Magnificent Exhibits," *Raleigh Gazette*, October 31, 1896, 3.

29 E. Murray, "North Carolina Industrial Association."

30 "Historical Note and Timeline," Charles N. Hunter Papers, David M. Rubenstein Rare Book and Manuscript Library, Duke University.

31 Andrews, *John Merrick*, 39–40.

32 Andrews, 34–45.

33 "County Ticket Named," *Durham Recorder*, October 8, 1896, 3.

34 "Historical Context for the Pope Family."

35 Sumner, "African American State Fair."

36 Mitchell, "Durham Colored Fair—Magnificent Exhibits," 3.

37 "The Colored State Fair," *Raleigh News and Observer*, November 10, 1896, 5.

38 "Visitors to the Fair," *Raleigh Gazette*, November 21, 1896, 3.

39 "Colored State Fair," 5.

CHAPTER THIRTEEN

1 Anderson, *Durham County*, 190.

2 "White Rock Baptist Church."

3 "Badly Burned," *Durham Sun*, July 4, 1896, 1.

4 "Malone Will Recover," *Durham Sun*, August 18, 1898, 4.

5 Moore Merrick interview.

CHAPTER FOURTEEN

1 C. M. Epps, "Bridgers-Dancey Nupitals" [*sic*], *Raleigh Gazette*, January 1, 1898.

2 Birth and death date chart, Israel Moore (A. M. Moore) family, Spaulding Family Papers, compiled by Luke Alexander, BESDA Archive.

3 Birth and death date chart, Israel Moore (A. M. Moore) family.

4 Moore Merrick interview.

5 March 1899, Columbus County, North Carolina, Court Minutes, Israel Moore Sr., Estate Division, 77, North Carolina Register of Deeds.

6 December 26, 1917, Columbus County, North Carolina, Dr. A. M. and Cottie Moore to David J. Williston, North Carolina Register of Deeds.

7 Crow, Escott, and Hatley, *History of African Americans in North Carolina*, 112–15.

8 Tyson and Zane, *Ghosts of 1898*, 7.

9 Crow, Escott, and Hatley, *History of African Americans in North Carolina*, 116.

10 Anderson, *Durham County*, 187.

11 Brown, *Upbuilding Black Durham*, 68–71.

12 Brown, 63.

13 Kendi, *Stamped from the Beginning*, 284.

14 Durden, *Dukes of Durham*, 101–5.

15 Brown, *Upbuilding Black Durham*, 55–56.

16 Toppin, *Biographical History of Blacks in America*, 144.

17 Toppin, 130.

18 Brown, *Upbuilding Black Durham*, 56–59.

19 Tyson and Zane, *Ghosts of 1898*, 9.

20 Alexander L. Manly, "Alexander L. Manly's Editorial of August, 1898, Goin' North," https://goinnorth.org/collections/show/12, Alex L. Manly Papers, East Carolina Manuscript Collection, J. Y. Joyner Library, East Carolina University, Greenville.

21 Crow, Escott, and Hatley, *History of African Americans in North Carolina*, 115.

22 Brown, *Upbuilding Black Durham*, 58–65.

23 Brown, 58–65.

24 Tyson and Zane, *Ghosts of 1898*, 11.

25 Crow, Escott, and Hatley, *History of African Americans in North Carolina*, 117; Tyson and Zane, *Ghosts of 1898*, 7.

26 Zogry, "House That Dr. Pope Built."

27 Burnett, "Alex Manly (1866–1944)."

CHAPTER FIFTEEN

1 "A Small Fire—Boston Team to Practice in Durham," *North Carolinian*, December 22, 1898, 3.

2 Mjagkij, "Grand United Order of True Reformers," 253–54.

3 Weare, *Black Business in the New South*, 12–13.

4 Kennedy, *North Carolina Mutual Story*, 4.

5 "North Carolina Mutual/Mechanics and Farmers."

6 Kennedy, *North Carolina Mutual Story*, 4–7.

7 "Chronological History," North Carolina Mutual Life Insurance Company Archives, David M. Rubenstein Rare Book and Manuscript Library, Duke University.

8 Anderson, *Durham County*, 187–88.

9 Andrews, *John Merrick*, 81–85.

10 Kennedy, *North Carolina Mutual Story*, 8.

11 Andrews, *John Merrick*, 64–66.

12 Andrews, 69–71.

13 Andrews, 69–71.

14 Andrews, 71.

15 Kennedy, *North Carolina Mutual Story*, 21.

16 Mitchell, "Aaron McDuffie Moore."

17 Kennedy, *North Carolina Mutual Story*, 18.

18 Andrews, *John Merrick*, 1–12.

CHAPTER SIXTEEN

1 Charles F. Meserve to Eastern Hospital for the Insane, Goldsboro, N.C., February 15, 1897, Meserve Correspondence, Shaw University Archives, Raleigh.

2 W. S. Armstrong, "Rocky Mountain Grits," *Raleigh Gazette*, January 2, 1897, 3.

3 "Cherry Hospital."

4 Quoted in Andrews, *John Merrick*, 47–48.

5 Andrews, 49–50.

6 Reynolds, *Durham's Lincoln Hospital*, 14–15.
7 Andrews, *John Merrick*, 15.
8 Wicker, *Voices*, 21.
9 Reynolds, *Durham's Lincoln Hospital*, 24.
10 Wicker, *Voices*, 21.
11 Reynolds, *Durham's Lincoln Hospital*, 70.
12 Brown, *Upbuilding Black Durham*, 160–163.
13 Wicker, *Voices*, 17.
14 Wicker, 12–13.
15 Moore Merrick interview.
16 Moore Merrick interview.

CHAPTER SEVENTEEN
1 "506 Fayetteville Street—The John Merrick House."
2 "Richard Fitzgerald House—'The Maples.'"
3 Quoted in Andrews, *John Merrick*, 32.
4 Andrews, 56–58.
5 Du Bois, "Upbuilding of Black Durham," 334–38.
6 C. Eileen Watts Welch remembers this from her childhood.
7 "Schools Days in Durham," Asa T. Spaulding Papers.
8 Wilson and Mullally, "In This Dark World and Wide," 69.
9 Anderson, *Durham County*, 187–90.
10 "Dr. Aaron Moore House—606 Fayetteville St."

CHAPTER EIGHTEEN
1 Wilson and Mullally, "In This Dark World and Wide," 70.
2 Andrews, *John Merrick*, 60.
3 "History of the Durham County Library."
4 North Carolina Department of Revenue, letter of inquiry on status of the Durham Colored Library, January 4, 1954, Raleigh.

CHAPTER NINETEEN
1 Wilson and Mullally, "In This Dark World and Wide," 70.
2 Klein, "10 Top Draws of San Francisco's 1915 World's Fair."
3 Moore Merrick interview.
4 Moore Merrick interview.
5 "D. W. Griffith's 'Birth of a Nation' Opens, Glorifying the KKK."
6 Churchwell, *Behold, America*, 58–61.

CHAPTER TWENTY
1 Mitchell, "Aaron McDuffie Moore."
2 Mitchell, 256.
3 Abel, "Persistence and Sacrifice."
4 Justesen, *George Henry White*, 437–38.
5 A. M. Moore to James Joyner, April 26, 1915, Department of Public Instruc-

tion Records, Superintendent of Public Instruction Correspondence, box 48, State Archives of North Carolina, Raleigh.

6 Branson to James Joyner, May 27, 1915, Superintendent of Public Instruction Correspondence, box 44.

7 Chief Clerk of James Joyner to E. C. Branson, May 29, 1915, Superintendent of Public Instruction Correspondence, box 44.

8 *Negro Rural School Problem Condition-Remedy: Let Us Reason Together*, James E. Shepard Memorial Library, University Archives, Records, and History Center, North Carolina Central University, Durham.

9 C. S. Brown, "Movement to Improve the Negro Rural Schools Launched at Meeting of Leaders at Winston-Salem," *Wilmington Morning Star*, June 26, 1915.

10 S. Smith, "From the Biographical Files of Charles Henry Moore."

11 "Report of Prof. Chas. H. Moore State Inspector of Negro Schools," made before the North Carolina State Teachers' Association assembled at Greensboro, June 23, 1916, C. C. Spaulding Papers, box 18.

12 "Report of Prof. Chas. H. Moore State Inspector of Negro Schools," 1–2.

13 "Report of Prof. Chas. H. Moore State Inspector of Negro Schools," 6–7.

14 S. Smith, "From the Biographical Files of Charles Henry Moore."

15 Dominguez, "Booker T. Washington's Death Revisited."

16 "Report of Prof. Chas. H. Moore State Inspector of Negro Schools," 8.

17 "Report of Prof. Chas. H. Moore State Inspector of Negro Schools," 14.

18 "Young Durham Couple United in Marriage," *New York Age*, November 30, 1916, 2.

19 Mitchell, "Aaron McDuffie Moore," 256.

20 "Young Durham Couple United in Marriage," 2.

21 Mitchell, "Aaron McDuffie Moore," 256.

22 "Report of Prof. Chas. H. Moore State Inspector of Negro Schools," Conclusion, 17.

23 Aaron McDuffie Moore will and probate document, C. D. Watts Family Papers, James E. Shepard, Memorial Library, University Archives, Records, and History Center, North Carolina Central University.

24 Moore Merrick interview.

CHAPTER TWENTY-ONE

1 Bryan, "Fighting for Respect."

2 This term refers to high-level executives who are asked to serve government organizations (often during wartime) for the salary of one dollar a year. It is illegal to serve as an unpaid volunteer.

3 U.S. Department of Labor, *Negro at Work*, 98.

4 U.S. Department of Labor, 99.

5 U.S. Department of Labor, 102.

6 U.S. Department of Labor, 103.

7 U.S. Department of Labor, 102–3.

8 Kendi, *Stamped from the Beginning*, 312–14.

CHAPTER TWENTY-TWO

1 Quoted in Andrews, *John Merrick*, 111–12.
2 Quoted in Andrews, 114–15.
3 Kennedy, *North Carolina Mutual Story*, 52.
4 Andrews, quoted in Kennedy, 53.

CHAPTER TWENTY-THREE

1 Murphy, "Depression You've Never Heard Of."
2 A. M. Moore to N.C. Mutual Agents, circa May 1922, C. C. Spaulding Papers.
3 A. M. Moore to N.C. Mutual Agents, quoted in Kennedy, *North Carolina Mutual Story.*
4 A. M. Moore to W. E. B. Du Bois, April 21, 1921, W. E. B. Dubois Papers, 1803–1999, Special Collections and University Archives, University of Massachusetts Amherst.
5 A. M. Moore to Cottie Moore on Battle Creek Sanitarium stationery, December 20, 1921, from the personal collection of C. Eileen Watts Welch. Two lines from this letter have been omitted due to the difficulty in deciphering his very tired handwriting.
6 Mudsills sit on top of the foundation of a building and are an important first step.
7 A. M. Moore to Lyda Moore Merrick (Mrs. E. R. Merrick) on Battle Creek Sanitarium Stationery, undated, from the personal collection of C. Eileen Watts Welch.
8 Reynolds, *Durham's Lincoln Hospital*, 18.
9 North Carolina State Board of Health, Bureau of Vital Statistics, Standard Certificate of Death, Dr. A. M. Moore, April 29, 1923.
10 Merrick interview.
11 Kennedy, *North Carolina Mutual Story*, 83.
12 "Durham, N.C., 1923."
13 Evidence of all of these tributes is in the C. C. Spaulding Papers, labeled simply "A. M. Moore."
14 Mitchell, "Aaron McDuffie Moore," 248.

BIBLIOGRAPHY

ARCHIVES
Amherst, Mass.
   Special Collections and University Archives, University of Massachusetts
      Amherst
      W. E. B. Du Bois Papers, 1803–1999
Chapel Hill, N.C.
   North Carolina Collection, Wilson Library, University of North Carolina
Durham, N.C.
   Benjamin and Elizabeth Spaulding Descendants Association (BESDA)
      Archive, privately held by Luke Alexander
      Spaulding Family Papers
   David M. Rubenstein Rare Book and Manuscript Library, Duke University
      Asa T. Spaulding Papers
      C. C. Spaulding Papers
      Charles N. Hunter Papers
      North Carolina Mutual Life Insurance Company Archives
   James E. Shepard Memorial Library, University Archives, Records, and
      History Center, North Carolina Central University
      C. D. Watts Family Papers
Greenville, N.C.
   East Carolina Manuscript Collection, J. Y. Joyner Library, East Carolina
      University
      Alex L. Manly Papers
Raleigh, N.C.
   Pope House Museum
   Shaw University Archives
      Meserve Correspondence
      Shaw University Medical, Pharmacy, and Law Catalogs
   State Archives of North Carolina
      Department of Public Instruction Records, Superintendent of Public
         Instruction Correspondence
      North Carolina Maps Collection
Washington, D.C.
   National Archives and Records Administration (NARA)
      U.S. Bureau of Refugees, Freedmen, and Abandoned Lands, Records of
      the Freedmen's Branch of the Adjutant General's Office, 1868

U.S. Bureau of the Census, Agricultural Schedule, 1850
U.S. Department of State, Passport Applications, 1795–1925

NEWSPAPERS AND PERIODICALS
Atlanta Journal-Constitution
Charlotte Democrat
Durham Globe
Durham Recorder
Durham Sun
Houston Post
New York Age
The North Carolinian (Elizabeth City, N.C.)
Raleigh Gazette
Raleigh News and Observer
Raleigh Signal
The Robesonian (Lumberton, N.C.)
Tobacco Plant (Durham)
Weekly Carolina Era
Wilmington Morning Star

ARCHIVAL AND PRIMARY SOURCES
1882–83 Catalog of the Officers and Students of Howard University. Washington, D.C.: Howard University, 1882.
North Carolina Department of Revenue. Letter of inquiry on status of the Durham Colored Library, January 4, 1954. Raleigh.
North Carolina Marriage Records. Marriage Register, A. M. Moore, Edgecombe, North Carolina, December 17, 1889. North Carolina, Marriage Records, 1741–2011, Ancestry.com.
North Carolina Register of Deeds. Columbus County, Deed Books. Whiteville.
North Carolina State Board of Health, Bureau of Vital Statistics. Standard Certificate of Death, Dr. A. M. Moore, April 29, 1923, Raleigh.

PUBLISHED AND ONLINE SOURCES
"Aaron McDuffie Moore, M.D., President of the North Carolina Mutual Life Insurance Company" [obituary]. *Journal of the National Medical Association* 16 (January–March 1924): 72–74.
Anderson, Jean Bradley. *Durham County: A History of Durham County, North Carolina.* Rev. and expanded ed. Durham: Duke University Press, 2011.
Andrews, R. McCants. *John Merrick: A Biographical Sketch.* Durham: Press of the Seeman Printery, 1920.
The Benjamin and Edith Spaulding Descendants Association. https://www.spauldingfamily.org.
"Black Codes." Encyclopedia.com. https://www.encyclopedia.com/history/united-states-and-canada/us-history/black-codes#3437700548.

"A Brief History of Gray's Anatomy." http://www.coursewareobjects.com
/marketing/standringtimeline.pdf.

Brooks, Walter H. "The Evolution of the Negro Baptist Church." *Journal of Negro History* 7 (January 1922): 11–22.

Brown, Leslie. *Upbuilding Black Durham: Gender, Class, and Black Community Development in the Jim Crow South.* Chapel Hill: University of North Carolina Press, 2008.

Bryan, Jami L. "Fighting for Respect: African American Soldiers in WWI." Army History Center, January 20, 2015. https://armyhistory.org/fighting-for -respect-african-american-soldiers-in-wwi/.

Burnett, Lucy. "Alex Manly (1866–1944)." Black Past. https://www.blackpast.org /african-american-history/manly-alex-1866–1944/.

Caldwell, A. B. *The American Negro and His Institutions, North Carolina Edition, Volume IV.* Atlanta: A. B. Caldwell Publishing, 1921.

"Cherry Hospital." Asylum Projects. http://www.asylumprojects.org/index.php ?title=Cherry_Hospital.

Churchwell, Sarah. *Behold, America: A History of "America First" and the "American Dream."* New York: Basic Books, 2018.

Coggins, Jennifer. "Human Dissection in the Early Years of Medical Education at UNC." *For the Record* (blog), April 27, 2016. http://blogs.lib.unc.edu /uarms/index.php/2016/04/human-dissection-in-the-early-years-of -medical-education-at-unc/.

Cohn, David V. "The Life and Times of Louis Pasteur." Louis Pasteur, http:// pyramid.spd.louisville.edu/~eri/fos/interest1.html.

Crow, Jeffrey J., Paul D. Escott, and Flora J. Hatley. *A History of African Americans in North Carolina.* Raleigh: North Carolina Division of Archives and History, 1992.

Dancy, John C. *Sands against the Wind: Memoirs of John C. Dancy.* Detroit: Wayne State University Press, 1966.

Davis, Lenwood G. *Selected Writings and Speeches of James E. Shepard, 1896–1946: Founder of North Carolina Central University.* Madison, N.J.: Fairleigh Dickinson University Press.

Dominguez, Alex. "Booker T. Washington's Death Revisited." *Washington Post,* May 5, 2006. http://www.washingtonpost.com/wp-dyn/content/article/2006 /05/05/AR2006050501345.html.

Du Bois, W. E. B. "The Talented Tenth." In *The Negro Problem: A Series of Articles by Representative American Negroes of To-Day,* by Booker T. Washington, 31–75. New York: James Pott, 1903.

———. "The Upbuilding of Black Durham: The Success of the Negroes and Their Value to a Tolerant and Helpful Southern City." *World's Work* 23 (January 1912): 334–38. http://docsouth.unc.edu/nc/dubois/summary.html.

Durden, Robert F. *The Dukes of Durham, 1865–1929.* Durham: Duke University Press, 1987.

"Durham, N.C., 1923." Cemetery Census. http://cemeterycensus.com/nc/durh/.

"D. W. Griffith's 'Birth of a Nation' Opens, Glorifying the KKK." History, February 9, 2010, https://www.history.com/this-day-in-history/birth-of-a -nation-opens.

Fairclough, Adam. *Better Day Coming: Blacks and Equality, 1890–2000.* New York: Penguin Random House, 2002.

Feldman, David. *How Does Aspirin Find a Headache?* New York: Harper Perennial, 2005.

Grun, Bernard. *The Timetables of History.* 4th ed. New York: Simon and Schuster, 2005.

"Historical Context for the Pope Family." City of Raleigh. https://www.raleighnc .gov/content/PRecRecreation/Documents/HRMPopeFamily.pdf.

"History of the Durham County Library." Durham County Library. https:// durhamcountylibrary.org/about/history/.

Horton, Clarence E., Jr. "Telephones." In *Encyclopedia of North Carolina*, edited by William S. Powell. Chapel Hill: University of North Carolina Press, 2006. https://www.ncpedia.org/telephones.

Illinois State Board of Health. *Annual Report of Illinois State Board of Health.* Springfield: The Board, 1883.

Jackson, David H., Jr. *Booker T. Washington and the Struggle against White Supremacy: The Southern Educational Tours, 1908–1912.* Basingstoke, UK: Palgrave Macmillan, 2008.

Jones, Dorothy Phelps. *The End of an Era.* Durham: Brown Enterprises, 2001.

Justesen, Benjamin R. *George Henry White: An Even Chance in the Race of Life.* Baton Rouge: Louisiana State University Press, 2001.

Kendi, Ibram X. *Stamped from the Beginning: The Definitive History of Racist Ideas in America.* New York: Bold Type Books, 2016.

Kennedy, William Jesse. *The North Carolina Mutual Story: A Symbol of Progress, 1898–1970.* Durham: North Carolina Mutual Life Insurance, 1970.

Kickler, Troy L. "N.C. Played Crucial Role at Civil War's End." North Carolina History Project. http://northcarolinahistory.org/commentary/n-c-played -crucial-role-at-civil-wars-end/.

King, William E. "Booker T. Washington Visits Trinity College." *Duke Dialogue*, March 27, 1991. https://library.duke.edu/rubenstein/uarchives/history /articles/booker-t-washington.

Klein, Christopher. "Top 10 Draws of San Francisco's 1915 World's Fair." History, August 22, 2018, https://www.history.com/news/10-top-draws-of-san -franciscos-1915-worlds-fair.

Lewis, J. D. "Bladen County, N.C.—1875–1880." Carolana. https://www.carolana .com/NC/Counties/bladen_1875_to_1880.html.

———. "Columbus County, N.C.—1878–1880." Carolana. https://www.carolana .com/NC/Counties/columbus_1878_to_1880.html.

Little, Ann Ward, and Columbus County Bicentennial Commission. *Columbus County, North Carolina: Recollections and Records.* Whiteville, N.C.: Columbus County Commissioners and Columbus County Public Library, 1980.

Locklear, Lawrence T. "UNCP's Founders." University of North Carolina at Pembroke. https://www.uncp.edu/about/history/uncps-founders.

Madden, Bridget. "December 1865: Henry Martin Tupper and the Founding of Shaw University." *North Carolina Miscellany* (blog), December 1, 2009. https://blogs.lib.unc.edu/ncm/index.php/2009/12/01/this_month_dec_1865/.

Maerker, Anna. "Dr. Auzoux's Papier-Mâché Models." Explore Whipple Collections. http://www.sites.hps.cam.ac.uk/whipple/explore/models/drauzouxsmodels/.

Majors, Gerri, and Doris E. Saunders. *Black Society*. Chicago: Johnson Publishing, 1976.

McKee, James Battle. "McKee, James." In *Dictionary of North Carolina Biography*, edited by William S. Powell. Chapel Hill: University of North Carolina Press, 1991. https://www.ncpedia.org/biography/mckee-james.

Medical Society of the State of North Carolina. *Transactions of the Medical Society of the State of North Carolina, Annual Session 8–11 May, 1888*. Fayetteville: Medical Society of the State of North Carolina.

Mégnin, Jean-Pierre. *La faune des tombeaux*. Paris: Gauthier-Villars, 1887.

Mitchell, Louis D. "Aaron McDuffie Moore: He Led His Sheep." *The Crisis*, August/September 1980, 248–57.

Mjagkij, Nina. "Grand United Order of True Reformers." In *Organizing Black America: An Encyclopedia of African American Associations*, edited by Nina Mjagkij, 253–54. New York: Garland, 2001.

Moore, Anne, and James I. Martin Sr. "Baptists." In *Encyclopedia of North Carolina*, edited by William S. Powell. Chapel Hill: University of North Carolina Press, 2006. https://www.ncpedia.org/baptists.

Moore, J. H. *Noble Ancestry and Descendants*. Wilmington, N.C.: Lin Print Company, 1949.

Murphy, Robert P. "The Depression You've Never Heard Of: 1920–1921." Foundation for Economic Education, November 18, 2009. https://fee.org/articles/the-depression-youve-never-heard-of-1920–1921/.

Murray, Elizabeth Reid. "North Carolina Industrial Association." In *Encyclopedia of North Carolina*, edited by William S. Powell. Chapel Hill: University of North Carolina Press. https://www.ncpedia.org/north-carolina-industrial-associati.

Murray, Pauli. *Proud Shoes: The Story of an American Family*. Boston: Beacon Press. 1999.

Nash, Betty Joyce. "Economic History: Tar and Turpentine; Tarheels Extract the South's First Industry." *Econ Focus (Federal Reserve Bank of Richmond)* 15, no. 4 (Fourth Quarter 2011). https://fraser.stlouisfed.org/title/3941/item/476954/toc/503576.

North Carolina State Board of Education. *Second Annual Catalogue of the North Carolina State Colored Normal Schools for 1905–'06*. Raleigh: E. M. Uzzell, 1906.

Outland, Robert B. *Tapping the Pines: The Naval Stores Industry in the American South*. Baton Rouge: Louisiana State University Press, 2004.

Perdue, Theda. *Native Carolinians: The Indians of North Carolina*. Raleigh: Division of Archives and History, North Carolina Department of Cultural Resources, 1985.

Pohanka, Brian C. "Fort Wagner and the 54th Massachusetts Volunteer Infantry: July 18, 1863." American Battlefield Trust. https://www.battlefields .org/learn/articles/fort-wagner-and-54th-massachusetts-volunteer-infantry.

Procter, Ivan Marriott. *One Hundred Year History of the North Carolina State Board of Medical Examiners, 1859–1959*. Raleigh: Board of Medical Examiners, 1959.

Raleigh Historic Development Commission. *Dr. M. T. Pope House Statewide Significance Report*. RHDC.org. https://rhdc.org/sites/default/files/Pope %20House%20SWS%20Report.pdf.

"Reconstruction." Encyclopedia.com. https://www.encyclopedia.com/history /united-states-and-canada/us-history/reconstruction#3401803536.

Reynolds, Pamela Preston. *Durham's Lincoln Hospital*. Mount Pleasant, S.C.: Arcadia, 2001.

Savitt, Todd L. "The Education of Black Physicians at Shaw University, 1882–1918." In *Black Americans in North Carolina and the South*, edited by Jeffrey C. Crow and Flora J. Hatley, 160–88. Chapel Hill: University of North Carolina Press, 1984.

———. *Race and Medicine in Nineteenth- and Early-Twentieth-Century America*. Kent: Kent State University Press, 2006.

———. "Training the 'Consecrated, Skillful, Christian Physician': Documents Illustrating Student Life at Leonard Medical School, 1882–1918." *North Carolina Historical Review* 75 (July 1998): 250–76.

Smith, Charles Lee. *The History of Education in North Carolina*. Washington, D.C.: Government Printing Office, 1888.

Smith, Sarah. "From the Biographical Files of Charles Henry Moore." The Consecrated Eminence: The Archives and Special Collections at Amherst College, December 14, 2011. https://consecratedeminence.wordpress. com/2011/12/14/from-the-biographical-file-of-charles-henry-moore/.

Stolze, Dolly. "Bodies in the Basement: The Forgotten Stolen Bones of America's Medical Schools." *Atlas Obscura*, January 22, 2015. https://www.atlas obscura.com/articles/bodies-in-the-basement-the-forgotten-bones-of -america-s-medical-schools.

Sumner, Jim. "The African American State Fair." *Tar Heel Junior Historian* 42, no. 1 (2002). https://www.ncpedia.org/anchor/african-american-state-fair.

Toppin, Edgar Allan. *A Biographical History of Blacks in America since 1528*. New York. David McKay, 1971.

Tupper, Henry Martin. "Educational Department, Shaw University." *Baptist Home Mission Monthly* 9–10 (1887–88): 25.

———. "The Leonard Medical School, Shaw University—Its Endowment a Necessity." *Baptist Home Mission Monthly* 7–8 (1885–86): 56–57.

Tyson, Timothy B., and J. Peder Zane, eds. *The Ghosts of 1898: Wilmington's*

Race Riot and the Rise of White Supremacy. Raleigh: News and Observer,
2006.

U.S. Bureau of the Census. *Eighth Census of the United States, 1860.*
Washington, D.C.: Government Printing Office, 1864.

———. *Ninth Census of the United States, 1870.* Vol. 1, *The Vital Statistics of the
United States.* Washington, D.C.: Government Printing Office, 1872.

———. *Twelfth Census of the United States, 1900.* Washington, D.C.:
Government Printing Office, 1972.

U.S. Department of Labor, Division of Negro Economics. *The Negro at Work
during the World War and during Reconstruction: Statistics, Problems, and
Policies Relating to the Greater Inclusion of Negro Wage Earners in American
Industry and Agriculture.* Washington, D.C.: Government Printing Office,
1921.

Ward, Thomas J., Jr. *Black Physicians in the Jim Crow South.* Fayetteville: The
University of Arkansas Press, 2003.

Washington, Harriet A. *Medical Apartheid: The Dark History of Medical
Experimentation on Black Americans from Colonial Times to the Present.*
New York: Doubleday, 2007.

Watson, Joseph W., and C. Franklin Grill. *The Historical Directory of Churches
in the North Carolina Conference.* Garner: North Carolina Conference
Commission on Archives and History, North Carolina Conference of the
United Methodist Church, 1984.

Weare, Walter B. *Black Business in the New South: A Social History of North
Carolina Mutual Life Insurance Company.* Durham: Duke University Press,
1993.

———. "Moore, Aaron McDuffie." In *Dictionary of North Carolina Biography,*
edited by William S. Powell. Chapel Hill: University of North Carolina Press,
1991. https://www.ncpedia.org/biography/moore-aaron-mcduffie.

Webster, Noah. *The Blue-Backed Speller and New England Primer.* New York:
American Book Company, 1880.

Wells, Warner. "Battle, Kemp Plummer, Jr." In *Dictionary of North Carolina
Biography,* edited by William S. Powell. Chapel Hill: University of North
Carolina Press, 1979. https://www.ncpedia.org/biography/battle-kemp
-plummer-jr.

Whitted, J. A. *A History of the Negro Baptists of North Carolina.* Raleigh:
Edwards and Broughton, 1908.

Wicker, Evelyn Pearl Booker. *Voices: Lincoln Hospital School of Nursing,
Durham North Carolina, 1903 ...* Fuquay-Varina, N.C.: Jones Booker
Publishing, 2013.

Wilson, Emily Herring (text), and Susan Mullally (photographs). "In This Dark
World and Wide: Lyda Moore Merrick, Durham." Chap. 7 in *Hope and
Dignity, Older Black Women of the South.* Philadelphia: Temple University
Press, 1983.

Wood, Thomas F., ed. *North Carolina Medical Journal,* vol. 12. Wilmington,

N.C.: Jackson and Bell Water-Power Presses, 1883. https://archive.org
/details/northcarolinamed121883jack/page/n5.

INTERVIEWS

Dial, Mary Ellen Moore. Interview by Adolph L. Dial. 1969.
Moore Merrick, Mrs. Lyda. Interview by Meredythe Holmes. Tape recording,
1983.

THESES AND DISSERTATIONS

Abel, Joanne. "Persistence and Sacrifice: Durham County's African American
Community and Durham's Jeanes Teachers Build Community and Schools,
1900–1930." M.A. thesis, Duke University, 2009.
Zogry, Kenneth Joel. "The House That Dr. Pope Built: Race, Politics, Memory,
and the Early Struggle for Civil Rights in North Carolina." Ph.D. diss.,
University of North Carolina, 2008.

INDEX

Page numbers appearing in italics refer to illustrations.

ABOUT DURHAM COLORED LIBRARY, INC.

Durham Colored Library, Inc. (DCL), is one of Durham's oldest nonprofit organizations, dedicated to the mission of lifting up stories about African Americans, both current and historical, to help create a more comprehensive picture of the American experience. Today, DCL publishes the *Merrick Washington Magazine*, a publication started in 1952 that brings news articles about and related to African American culture and history to a sight-challenged population who do not readily have access to braille or large-print editions of major publications.

DCL was founded and chartered in 1918, and at that time, its board oversaw the management of the library's staff and facilities. The historic DCL System remained under DCL's management until 1969, when the Durham County Public Library system opened its doors to all residents of Durham, thereby desegregating Durham's public library services. In the process, the DCL Stanford L. Warren branch, as well as DCL's other branches and bookmobile, continued to function as a part of the newly integrated public library system. Today, the historic Stanford L. Warren facility is still standing as a branch of the Durham Public Library system.

C. Eileen Watts Welch,
president and CEO of
Durham Colored Library, Inc.
Photo courtesy of Anthony Farrell.

Durham Colored Library, Inc.